Hana Horáková, Stepł

C000151122

Global Challenges a
Czech Republic ὶ

Global Challenges and Local Reactions: Czech Republic and South Africa

edited by

Hana Horáková and Stephanie Rudwick

LIT

Scientific reviewers: Tommaso Milani, Martin Riegl, Tereza Hyánková

Cover design: Hana Novotná

English language editor: Akiva Zasman

Technical editorial work: Jiří Procházka

This book is printed on acid-free paper.

Bibliographic information published by the Deutsche Nationalbibliothek
The Deutsche Nationalbibliothek lists this publication in the Deutsche
Nationalbibliografie; detailed bibliographic data are available in the Internet at
http://dnb.d-nb.de.

ISBN 978-3-643-90591-8

Acknowledgements

This volume grew out of a workshop held at Metropolitan University Prague, in November 2013, where most of these chapters were presented. We would like to thank Metropolitan University Prague for its generous funding of this workshop and the participants for their time and efforts. We also thank several anonymous reviewers for their work on the separate chapters.

Financial support for the research and publication of this book was provided by the Internal Grant System of Metropolitan University Prague, project number MVES/18/2013, A10-21.

Contents

Notes on contributors

Petra Ahari graduated from Metropolitan University Prague, the Department of International Relations and European Studies, where she is currently completing her Master's thesis. Her main interests are democratisation, political institutions and party systems as they are applied in the third wave African democracies.

Hana Horáková is an African Studies scholar and social anthropologist teaching at Metropolitan University Prague. She received her Ph.D. in African Studies from Charles University in Prague. Her professional interests include anthropology of sub-Saharan Africa, theories of culture, ethnicity and nationalism. She has published and edited several books and other texts in the fields of African studies and social anthropology.

Júlia Lampášová is a Ph.D. candidate at the Department of International Relations and European Studies, Metropolitan University Prague. She focuses on the security impacts of HIV/AIDS and other epidemics worldwide. Her fields of interest also include Human rights and International law. She has presented papers at numerous conferences on Africa in the Czech Republic.

Thabo Msibi is a senior lecturer in curriculum studies in the School of Education at the University of KwaZulu-Natal, where he is also Cluster Leader for the Education Studies Academic Cluster. The scope of his work falls within the wider area of Gender and Education, with his primary focus being on same-sex desire and schooling. Thabo has published research in South African and international journals and books.

Mvu Ngcoya is a senior lecturer in the Development Studies programme at the University of KwaZulu-Natal. Thanks to his background in International Relations (IR), he has a strong interest in decolonial methodologies in international relations. Thus his current research examines subjugated knowledge (for example ubuntu) and thinkers in the discipline of IR. He is currently working on a project on the relevance of Frantz Fanon in international relations.

Stephanie Rudwick received her M.A. in social anthropology from Ludwig-Maximilians University, Munich and her Ph.D. in Linguistics from the University of KwaZulu-Natal. She currently holds a research position at the *Afrikanistik* Institute at Leipzig University, funded by the German Research Foundation (DFG). Stephanie has published on a wide range of ethnolinguistic and socio-anthropological topics. Most recently, her main research interest has shifted towards the theme of language and ethnicity in South African higher education.

Vilém Řehák graduated from African Studies, Political Science, and International Relations at Charles University in Prague. Currently he is a Ph.D. student at the Department of International Relations, Faculty of Social Sciences, Charles University in Prague. His main research interest lies in the modern history of Africa, particularly with respect to economic integration, trade regimes in sub-Saharan Africa, and the position of Africa in the global economy and multilateral trade negotiations.

Hana Synková is a lecturer in social anthropology at the University of Pardubice, Czech Republic. Her research focuses on strategies of survival of NGOs that work with Roma, professionalisation of social work and legitimisation struggles about access to social work profession. She gained her Ph.D. at the Institute of Ethnology at Charles University in Prague. She also coordinates applied research on state and municipal social policies and situation of marginalised, predominantly Romani, groups at the Agency for Social Inclusion within the Office of the Government of the Czech Republic.

Kateřina Werkman, Ph.D. is a lecturer in International Relations at the Faculty of Social Sciences at Charles University in Prague. She teaches and researches on the fields of Transitional Justice, Post-Conflict Reconstruction and Security in African contexts. Most of her recent projects focused on the reconciliation process in Sierra Leone and on the role of 'local' practices and techniques of reconciliation and reintegration in transitional justice in Africa.

Introduction: Rethinking and revising post-transitional South Africa and Czech Republic

Hana Horáková and Stephanie Rudwick

Introduction

Drawing comparisons between the Czech Republic and South Africa, two apparently different countries in terms of history, geopolitical position, political and social development, demography, etc. is an uncommon task. It is not surprising that there have been very few comparative studies of the two countries so far. Some achievements in this respect include Amselle's (1992) text written for the conference *The relationship between state and civil society in eastern Europe and Africa held at Bellagio,* Italy (February 1990); Van Beck's (1995) proceedings from the Polish-South African symposium organised in Pretoria by the Human Sciences Research Council; and (2005b) volume *Negotiated Revolutions: The Czech Republic, South Africa and Chile* focusing on the study of radical political and socio-economic change, presenting a comparative analysis of three transformations from authoritarian rule to market democracy. This book is a kind of follow-up of Skalník's edited volume *Transition to Democracy: Czech Republic and South Africa Compared* published in 1999. Why, some readers may wonder, have we decided to tackle this comparative study again, almost fifteen years after the first comparative volume on the two countries was published? The answer is simple: Because we are convinced, that central issues of South African and Czech liberal democracy, after twenty, twenty-five years respectively, should be "revisited, reviewed and, where necessary, revised" (Alexander 2012: 1). Also, our volume differs in at least three important features from that of Skalník.

First, the scope of time is different. While Skalník's book focused on the very process of transition from authoritarian to democratic social orders, covering five to ten years of the 1990s, our focus is more comprehensive and more current. Although a number of chapters discuss issues that were prevalent during the respective oppressive regimes, they all primarily focus on the developments of the past two decades.

Second, we seek to cover a broader perspective on the two young democracies. While Skalník's volume features merely five contributions, our volume includes ten chapters and presents a significantly wider and inter-disciplinary scope of analysis. Some issues addressed here, such as gender and language, find no mention in the previous volume. Additionally all, except two chapters in this volume include perspectives on both countries rather than the single perspective articles in Skalník's volume.

A third and important difference between Skalník's work and ours is the nature and positions of our contributors. While in Skalník's book all five scholars are established scholars in their respective research areas, our volume comprises a few contributors who can count their chapter as a first publication. Although established scholars wrote most of the chapters, there are some that constitute post-doctorate work and one that is written by a post-graduate student.

Conceptual framework

Our concern is to examine some aspects of the large-scale processes of socio-economic and political change of the two 'young' democratic societies, the South African postapartheid[1] state and the postsocialist Czech Republic under a common rubric but within the context of global developments. The political transition in both countries coincided with the intensified effects of globalisation, especially with the advent (and the immediate hegemony) of neoliberal economic ideologies and policies (Wood 2006) that further implicated political organisation, all manners of social institutions, systems of meaning, as well as issues of social homogeneity, individuation, and inequality (Verdery 1996: 230). The hegemony of neoliberal thinking and practice affects even seemingly distant realms of social reality, such as the newly contested issues concerning state, territory, citizenship, nation, property, and democracy. Neoliberalism is a "pervasive form of political rationality whose formal and 'global' character is allowing it to enter into novel relationships with diverse value orientations and political positions" (Collier and Ong 2005: 17).

The transformation processes, both in South Africa and the Czech Republic, bear the mark of global developments and conditions and they are not reducible to internal social or cultural determinations. The advent of the 'new world order' (after the neoliberal turn) in the early 1990s, characterised by the complex web of interconnectedness of ideology and practice, meant limited sovereignty of national polities moulded by subnational and supranational bodies. The ability of governments to set policy has been diminished through the growing strength of both transnational institutions such as the European Union (EU) and International Financial Institutions

---

[1]We purposely drop the commonly employed hyphen between 'post-apartheid' and 'post-socialist' in order to emphasize that the previous orders continue to be part of the current states and in order to stress the continuous repercussions of apartheid and socialism.

(IFIs), and through the operation of the international financial services sector (Wood 2006). Neoliberalism as an epochal shift in relations among capital, labour, consumption and place has transformed the relationship between state and economy so that at present it is the market (economy) that becomes the organising and regulative principle underlying the state (Comaroff and Comaroff 2008). The results – widening disparities of wealth, exacerbated by mass unemployment and social protests – are being felt, albeit in varying degrees, among the citizens of both countries, South Africa and the Czech Republic.

As both countries continue participating in the dynamics of an expansive political and economic order that is essentially internationalist in character (Thomas 2009: 203), there are many reasons to believe that we can regard both cases as part of a common (transnational, transitive) 'post-ish' development. Our interest is driven by the desire to describe and analyse the particular place(s) South Africa and the Czech Republic occupy in this context and we aim to interrogate which particular issues they face in the dual processes of internationalisation and globalisation. So far, both transitions under study represent more an attempt to catch up with the 'mature' democracies than to embark on a totally new form of governance. At the same time, the changes in the two countries did represent a partial contesting of the existing international economic order (Wood 2006; Lawson 2005b) and this ambivalence is reflected in our conceptual framework.

The relationship between globalisation, postcolonialism/postapartheid and postsocialism is extremely complex and in flux. The process of social change is one of continuity, incremental development, hybridisation and rupture (Boyer 2006). Although both countries rejected the preceding political orders, the long afterlife of the repercussions of the previous orders paradoxically keeps them alive. Noteworthy, the common linear model of 'transition' from a previous order to a firm endpoint does apply nicely to neither the postsocialist, nor the postapartheid state. Our understanding of 'transition' as neither a complete break with the past, nor a predictable historical process is a counterpoint to the perspective of transitology (Hörschelmann and Stenning 2008: 345). Accordingly, we try to avoid the general framework of 'transitology' according to which comparison ranks different post-countries along externally derived and allegedly universal metrics of, for instance, freedom, corruption, marketisation, or the development of civil society (Lawson 2005a, b). The transition concept presupposes standardisation of social values, representations and practices and it ultimately denies the concept of 'multiple modernities' (Eisenstadt 2002). Moreover, the emphasis on unilineality of a process is deeply ethnocentric by nature as it is based on the assumption that the Western transitional model is the only option, and also the best possible one. This notion of transition implies a theory of deficit, in other words, both Czech and South African democracies are 'young' and 'unfinished' as they continue to lack important democratic values and virtues, organisational structures and the 'right' political culture. While there is some merit in this understanding, our approach is slightly different. To avoid the epistemological flaws of the deterministic and neo-evolutionist paradigm of 'transition' that was developed and upheld by Western social and political sciences (Giordano 2009: 299), our volume prefers a more ethnographic approach and broader contextualising of the topic. By challenging, in particular the idea that only one 'road' leads to development, we want to show the various multi-linear responses to global challenges exercised by the societies under study. Our focus is on the processes and meanings of postsocialist and postapartheid transformation as it is lived, experienced and negotiated on a grassroots level every day.

Commonalities and differences

There is neither a single set of unique conditions nor a shared model in terms of which the processes of democratisation in South Africa and the Czech Republic could possibly be compared (Wood 2006: 241; Coetzee 1999: 21). This does not imply, however, that certain links and similarities do not exist. The Czech Republic and South Africa exhibit a number of common features and parallel developments in their respective transitions and post-developments. In both countries the regime transitions occurred when the dissolution of the old political structure took place and a new political dispensation was established. Transformations from authoritarian (South African case) and totalitarian (Czech case) rule triggered by the end of apartheid in South Africa, and the collapse of state socialism in the Czech Republic, happened approximately at the same time – towards the end of the 1980s and beginning of the 1990s, and in both countries these transformations occurred peaceful.

Both countries are 'young democracies', though no more teenagers (cf. Shapiro and Tebeau 2012b). During the Velvet Revolution in November 1989 the slogan "We are not like them" was widely popularised, implying that people wanted to say that they are not like the communists. It was an attempt by the population to separate themselves from the former oppressors without reprisal. Following the 'velvet divorce' in January 1993 (Musil 1995), Czechoslovakia split into two independent countries, the Czech Republic and Slovakia. In South Africa, Fredrik W. de Klerk in 1989, the 'South African Gorbachev', largely precipitated the change of regime. The new order had its decisive moment in the first competitive and fair elections (Wood 2006: 238) and in 1994 the first 'multiracial' national election took place in South Africa and brought the African National Congress (ANC) under the leadership of Nelson Mandela to power. The international community widely endorsed the regime changes in South Africa and the Czech Republic. While South Africa was described as a "text-book case of well-crafted transition" (Jung and Shapiro 1995: 269–308) and the process of change widely hailed as a "small miracle", the Czech Velvet Revolution was also positively evaluated particularly for its peaceful, non-violent character.

Negotiated revolution

Transitions from authoritarian rule to multi-party democracy are open-ended and assume many different forms. The transitions that took place in the two countries took the form of negotiated revolutions (Lawson 2005a, b).[2] As for the Czech Republic, the term is used in a 'maximum' sense because of the systemic transformation of its principal political, economic and social institutions since 1989, as opposed to the label 'minimum' transformation in the South African case, which indicates the continuity of some of the structures inherited from the apartheid regime, in particular economic institutions (Lawson 2005a: 477). In South Africa, a negotiated revolution/transition meant that the security of tenure was ensured for the white-dominated bureaucracy (Coetzee 1999: 23).

The inherent open-endedness and complexity of the transformation processes in the Czech Republic and South Africa is acknowledged by the scholarly use of multiple labels for these young democracies today. Proponents of the unilineal character of democratisation processes claim that both regime transitions have not led to 'full democracy', to not (yet) standard democracies of the Western type. Other scholars assert that the protection of the interests of some members of the society and the pact between the adversarial elites of the previous and the current regimes, has led to a kind of "limited democracy" (Coetzee 1999: 22).

South African democracy has been labelled as an "awkward democracy" (Giliomee 1996), as well as an "uncommon democracy" (Pempel 1990). One of the many reasons behind this 'awkwardness' of South Africa's democracy is that South African politics continue to constitute racial politics. Most South

---

[2]The phrase "negotiated revolution" was initially used in a book edited by Heribert Adam and Kogila Moodley (1993). It was further popularised in South Africa by Allister Sparks (1995), who used it as the subtitle of his investigation into the secret talks between the apartheid regime and ANC leaders prior to the release of Nelson Mandela in 1990.

Africans vote along ethnic or racial lines and the country continues to be
segregated along racial lines. Thus, the possibility of political change in terms
of alternatives to the ANC is rather minimal (Skalník 1999: 12).[3] One of the
negotiated revolution's objectives is the establishing of a mechanism that
deals with the injustices of the old order. The Truth commissions into past
violence (also see Werkman's chapter in this volume), often drawing on
a human rights model, are set up not only to confirm the authority and
legitimacy of the incoming regime but also to provide an institution for
people's sense of outrage and thirst for revenge (Lawson 2005a). The
character and the outcomes of these truth commissions confirm the essentially
ambivalent nature of negotiated transitions. On the surface, it appears that
South Africa found a better way to deal with the past by introducing the
concepts of self-reflection, reconciliation and healing. Nelson Mandela's
reconciliatory and integrative policy was instrumental in setting up a truth
commission which was viewed as a valuable symbolic tool representing the
birth of a new nation. The Truth and Reconciliation Commission (TRC)
established in 1995 with the aim to, non-violently, "put the past behind" (Ross
2008: 244) was met, on the one hand, with vast societal approval, and, on the
other hand, with harsh criticism on the other that revolved around the
argument that there is a fundamental difference between the Commission's
'truth' and the many other 'truths' that circulate in local discourses (ibid.).
By 1999, the TRC came to an end with expected controversial results that
provoked further disapproving reactions. While many white South Africans
consider the efforts of the TRC to be manipulated and unfair, some Africans
are convinced that an apology does not suffice (Hulec 1999: 52). The outcome
was, according to many critics, messy and violent, initiating a new wave of
investigation into the apartheid years, this time by using 'standard' judicial
institutions as well as international law (Ross 2008).

In the Czech Republic a political and public discourse of 'break' or 'thick
line' between the present and the past has characterised the process of
reconciliation. Coming to terms with the totalitarian past was also modelled
along the Velvet Revolution's rallying cry: "We are not like them"; the other
being the former communist bosses (Hulec 1999: 54). The outcome was as
uncertain and limited as is the South African case; the largely ineffective
political redress of past wrongdoings was being addressed both judicially and
by a public institution. The former was embodied by the law based on
lustrace,[4] which has, however, failed to provide a sense of resolution between

---

[3]There are of course, exceptions to this, such as the large number of coloured people in the
Western Cape who voted for the New National Party in the first democratic elections.

the autocratic past and a democratic future (Williams 2003; Lawson 2005a: 487). The latter was the Office for Documenting and Investigating the Crimes of Communism (ÚDV), which was established in 1995. Similarly to the TRC, the office did and continues not to have any legal powers and thus cannot punish the offenders by law. The Czech justice follows suit – so far, only a sporadic number of political proceedings have taken place; only one political crime was punished (the communist prosecutor who contributed to sentence Dr. Milada Horáková to death[5]). The offenders who collaborated with the Soviet occupiers of 1968 and who even requested the former Soviet Union to order its army to take steps against Dubček's leadership have not been punished to this day. A copy of the 'letter of invitation' kept in Russian archives is presently in the hands of Czech judges (Hulec 1999: 57). Many Secret Police investigators and warders have never been sentenced. There has not been sufficient political will in this respect – and until now, there is scarcely any public demand for reconciling with the past in the Czech Republic.[6]

Double transitions

Both countries have dealt and continue to deal with the predicament of 'double transitions' (Wood 2006; Boyer 2000). The pronouncement of the neoliberal model of market economy brought about the 'trauma' of the transitions (Weiss 2003). The central contradiction lies in the interconnectedness between the political and the economic spheres after the neoliberal turn. Citizens' degrees of satisfaction with democracy depend on their economic success (Weiss 2003). The social change that characterised the political democratisation in the late 1980s and early 1990s brought to light a dichotomy. On the one hand, political democratisation brought the benefits positively endorsed by the citizens, such as freedom of political expression and participation, human rights, etc. On the other hand, the effects of neoliberal reforms triggered large-scale job losses, the decline of agriculture and industry, and a subsequent lack of social cohesion marked by increased social inequality and accompanied by social unrest, xenophobia and racism. The contradictory effects of 'double transition' imply that political freedom

---

[4]*Lustrace* implies the laws accepted in some post-communist countries that ban the former power elites to espouse chosen posts in public administration and armed forces.
[5]Dr. Milada Horáková was a Czech politician executed during the communist political processes of the 1950s for alleged conspiracy and treason.
[6]Quite the opposite is the case: Current polls show people's inclination to tolerate the Communist Party and a fairly stable percentage of people (11 to 15 percent) gives Communists their vote in general elections (http://www.stem.cz/clanek/2970).

has often coincided with persistent economic volatility and social inequality (Wood 2006). This assessment holds true, at least to some extent, for both countries under study. However, in South Africa, the persistent racial division of wealth, unemployment, and social unrest are significantly more pronounced than in the Czech Republic. Socio-economic disparity is somewhat less palpable in the Czech Republic due to the less starkly lop-sided wage distribution (Wood 2006). Yet, a significant racial dimension of the socio-economic disparity is evident with Roma people who are at the bottom of the socio-economic ladder.

In both countries the Janus-face of the transition revealing highly contentious aspects of the political and economic transformation has fully come to light during the second decade characterised by a great deal of disillusionment and pessimism in Czech and South African society. More and more sectors of populations have realised that the movement towards change was not as smooth and inevitable as predicted by the postsocialist and postapartheid power elites. Democratisation seems to remain an unfinished business in South Africa (Bell and Ntsebeza 2003), but also in the Czech Republic. In the past decade, both societies had to deal with a fundamental change in public moods. During the first ten years of democracy, political narratives exuded optimism that was largely shared with the broader public. However, as the overall situation has worsened, signs of a transition from an 'age of hope' to an 'age of uncertainty' are reported (Roberts et al. 2010: 1). A lot of the hope and enthusiasm that accompanied the birth of the two democracies has now evaporated.

The shift from the age of hope to the age of uncertainty is apparent from the use of keywords and key concepts that have become central to public and political discourses in postapartheid South Africa and post-November 1989 Czech Republic. They largely reflect the current socio-economic develop-ment in both societies. However, they also represent some 'troubling' continuities between the apartheid/socialist and postapartheid/ postsocialist periods. Due to the different historical and socio-political trajectories, the keywords may bear different meanings, not only between the Czech and South African case but also within the individual historical trajectories. For instance, the concept of 'development' used under apartheid assumes a new meaning in the new South Africa (also, see Ngcoya's chapter in this volume). Together with Shepherd and Stevens who edited *New South African Key-words* (2008) one can ask how 'new' the new South Africa is, which continuities with the former apartheid regime persisted, and what actually has changed.

Questioning the nature of socio-political change is equally pertinent for

Czech society that too underwent a profound change regarding the understanding of key terminologies and concepts. In the 1990s, keywords such as 'civil society', 'democracy', and 'return to Europe' were prevalent. The 1990s political and public discourse of the 'return to Europe' favoured rapid access to the EU – emphasis was put on a free market, privatisation, democracy, and smoother enforcement of the rule of law and human rights. As the Czech economy has spawned new socio-economic classes, the *nouveau riche*, the new poor, businessmen, and the unemployed (Esparza 2010: 418), the current discourse is replete with notions such as 'corruption', 'social security and social welfare state', 'socio-economic inequality' and the 'un-adaptable', which is a label for Roma people in public discourse, among others. Dominant topics of the internal politics and public life revolve around affairs such as a reform of the public health system, tax reform or corruption cases.

The feeling that "nothing is as it was expected to be" (Verdery 1996: 219) is exacerbated by apparent discontinuities and unexpected developments since the fall of apartheid and state socialism. They are associated with concerns about mounting violent crime (exclusively in South Africa), increasing unemployment and persistent poverty as well as with widespread corruption. The erosion of trust in public institutions and political actors and their disability to deliver on expectations, as well as increasing social and racial polarisation has been reported in South Africa (Kagwanja 2009), and the Czech Republic. Also, in South Africa, the most unexpected postapartheid development was linked to the HIV-AIDS pandemic which experienced a steep rise in the 1990s, from less than one percent infection rate in 1990, to 22.8 percent in 1998. By 2000 the country had the highest number of HIV infected people in the world (Marks 2002, cited in Posel 2008: 21). South Africa's controversy around HIV/AIDS during the late 1990s, captured by Thabo Mbeki's lead 'AIDS denialism' deeply affected the country. The reason of the AIDS epidemic lay, according to the 'denialists', in the debilitating effects of poverty on the body's immune system, not in the common explanation of AIDS as a primarily sexually transmitted disease. In order to explain the controversy and reveal why the AIDS pandemic became a matter of heated political debates, Posel (2008) refers to the symbolic politics of Thabo Mbeki's governance between 1999 and 2008. Accordingly, Mbeki's concept of the 'African Renaissance' created the ethos that South Africa's moral regeneration could not have been contaminated by the conviction, that AIDS, being primarily of heterosexual type in South Africa, could have anything to do with South African 'culture' or morality. By replacing the centrality of sex in the epidemic with poverty, Mbeki strove to represent South

Africa as an essentially moral site, negatively affected by poverty as a legacy of colonialism and apartheid.

The second largest unexpected development in postapartheid South Africa is linked to crime. After 1994, irrespective of Mandela's own example of non-vengeance and his dedication to national reconciliation, there was a massive rise in crime on all levels; crime was becoming more violent with murder, armed robbery, car hijacks, and rape. South Africa has been crowned as the "rape capital of the world" (Coetzee 1999: 38). For the first time in the history of the country, violent crime reached white suburbs. Many whites believed that crime represents a "toxic expression of vengeance", though the statistics did not pin down whites as primary crime victims (Steinberg 2008: 27). Crudely expressed, while 1 in 9 South Africans is white, 32 out of 33 murder victims are non-whites (ibid.). Violent forms of crime are primarily associated with South African townships and rural 'shanty-towns' where most of the poor live.

The decline of post-revolutionary enthusiasm, replaced by disillusionment and lost expectations is equally experienced in the present-day Czech Republic. It can be traced back to the so-called Opposition treaty between the Civic Democratic Party (ODS) and the Czech Social Democratic Party (ČSSD) between 1998 and 2002. This highly pragmatic, even cynical, treaty allowed the ČSSD minority government to rule within the limits set by the ODS (Skalník 2009: 241). It brought the vast abuse of power by the politicians who adopted laws that enabled them to gain access to financial packages. The widespread embezzlement and corruption reinforced the infamous communist slogan "the one who does not steal, robs from his/her family" (Skalník 2009). In response to the negative impact of the Opposition treaty on Czech society, the then president Václav Havel warned that Czech society developed a "mafia-like concept of capitalism" (Havel 2002). In his famous speech he spoke about the "political jungle of post-communism" in which the new power bloc of politicians and managers were like parasites on the state. The social democratic minority government that came to power after the Opposition treaty followed suit. Nosál (2004) added that the new political class (the post-communist ruling elite) emerged from three basic elements – the managerial elite, the politicians and a section of the humanist intelligentsia.

In the Czech Republic, the development after the end of the Opposition treaty in 2002 witnessed a number of elections, yielding both standard (right-and left-wing), and premature and clerical (caretaker) governments; a change in presidency from Havel to Klaus. Havel's death in December 2011 was experienced as a great loss, both inside and outside the country. There was an emergence of new short-lived political parties and movements, a deterioration of the economic situation due to the global recession, and a contestation over the nature of the socialist past, particularly the 'really existing socialism' of the 1970s and 80s. By and large, the widespread anti-communist climate of the 1990s has now turned into the relativist discourse that even challenges the view of the communist regime as totalitarian. In the media, public sphere and politics, there are numerous examples. One such illustrative example is the collapse of the Institute for the Study of Totalitarian Regimes' scientific committee and it substitution with people who reject to call the 1980s the totalitarian regime. The contempt over the powerful slogan of the 1990s – 'invisible hand of the market' – triggered by widespread corruption, brought about scepticism towards the enforcement of law, and lack of trust in public institutions. First, people tended to set up a contrast with the form of government under socialism and blame the current politicians whose ruling practices were sometimes found similar, or even worse, to those of socialism's state. Second, as the economic situation continues to deteriorate for many people, appeals to paternalist state are more vociferous, particularly among the poor segments of the population. Recent surveys show that about a third of the Czech population is against the contemporary regime, favouring security to freedom. Overall public resentment has led to the upsurge of public protests, the communist re-entry into regional politics, the emergence of populist political formations or quasi-parties such as VV (Public Affairs), LIDEM (People's Democracy), and many others. Newly emerging social protest movements and institutions demand socio-economic equality, a large social welfare state, and direct democracy.

One of the events of the 2000s that looms over others is the accession of the Czech Republic into the European Union in 2004. The need to access the EU modelled along the slogan 'A Return to Europe' was first articulated by Václav Havel in the 1990s. As Esparza (2010) explains, Havel emphasised the democratic values of the EU – of the 'West' and the 'Euro-Atlantic area' freedom and respect for human rights. Europe and the EU were presented as positive Other; the prospect of joining the EU was perceived as the engine of democratisation and transformation. For Václav Klaus, who became president in February 2003, the perceptions and attitudes towards the EU were quite different, 'Eurorealistic', as he himself prefers to term it (Esparza 2010: 422). Though he signed the application form of the Czech Republic to the EU, he opposed the processes of increasing political integration of the EU embodied by the EU Constitution and the Lisbon Treaty. Irrespective of the differing ways of imagining the EU represented by two leading politicians – Havel and Klaus, the majority of the Czech population held positive attitudes to the EU. In the EU referendum of 2003, 77 percent voted in favour of the Czech

Republic's accession to the EU. Still in 2007, 61 percent of Czechs believed that the EU was more positive than negative (Eurobarometer 67). However, after the advent of global recession in 2008 which brought a decline in the Czech economy, accompanied by the decrease in the standard of living for many citizens, the attitudes towards the EU started to change quite significantly. Data taken from Eurobarometer (EB79.5) indicate a downward trend in the loyalty towards the EU – to only 38 percent in 2012 to even less 34 percent in 2013. The Czech membership in the EU is positively endorsed only by 31 percent of Czech citizens. Data confirming the extremely low participation in the EU elections held in May 2014 only support these trends. The turnout dropped to a record low of 18.2 percent, confirming that the attitudes towards the EU are largely of 'indifferent' nature.

When reviewing the post-transition period in South Africa, an insight into the relative successes of the country's first democratic government must be contrasted with the more pessimistic second phase of South African democracy that brought a whole host of disappointments: lingering poverty, ever increasing socio-economic inequality, slow pace of economy, high unemployment rate,[7] enormous levels of corruption; the HIV/AIDS pandemic, high rates of violent crime and the failures in local infrastructure and service delivery. Economic growth in South Africa has only marginally improved racial inequalities and the public service transformation has been uneven which contributes to South Africa's transition being seen as "still incomplete" (Wood 2006: 237). The widespread disillusionment with the postapartheid period manifested itself in the wave of mass protests and violent demonstrations against poor delivery failure, food price inflation and the cost of living. Turbulent forces that erupted over the decade of the 2000s saw the emergence of new urban-based oppositional social movements such as the Anti-Privatisation Forum, or the Landless Peoples' Movement, which was launched in 2001 in Johannesburg to fight against the slow pace of land reform embedded in the frame of a 'willing buyer, willing seller' (Hart 2013). They opposed the rising costs of basic services (Hart 2013: 31). Expressions of popular discontent take shape in service delivery protests which erupted after the national election in April 2004 and by now represent a feature of everyday life in black townships and shack settlements (Hart 2013). There was a sharp increase, from ten events in 2004, to 173 in 2012 (Municipal IQ, Hotspots Monitor, June 2013). Expressions of popular discontent in the 2000s were accompanied by the shift in official discourses and practices, from structural

---

[7]Unemployment rate in South Africa increased to 25.20 percent in the first quarter of 2014 from 24.10 percent in the fourth quarter of 2013 (Statistics South Africa 2014).

adjustment in the first phase of the postapartheid era (1994–2000) to 'pro-poor' and 'development' discourse (Hart 2013: 4). Pro-poor measures, however, are inflaming the popular anger they were designed to contain (Hart 2013: 22).

The gap between citizens and the political elite has deepened and brought new issues of political accountability and legitimacy to the forefront of public debate. The public is disgusted by the widespread corruption occurring at all levels of public administration. Though on paper, South African can boast of impressive anticorruption legislation, in practice, the law functions fairly ineffectively. South African legislature has not been able to resolve several high-profile corruption scandals, including the arms deal and Travelgate scandals (Camerer 2012). At present, the most serious scandal, provoking public outrage, deals with the abuse of public money for the reconstruction of Jacob Zuma's private home in Nkandla. Widespread disenchantment of people from politics has resulted in substantial changes in the political life. The major change concerns the credibility of the 'traditional', established political parties. Politics in terms of representative democracy seems to become repulsive for the Czech constituency. A clerical, caretaker form of government is most valued, while politicians are viewed as spurious. A desire for 'unpolitical politics'[8] and the Janus-face of the transition have paved way for the emergence of populist and extremist political formations and movements (often led by celebrity figures – wealthy entrepreneurs, such as Andrej Babiš or Tomio Okamura in the Czech Republic) which have entered the political arena with the aim of winning the votes of those who have been disappointed by the policies of the established political actors such as the ANC in South Africa, and ODS and ČSSD in the Czech Republic. In South Africa, these new formations include the Congress of the People (COPE), the civic movement AGANG led by Mamphela Ramphele and the Economic Freedom Fighters (EFF) led by Julius Malema. In the Czech Republic, these new parties include ANO (lit. translated 'YES') and ÚSVIT (Dawn) which are both led by successful and socio-economically powerful entrepreneurs, who make appeal to a return of morals into politics while distancing themselves from the hitherto widespread immoralities in governance (Skalník, an unpublished paper). The passive political behaviour of the Czech constituency contrasts with the success of the ANO movement which has witnessed a remarkable increase in votes. The movement even won the European election in 2014. Furthermore, Czech extreme populist politics exemplified by Tomio Okamura express overt racial politics particularly towards the most

---

[8]Havel thought that leaders should be intellectuals instead.

significant Other; that is Roma who are blamed for their own bad economic situation and social exclusion. South African populist politics is embodied by Julius Malema's EEF who demands 'economic freedom in our lifetime' – nationalisation of the mines and expropriation without compensation of land 'stolen by whites'. The rise of populist politics in South Africa in the first decade of the new millennium went hand in hand with proliferating expressions of nationalism (Hart 2013: 4). The ANC-led multiple efforts to produce the postapartheid 'nation' have shifted from Mandela's reconciliatory discourse of the rainbow nation, over Mbeki's African Renaissance to the 'Fortress South Africa' that is highly exclusivist and more and more racialized (see Horáková's chapter in this book).

Review

It is nonetheless our contention, that by reflecting on the past twenty, twenty-five years respectively, one can credit the new South Africa and postsocialist Czech Republic with many diverse achievements.

South Africa is viewed as one of the most fundamentally transforming societies in modern times (Sparks 2003: 96). Despite the history of apartheid and inherited socio-economic inequality, its progress toward democracy is remarkable (Shapiro and Tebeau 2012). The country has witnessed major achievements in South Africa's macroeconomic governance and performance since 1994 (Aron 2012). Millions of people gained access to clean water and electricity. Between 1996 and 2010 the proportion of people living on less than $2 a day fell from 12 to 5 percent (South Africa: Over the rainbow 2012). The racist legislation of apartheid is abolished, and all major democratic institutions have been successfully installed, at least on paper. The South African Constitution of 1996 is hailed as one of the most liberal constitutions in the world.

Among the other Central and East European (CEE) countries, the Czech Republic showed the strongest orientation towards the 'Western model' of social and economic organisation (Weiss 2003). Postsocialist change was viewed as a one-way process of transition (Hörschelmann 2002). In this logic, the Czech Republic belonged to the 'successful' CEE countries, together with Hungary, Slovakia, Poland and Slovenia (Hann 2002). In the first stage of the transformation, the Czech Republic served as a prime example of a post-communist country where 'democracy' and 'capitalism' coexisted in relative harmony yielding political stability and sustained economic growth (Bunce 1999).

The second stage of transformation however confirmed Burawoy and

Verdery's assumption (1999) that the postsocialist transition is not a single prescribed road to an objective phase of Western-style capitalism. It is an uncertain process enmeshing new rights and rules with old values and interests. Hence, general feelings of uncertainty and disillusionment tend to be a distinctive feature of any wide-ranging process of transition. In the Czech Republic, the process revealed the complexity and conflictual nature of societal transformations, yielding ambivalent assessments by the population. For some people, postsocialism is a time of uncertainty, rapid transformation, economic anxiety, and instability. In Czech public discourse people tend to stress the negative sides of transformation, such as sharp social and economic rifts, massive unemployment, austerity measures, a diminishing welfare state, insecurity and ubiquitous corruption. For others, however, postsocialism continues to fulfil dreams as a result of political and economic freedom.

Though South Africa is a relatively successful example of conflict resolution (mainly due to Nelson Mandela's reconciliatory and integrative politics), it is still a fragile democracy and significant drawbacks are apparent throughout all layers of social landscape. After many years of poor economic policy, South Africa has lost its position as sub-Saharan Africa's largest economy. One of the most pertinent reasons is the 25 percent unemployment rate – one of the highest in the world, coupled with a dysfunctional education system and skills shortage.

The postsocialist and postapartheid condition shows a wide array of similar features. Arrival of political and economic freedom made space for opportunists and in the case of the Czech Republic, interconnection between politics and business means that the business community seeks political patronage and is thus closely tied up with the state, especially with the two biggest political parties: ODS and ČSSD. In the new South Africa, the new class is termed 'tenderpreneurs', that is a class created by the ANC that gets state contracts using their connections in government. A rise in lawlessness, embezzlement and corruption resulted in substantial public dissatisfaction with the performance of political leaders and the newly created political and economic institutions (Bunce 1999). In both countries, there is a lack of accountability and political legitimacy and this is mirrored by increasing disrespect for politicians and their parties.

Accelerating social differentiation and fragmentation processes have given rise to new hierarchies, new identities, and new inequalities. This is also the case in both South Africa and the Czech Republic. In the latter case, new types of cleavages are being formed under postsocialism. While in the socialist period fragmentation went along the main fissure between the party elite (Them) and the masses (Us),[9] the postsocialist period is marked by the new dichotomies between Us, ordinary people and Them represented diversely by corrupt politicians, managers of foreign companies/large corporations/parastatals and dubious entrepreneurs, the EU as the new 'outside' Other, and Roma people as the most significant domestic Other. Czech society, while opening to the world witnesses the re-emergence of racist thought and practices, primarily directed towards Roma people, but also towards Vietnamese or Muslims.

According to Hart (2013), key markers of postapartheid South Africa in the new millennium are: coercive rule of the postapartheid state; a rise of new social movements representing expressions of popular discontent towards the ANC; and the emergence of so-called service delivery protests. The first marker can be exemplified by the Marikana massacre. In August 2012 police shot dead 34 miners on strike at the platinum mine near Marikana in the North West province. The second and third aspects are associated with the ANC government's failure to significantly redress the extreme levels of poverty and inequality in South Africa perpetuated by high unemployment rates and a low quality educational system (Seekings 2012). The gap between the rich and the poor is widening. After twenty years of democracy, South Africa has one of the most unequal societies in the world. As a result, support for the democratic regime is relatively weak (Mattes 2012). Scholars point to the decline of trust in public and state institutions as well as in the 'traditional' political parties (Kagwanja 2009). Yet, the ANC as the major political post-apartheid player which has been in power uninterruptedly since 1994 confirmed its victorious position in the latest national election of 2014 (62.15 percent) (2014 National and Provincial Election Results). The persistent support for the ANC is partly due to its liberation credentials and partly due to the way race continues to matter in South Africa. Poor black South Africans have benefited from social grants, the working class from the party's pro-labour stance and the power of the unions, and the middle and upper classes from its policy of Black Economic Empowerment (BEE) (South Africa: Over the rainbow 2012).

Despite the substantial electoral gain made by the biggest opposition party – the Democratic Alliance (DA), from almost 17 percent in 2009 to 22 percent in the general election of 2014 (2014 National and Provincial Election Results), there is little chance/hope for change. Hence, two decades after the demise of apartheid, South Africa remains a de facto one-party state.

---

[9]Such a differentiation was far from absolute. There were diverse ways to deal with this, through dissidence, informal networks, second economy, retreat into the private sphere, jokes, etc. (Sampson 2002).

Democratic scholars (e.g. Gumede 2014) warn against the danger in the lack of effective political opposition, necessary for ensuring a healthy democracy.

Legacies

Both countries are gravely afflicted by the legacies of the past – of the 'really-existing socialism', and of colonial and apartheid past – that co-determine the space available for transformation. The persistence of specific thought patterns and practices, organisational structures and social ties are essential features of these transitions.

One of the key factors that continue to inform the new South Africa is the legacy of the dichotomising of social identities, and their inherent race prejudice. Race thought has been a central element of the South African experience and it continues to be so (Maré 2005: 509). The transformation from apartheid to a supposedly non-racial society has not brought any substantial progress in this regard as most social categories are still starkly defined in racial terms (Shapiro and Tebeau 2012). Survey data suggest that younger South Africans who grew up in the postapartheid society, the so-called 'born-frees', do not significantly distinguish themselves in terms of racial intergroup relations from their older compatriots (Durrheim and Dixon 2010: 286). South Africa needs another kind of transformation that would lead to "freedom from race" (Mbembe 2008: 18). Racism has always been and continues to be an inseparable feature of South African society (Dubow 1995; Horáková 2011). Moreover, the past decade of transformation has witnessed a recrudescence of racism. Besides the continued white racism, new forms of racism are on the increase in the new in South Africa. 'Black racism' towards whites, especially among the members of the black new elite, who wield blackness like a weapon as they climb the ladder of privilege (Sparks 2003), and black racism towards the black immigrants from other African countries are continuously on the rise. Xenophobic practices have been reported as a common feature of life in postapartheid South Africa (Harris 2001; Neocosmos 2008, 2010).

Another point of comparison is that at present, the majority of people in both countries expect the government to provide solutions to problems of economic and social nature rather than taking initiatives themselves (Coetzee 1999: 33–4). South Africans and Czechs, quite alike, tend to expect the state to provide housing, education, health, security, etc. (Coetzee 1999: 32). In the Czech Republic, part of the communist legacy looms over the role of state in the economy. In the past, many Czechs got accustomed to the presence, subsidies, and interventions of socialism's paternalistic state (Verdery 1996).

Numerous social groups who profited from the 'really-existing socialism', including its inherent part, 'second economy',[10] now articulate their nostalgia for the past regime calling for a return of socialist egalitarianism and homo-genisation. The stable electoral gains of KSČM (and those left-wing political parties that 'promise to deliver') show that the ideology based on paternalist, protective and redistributive state is still alive. Most of the Czech population having been used to redistribution of material goods by the socialist state did not understand the building of an open society as its own responsibility (Skalník 1999: 14). Contestation takes place between socialist values of equality and welfare, the central symbols in socialist political discourse, and new notions of prosperity, individual initiative and success. The perseverance of values from before also determines a lack of active civil society that could interrogate the state, its legitimacy and accountability. As Mandel (2002: 282) rightly points out, the idea of civil society is to occupy a critical space *outside* the realm of the state, which was absolutely impossible under socialism – all social activities had been linked to the state ideology of socialism. The socialist state monopolised formal organisational activity with the attempt to direct and control cultural expressions for political purposes. Under socialism, initiatives from below were viewed as inappropriate, even dangerous. After 1989 there was a slow rise of civil society despite the assumption of some leading 'liberal' Czech politicians, including President Klaus, that civil society and grass-roots initiatives have no place in a representative democracy. The legacy of passive citizenry corresponds with the lack of confidence in the state and limited trust towards its institutions.

Trust between citizens and state is limited to those situations in which the citizen is authorised to gain personal benefits from the state (Giordano and Kostova 2002: 75). The state and its representatives are perceived as distant and alien. The disharmony between legality and legitimacy, and the precariousness of legal power contribute to the social production of mistrust (Giordano and Kostova 2002). South Africa's civil society has been more developed than its Czech counterpart, due to both the preservation of a 'Herrenvolk' democracy among whites, and the struggle of non-racial NGOs and trade unions against apartheid (Skalník 1999: 14). Under apartheid, diverse forms of anti-apartheid social protests took place; there were several instances of mobilisation against the apartheid regime. Many ended in blood-

---

[10]Profiting from socialism meant *inter alia* outwitting the state: through the theft of public (state) property and laxity in work discipline (Verdery 1996: 42). Second economy under socialism implied income-generating activities carried out by workers outside their formal jobs, while often using equipment, time, or physical premises of their formal jobs unofficially and/or illegally (ibid. 214).

shed such as Sharpeville in 1960, and the Soweto uprising of 1976. In the past it was possible to mobilise black people in South Africa around neatly demarcated campaigns such as human rights abuse, influx control, Bantu education, etc. Under postapartheid it is much more difficult to gain support around long-term ideals of democracy (Coetzee 1999: 37). Postapartheid 'voices of protest' (Ballard, Habib and Valodia 2006) are largely directed against (a) various local government policies, such as the GEAR (Growth, Employment and Redistribution) strategy; (b) local government's failures in meeting basic needs and addressing socio-economic rights, such as the Landless People's Movement and the Treatment Action Campaign; or (c) local, provincial and national governments' attempts to repress the existing socio-economic rights, such as the Soweto Electricity Crisis Committee of the Anti-Eviction Campaign (Ballard et al. 2006).

Chapter outline

The authors of this volume represent different academic disciplines: Economics, Sociology, Social Anthropology, Political Science, International Relations, Gender Studies and Linguistics. Accordingly, the chapters examine and analyse socio-political, socio-economic, cultural, gendered and linguistic aspects of the two countries on focus. Although not all authors have been in a position where they could compare and contrast the two young democracies most have tried to do exactly that. The two chapters that deal with Gender, i.e. Msibi and Ahari, are written only from a single country perspective, but on the basis of having read both chapters, the reader is able to compare some of the pertinent issues concerning women in both young democracies. Our aim, among other things, was to showcase work done by a new generation of scholars together with some more established authors, both in the Czech Republic and in South Africa. The chapters that follow are innovative, interdisciplinary and include a variety of different approaches to the main subject. This book provides some new insights to scholars who are interested in either one of the young democracies but it should be particularly valuable to scholars who have interests in both countries and appreciate the comparative perspective.

In the first chapter, **Mvu Ngcoya** looks at international aid behaviour of the two young democracies and thoroughly discusses the most significant trends in the development policies and practices of both countries over roughly the past two decades. His work shows that the Czech system has aimed to adapt the more traditional Development Assistance Committee (DAC) model while the South African model is founded on what he terms the Bandung model of development partnership. He concludes that despite great differences between the two countries, they both approach development aid in more sensitive ways than other donors because they are not only in a position of 'givers' but also of 'receivers'. However, he also warns that both countries need to transform their 'language of partnership' into something more than just window-dressing in order to avoid the "messianic complex and moral superiority that are at the heart of the development industry".

Vilém Řehák's study comprehensively discusses the political pheno- menon of new regionalism as a response of modern nation states to firstly, globalization and secondly, the deadlock in multilateral trade negotiations in the second chapter of this volume. While the first part of his chapter is theoretical, the second part is largely empirical and describes in great detail the economic transformation of post-communist Czechoslovakia/Czech Republic and post-apartheid South Africa within the framework of global economy. In the third part the author compares both countries along their role of regional trade agreements, and regionalism within the context of their respective economic transformations. Řehák ultimately argues that "although both countries pursued rather different goals, both used regionalism as their principal strategy when they searched for their place in the modern global governance system". The issue of regional and dichotomised identities are later also picked up by two other scholars, Synková and Werkman.

In the third chapter, **Hana Horáková** compares the nation-making processes in the two republics by examining issues of nationalism in postsocialist Czech Republic and postapartheid South Africa. She argues that attention needs to be paid to the deeper meaning of nationalist rhetoric constructed by the dominant political actors – the ANC and the Czech postsocialist political elite in order to find out how competing discourses of nationalism impact political and social transformation. Horáková argues that there has been a gradual shift from Mandela's initial vision of a non-racial society to new nationalisms, Afro-radicalism and extreme populism under the Zuma presidency. Similarly to some extent, new nationalistic, anti-EU discourse and practices are already latent in some sectors of Czech society and right-wing politics with racial undertones, particularly in the form of increasingly prevalent Roma xenophobia.

In the fourth chapter, **Hana Synková** discusses in great detail the socio- economic, political and cultural situation of Roma people in the Czech Republic by drawing some comparison to the discriminatory strategies of the apartheid government. She meticulously describes the primary discursive mechanisms used in politics and public dealings with Roma people in the previous Czechoslovakia and later in the Czech Republic. She argues, among other things, that in comparison to the historical development and institution-alisation of racism in South Africa, the discriminatory elements and racism behind Czech strategies towards Roma take on a more subliminal and concealed discursive form. However, its impact and effects are arguably no less humiliating for those affected.

The exploratory chapter by **Stephanie Rudwick** focuses on a specific ethno-linguistic dynamic in the two young democracies, i.e. that of the potential of a 'language of the oppressor'. She argues that language issues and socio-politics are intertwined in most countries and that both Russian and Afrikaans acquired negative stigmas during the respective oppressive regimes (Soviet-style communism vis-á-vis apartheid), albeit in different ways and with varying degrees. In South Africa, Afrikaans has widely been portrayed as a 'language of the oppressor' *par excellence*, but in socialist Czecho-slovakia, the status of Russian as the 'language of the oppressor' was not clear-cut, and more latent, covert and sublime. Rudwick describes the socio-historical background of the two languages in the respective countries and later hypothesises in how far language stigmas may persist to any degree in the young democracies. She ultimately argues that despite liberation and transition in both countries, there nonetheless persists a stigmatisation of both languages and their speakers, at least among a segment of the population. While the negative connotation with Afrikaans are much more overt in South Africa, there are also many Czech people who associate negative feelings with Russian.

Of course, both Czech and South African citizens suffered oppression in decade long regimes in most of the second half of the twentieth century. Hence, in chapter VI, **Kateřina Werkman** examines how the Czech Republic and South Africa have dealt with the legacy of communism and apartheid respectively. While she argues that the methodologies countries use in addressing the past depend largely on the specificities of the local context, she also aptly demonstrates that a number of general goals of transitional justice processes can be identified. Among those, are truth-telling and truth-finding, accountability and punishment, and victims' compensation. Although the Czech Republic and South Africa exhibit stark differences in the processes of transitional justice, there are also certain similarities. Werkman, for instance, argues that in South Africa as well as the Czech Republic, the instrumental use of collective identities based on dichotomous categories of 'us' (i.e. anti-communists/liberation/fighters/blacks) versus 'them' (i.e. communists/agents/perpetrators/ whites) are highly prevalent. These have roots in the past but continue to be successfully applied for mobilisation in the young democracies. Werkman concludes that "powered by present-day realities, such as the disillusionment with the results of transformation in the Czech Republic or worsening socio-economic conditions for the majority of the population in South Africa, these discourses contribute to the polarisation of the societies and are a reminder that the reckoning with the past is a long term process that is not quite finished yet".

There are two chapters dealing with Gender issues, the one by **Petra Ahari** focuses on the Czech Republic while the one focusing on South Africa is written by Thabo Msibi. Ahari examines how women's position as citizens and as workers has changed since the collapse of state socialism. Her central question is what precisely has changed for Czech women and what are the consequences of the political transition of 1989 in terms of the development of gender inequality? To find answers to this complex question, she focuses on three main themes, namely women's employment, remuneration and work-family-life balance and addresses these within a socio-historical framework. Her analysis suggests that although women's work force participation remains relatively high in the Czech Republic it is still characterised by horizontal and vertical job segregation which is also reflected in remuneration packages and responsibilities in the family. This means, among other things, that it continues to be necessary to increase the under-representation of women and men in occupations and men's domination of the highest status jobs. Ahari suggests that reducing the gender job segregation and discriminatory treatment in work places, and calling for wage transparency in companies along with gender neutral job classification should lead to a narrowing of the gender pay gap.

In his chapter on the position of women in South African **Thabo Msibi** focuses on the contrast between what is on paper (i.e. in the constitution) and what actually happens on the ground. More specifically, he closely examines the extent to which discourses that political leaders apply to women cohere with the official South African gender policies. He concludes that at a political level, traditional tactics of gender which undermine women take on more covert forms. Msibi demonstrates that such tactics are driven by the competing tension between constitutional democracy and traditional values, and that the political space offers much room for "spectacles and theatrics". He suggests that for radical transformation to occur within the South African's political space, focus has to shift away from developmental gender politics of representation, to politics of personal and structural transformation.

While on first sight, South Africa and the Czech Republic seem to have nothing in common when it comes to the pandemic of HIV/AIDS, **Júlia Lampášová** attempts to compare and contrast the two countries in the last chapter of this volume. Despite the stark differences in the percentage of

HIV/AIDS prevalence, both countries can claim to be examples of grassroots level engagement. Lampášová also interrogates whether the health security strategy in South Africa could be successfully applied to other countries outside the continent and comes to the conclusion that "the epidemiology patterns in sub-Saharan Africa are too specific to give researchers a chance to elaborate widely applicable measures of a global security strategy".

This volume shows that while the Czech Republic and South Africa are vastly different, there are also significant commonalities. There are certain themes and issues that are recurring throughout this volume, in particular in terms of identity politics. Several scholars (Horáková, Werkman, Synková, Řehák) have carved out that dichotomisation of local identities and the problematic development of radical politics at the point of disappointment with the 'new' political leadership. Horáková aptly demonstrates that xenophobia is prevalent in both countries, albeit with varying facets and constituents. There are also chapters (Rudwick, Ahari) that suggest that citizens of both countries continue to "grapple with the past" and the ongoing effects of apartheid and communism. We argue that the "ghost of the past" (Jansen 2002) continues to be present.

Conclusion

Transitions and transformations remain open-ended and contested processes that produce their own social systems, unprecedented in many respects (Illner 1996). Therefore it would be premature to predict any 'final' shape of the still young democracies the Czech Republic and South Africa constitute. Their transformations are 'unfinished' and their emerging societies defy any easy categorisation. While the fundamental socio-political changes in both countries on focus here have been extremely complex, it is also obvious that the democratisation process in both countries still has a long way to go.

A volume such as ours can never claim to be complete but we hope, at least, to offer diverse platforms on which South Africa and the Czech Republic are worth to be examined. The limitations are determined both by our own interests and disciplinary background, and by the selection of contributors. It has proved extremely difficult for us to find scholars with a 'double' expertise. Some of the authors offer perspectives on the societies from first-hand local observations that differ considerably from those written by authors of 'macro-scenarios' (Hannerz 2003: 174). While this volume cannot claim to be all encompassing, the contributions demonstrate both a wide and narrow focus on socio-political, cultural and linguistic dynamics in the Czech Republic and South Africa. We hope the book will offer a sufficient scope for understanding the current processes of transformation in the countries under study.

References

Adam, H. and K. Moodley (1993), *Negotiated Revolution: Society and Politics in Post-Apartheid South Africa*, Johannesburg: Jonathan Ball.

Alexander, N. (2012), After Apartheid: The Language Question, in: I. Shapiro and K. Tebeau (eds.), *After Apartheid: Reinventing South Africa?* Charlottesville and London: University of Virginia Press, pp. 311–332.

Amselle, J.-L. (1992), La corruption et le clientélisme au Mali et en Europe de l'Est. *Cahiers d'Etudes Africaines* XXXII, Vol. 4, pp. 629–942.

Aron, J. (2012), Macroeconomic Policy and Its Governance after Apartheid, in: I. Shapiro, and K. Tebeau (eds.), *After Apartheid: Reinventing South Africa?* Charlottesville and London: University of Virginia Press, pp. 136–178.

Ballard, R., A. Habib and I. Valodia (eds.) (2006), *Voices of Protest: Social Movements in Post-Apartheid South Africa*, Durban: University of KwaZulu-Natal Press.

Baptist, S. South Africa: Strike over, in: *Economist Intelligence Unit*, online: simonjbaptist.eiu.com (accessed 26.5.2014).

Bell, T. and D. B. Ntsebeza (2003), *Unfinished Business: South Africa, Apartheid and Truth,* Verso.

Boyer, R. (2000), The Great Transformation, in: B. Jessop (ed.), *Regulation Theory and the Crisis of Capitalism*, Volume 4: Country Studies, London: Edward Elger.

Boyer, R. (2006), How do Institutions Cohere and Change? in: P. James and G. Wood (eds.), *Institutions and Working Life*, Oxford: Oxford University Press.

Bunce, V. (1999), *Subversive Institutions: The Design and the Collapse of Socialism and the State,* Cambridge: Cambridge University Press.

Burawoy, M. and K. Verdery (1999), *Uncertain Transition. Ethnographies of Change in the Postsocialist World*, Rowman & Littlefield.

Camerer, M. (2012), Anticorruption Reform Efforts in Democratic South Africa, in: I. Shapiro and K. Tebeau (eds.), *After Apartheid: Reinventing South Africa?* Charlottesville and London: University of Virginia Press, pp. 269–294.

Collier, S. J. and A. Ong (2005), Global Assemblages, Anthropological Problems, in: S. J. Collier and A. Ong (eds.), *Global Assemblages: Technology, Politics, and Ethics as Anthropological Problems,* Malden, MA: Blackwell, pp. 3–21.

Comaroff, J. and J. L. Comaroff (2008), Faith, in: N. Shepherd and S. Robins (eds.), *New South African Keywords,* Johannesburg: Jacana, pp. 91–103.

Coetzee, J. K. (1999), The way towards democracy: The South African experience, in: P. Skalník (ed.), *Transition to Democracy: Czech Republic and South Africa Compared,* Prague: Set Out, pp. 17–43.

Dubow, S. (1995), *Scientific Racism in Modern South Africa,* Cambridge: Cambridge University Press.

Durrheim, K. and J. Dixon (2010), Racial Contact and Change in South Africa, in: *Journal of Social Issues,* Vol. 66, No. 2, pp. 273–288.

Eisenstadt, S. (ed.) (2002), *Multiple modernities,* New Brunswick, NJ: Transaction.

Esparza, D. (2010), National identity and the Other: imagining the EU from the Czech Lands, in: *Nationalities Papers,* Vol. 38, No. 3, pp. 413–436.

Eurobarometer 67. Veřejné mínění v zemích Evropské unie. Národní zpráva Česká republika (2007), online: http://ec.europa.eu/public_opinion/archives/eb/eb67/eb67_en.htm (accessed 17.8.2014).

Eurobarometer 79.5. One year to go to the 2014 European elections (2013), Brussels, online: http://www.europarl.europa.eu/pdf/eurobarometre/2013/election3/SyntheseEB795ParlemetreEN.pdf (accessed 17.8.2014).

Giliomee, H. (1996), *Liberal and Populist Democracy in South Africa: Challenges, New Threats to Liberalism,* Johannesburg: SAIRC.

Giordano, Ch. (2009), Afterword – Under the Aegis of Anthropology: Blazing New Trails, in: L. Kürti and P. Skalník (eds.), *Postsocialist Europe. Anthropological perspectives from home,* New York, Oxford: Berghahn Books, pp. 295–304.

Giordano, C. and D. Kostova (2002), The social production of mistrust, in: C. M. Hann (ed.), *Postsocialism. Ideals, Ideologies and Practices in Eurasia,* Oxford, New York: Routledge, pp. 74–92.

Gumede, W. (2014), The DA as an opposition: Lessons from 20yrs of democracy, in: *The Journal of the Helen Suzman Foundation.* Focus 72 – Democracy and its discontents, issue 72, April 2014, pp. 25–33, online: http://hsf.org.za/resource-centre/focus/focus-72-democracy-and-its-discontents/focus-72-democracy-and-its-discontents/view (accessed 15. 5.2014).

Hann, C. M. (ed.) (2002), *Postsocialism. Ideals, Ideologies and Practices in Eurasia,* Oxford, New York: Routledge.

Hannerz, U. (2003), Being There …and There … and There! Reflections on Multi-Sited Ethnography, in: *Ethnography,* Vol. 4, pp. 229–44.

Harris, B. (2001), A Foreign Experience: Violence, Crime and Xenophobia during South Africa's Transition, *Centre for the Study of Violence and Reconciliation,* Violence and Transition Series, Vol. 5, online: http://www.csvr.org.za/

index.php/publications/1646-a-foreign-experience-violence-crime-and-xeno-phobia-during-south-africas-transition.html (accessed 17.12. 2013).

Hart, G. (2013), *Rethinking the South African Crisis. Nationalism, Populism, Hegemony*, Durban: University of KwaZulu-Natal Press.

Havel, V. (2002), Volební rok 2002 bude přelomový. Novoroční projev prezidenta České republiky Václava Havla [Election year 2002 will be critical. Václav Havel's New Year's address], *Lidové noviny*, 2.1.2002, p. 8.

Horáková, H. (2011), Non-racialism and nation-building in the new South Africa, in: *The Annual of Language & Politics and Politics of Identity*, Vol. 5, pp. 109–124.

Hörschelmann, K. (2002), History after the end: post-socialist difference in a (post)modern world, in: *Transactions of the Institute of British Geographers*, Vol. 27, No. 1, pp. 52–66.

Hörschelmann, K. and A. Stenning (2008), Ethnographies of postsocialist change, in: *Progress in Human Geography*, Vol. 32, No. 3, pp. 339–361.

Hulec, O. (1999), Coming to terms with the cruel authoritarian past in South Africa and in the Czech Republic: a comparison, in: P. Skalník (ed.), *Transition to Democracy: Czech Republic and South Africa Compared*, Praha: Set Out, pp. 45–60.

Illner, M. (1996), Post-communist transformation revisited, in: *Czech Sociological Review*, Vol. 4, pp. 157–169.

Jansen, J. (2002), *Knowledge in the Blood*, Stanford University Press.

Jung, C. and I. Shapiro (1995), South Africa's negotiated transition, in: *Politics and Society*, Vol. 23, pp. 269–308.

Kagwanja, P. (2009), Introduction: Uncertain democracy – elite fragmentation and the disintegration of the 'national consensus' in South Africa, in: P. Kagwanja and K. Kondlo (eds.), *State of the Nation, South Africa 2008*. Cape Town: HSRC Press.

Lawson, G. (2005a), Negotiated revolutions: the prospects for radical change in contemporary world politics, in: *Review of International Studies*, Vol. 31, No. 3, pp. 473–493.

Lawson, G. (2005b), *Negotiated Revolutions: The Czech Republic, South Africa and Chile,* Aldershot: Ashgate.

Mandel, R. (2002), Seeding civil society, in: C. M. Hann (ed.), *Postsocialism. Ideals, Ideologies and Practices in Eurasia*, Oxford, New York: Routledge, pp. 279–296.

Maré, Gerhard (2005), Race, Nation, Democracy: Questioning Patriotism in the New South Africa, in: *Social Research*, Vol. 72, No. 3, pp. 501–530.

Marks, S. (2002), An Epidemic Waiting to Happen, in: *African Studies*, Vol. 61, No. 1, pp. 13–26.

Mattes, R. (2012), Forging Democrats: A Partial Success Story?, in: I. Shapiro and K. Tebeau (eds.), *After Apartheid: Reinventing South Africa?*, Charlottesville and London: University of Virginia Press, pp. 72–104.

Mbembe, A. (2008), Passages to Freedom: The Politics of Racial Reconciliation in South Africa, in: *Public Culture*, Vol. 20, No. 1, pp. 5–18.

Municipal IQ, Hotspots Monitor, June 2013, online: http://www.municipaliq.co.za/publications/press/201306141533398805.docx (accessed 16.6.2014).

Musil, J. (ed.) (1995), *The End of Czechoslovakia*, Budapest: Central European University Press.

Neocosmos, M. (2008), The Politics of Fear and the Fear of Politics: Reflections on Xenophobic Violence in South Africa, in: *Journal of Asian & African Studies*, Vol. 43, No. 6, pp. 586–594.

Neocosmos, M. (2010), *From "Foreign Natives" to "Native Foreigners": Explaining Xenophobia in Post-apartheid South Africa: Citizenship and Nationalism, Identity and Politics*, 2nd ed., Dakar: CODESRIA.

Nosál, I. (2004), Zrození české postkomunistické politické kultury [The birth of Czech postcommunist political culture], in: P. Skalník (ed.), *Politická kultura: antropologie, sociologie, politologie*, Prague: Set Out, pp. 71–88.

Pempel, T. J. (1990), *Uncommon Democracies: The One-Party Dominant Regimes*, Ithaca: Cornel UP.

Posel, D. (2008), AIDS, in: N. Shepherd and S. Robins (eds.), *New South African Keywords,* Johannesburg: Jacana, pp. 13–24.

Roberts, B., M. wa Kivilu and Y. D. Davids (2010), Introduction: Reflections on the Age of Hope, in: B. Roberts, M. wa Kivilu and Y. D. Davids (eds.), *South African Social Attitudes*, Cape Town: HSRC Press, pp. 1–16.

Ross, F. (2008), Truth and Reconciliation, in: N. Shepherd and S. Robins (eds.), *New South African Keywords,* Johannesburg: Jacana, pp. 235–246.

Sampson, S. (2002), Beyond transition: rethinking elite configurations in the Balkans, in: C. M. Hann (ed.), *Postsocialism. Ideals, Ideologies and Practices in Eurasia*, Oxford, New York: Routledge, pp. 297–316.

Seekings, J. (2012), Poverty and Inequality in South Africa, 1994–2007, in: I. Shapiro and K. Tebeau (eds.), *After Apartheid: Reinventing South Africa?* Charlottesville and London: University of Virginia Press, pp. 21–51.

Shapiro, I. and K. Tebeau (2012a), Introduction, in: I. Shapiro and K. Tebeau (eds.), *After Apartheid: Reinventing South Africa?* Charlottesville and London: University of Virginia Press, pp. 1–18.

Shapiro, I. and K. Tebeau (eds.) (2012b), *After Apartheid: Reinventing South Africa?* Charlottesville and London: University of Virginia Press.

Shepherd, N. and S. Robins (eds.), *New South African Keywords,* Johannesburg: Jacana.

Skalník, P. (ed.) (1999), *Transition to Democracy: Czech Republic and South Africa Compared*, Praha: Set Out.

Skalník, P. (2009), Political Anthropology of the Postcommunist Czech Republic: Local-National and Rural-Urban Scenes, in: L. Kürti and P. Skalník (eds.), *Postsocialist Europe. Anthropological perspectives from home,* New York, Oxford: Berghahn Books, pp. 227–252.

Skalník, P. (2014), *Political differentiation in the present-day South Africa and Czech Republic*, an unpublished paper.

South Africa: Over the rainbow (2012), The Economist, *online: http:// www.economist.com/news/briefing/21564829-it-has-made-progress-be-coming-full-democracy-1994-failure-leadership-means (accessed 14.7.2014).*

South Africa Unemployment Rate, online: http://www.tradingeconomics.com/ south-africa/unemployment-rate (accessed 2.7.2014).

Sparks, A. (1995), *Tomorrow is Another Country: The Inside Story of South Africa's Negotiated Revolution,* London: Heinemann.

Sparks, A. (2003), *Beyond the Miracle. Inside the New South Africa*, Chicago: The University of Chicago.

Statistics South Africa (2014), online: http://beta2.statssa.gov.za (accessed 17.8.2014).

Steinberg, J. (2008), Crime, in: N. Shepherd and S. Robins (eds.), *New South African Keywords,* Johannesburg: Jacana, pp. 25–34.

STEM – středisko empirických výzkumů [Centre for Empirical Research]. Stranické preference, online: http://www.stem.cz/clanek/2970 (accessed 2.10.2014).

Thomas, P. D. (2009), *The Gramscian Moment: Philosophy, Hegemony and Marxism*, Leiden: Brill.

Verdery, K. (1996), *What Was Socialism, and What Comes Next?* Princeton University Press.

Weiss, H. (2003), A Cross-National Comparison of Nationalism in Austria, the Czech and Slovak Republics, Hungary, and Poland, in: *Political Psychology*, Vol. 24, No. 2, pp. 377–401.

Williams, K. (2003), Lustration as the Securitization of Democracy in Czechoslovakia and the Czech Republic, in: *Journal of Communist Societies and Transition Politics*, Vol. 19, No. 4, pp. 1–24.

Wood, G. (2006), Review Essay. Negotiated revolutions or evolutionary regime transitions? The Czech Republic, South Africa and Chile, in: *African Sociological Review*, Vol. 10, No. 1, pp. 234–243.

2014 National and Provincial Election Results, online: http://www.elec-tions.org.za/resultsnpe2014/default.aspx (accessed 15.7.2014).

The Czech Republic and South Africa as emerging donors

Mvuselelo Ngcoya

Introduction

At face value, the connections between South Africa and the Czech Republic are tenuous, however, as the contributions to this volume show, there is a wealth of comparative material that enriches our analyses of trends in both countries. In 2014, while South Africa is celebrating twenty years of democracy, the Czech Republic celebrates its tenth anniversary of membership in the European Union (EU). During these respective timeframes, both countries have become respected players in their regions and have sought to breathe their hard-won freedoms into their international relations. Indeed, in the last quarter century the international profiles of the Czech Republic and South Africa have been fundamentally transformed.

Following their emergence from the chrysalis of communism and apartheid respectively, both countries have carved critical roles for themselves in the international arena and have often punched above their weight. There was veritable zeal to turn from pariah to messiah in a short period. That has been accomplished with immense political dexterity and ideological acrobatics, oftentimes, producing Gordian conundrums. For example, both countries share the enigmatic position of having been both donors and recipients of aid in the last two decades, the subject of this chapter. A few vignettes illustrate this paradoxical position and the concomitant challenges raised by the role of both countries in development aid.

In the heat of the invasion of Iraq by the United States of America (and its allies), Lawrence Anthony crossed the border into the Iraq-Kuwait border as part of the US military convoy. Anthony, founder of the Royal Zulu Biosphere project, was headed to the Iraqi National Zoo with a team of South African zoologists and veterinary experts. In his appeal to the South African public for support, he was quoted in the media as saying:

We don't know what the exact circumstances are in the Iraqi zoos. But from media reports and conversations with members of the US military, we're assuming the situation is dire. Even with some supplies of meat and other foodstuff getting through, there is still no refrigeration facility, which means that any food we bring along will have to be distributed to the animals immediately, leaving us with absolutely no reserves… We simply cannot stand

*by and allow animals to die in large numbers because of human
political machinations* (Panther 2003: 10).
At about the same time, the Czech government was involved in high-level
discussions with the so-called coalition of the willing, Australia, Britain,
Poland, Spain and the United States, regarding a humanitarian aid programme
for Iraq. The Czech aid package would include over 300 million crowns
[about US$15 million] and sending dozens of Czech experts to help with
reconstruction. Then Foreign Minister Cyril Svoboda was quoted as saying:

> *We would like to see, as soon as possible, Iraq become a normal
> country and give it back into the hands of Iraqis. Regarding
> business we are interested in the reconstruction of Iraq and we
> want our firms to get a chance to participate. But what is most
> important to us are the people of Iraq. First is humanitarian aid*
> (Hrobský 2003).

As these vignettes demonstrate, the world of development assistance is
a complex one. It involves bilateral, multilateral, and trilateral relationships
with other states, multilateral agencies, non-governmental organisations
(NGOs), business, individuals, etc. It is world of fantasy often established
upon foundations of ignorance ("we don't know what the exact circumstances
are in the Iraqi zoos") and, oftentimes, as Czech involvement in Iraq shows,
it is tied up in the iniquities of international relations. Due to the paucity of
space, this chapter will tease out some of the most significant trends in the
development assistance policies and practices of both countries over the last
two decades or so. It draws a profile of trends, key players, and challenges in
both countries. Using the example of these countries, this chapter essentially
asks whether it is possible to conceive of a development assistance diet that
is different from the staple of traditional development aid. I show that as
a member of the Organisation of Economic Cooperation and Development
(OECD), the Czech system seeks to adapt the more traditional Development
Assistance Committee (DAC) model while the South African model is
founded on what I have termed the Bandung model of development partnership. In light of the growing number of new non-DAC donors, a comparative
analysis of trends in the Czech Republic and South Africa can be useful
beyond these countries and help us understand motive and trends among the
so-called emerging donors. The penultimate section therefore compares these
two models. I conclude by saying that although much of what is called
development assistance (traditional or otherwise) is often conditioned by
both normative and instrumental considerations, I argue that when stripped
down to its core, and viewed as mere giving, we can indeed conceive of
development assistance programmes that are more horizontal and challenge

the dominant conception of development aid. But first, it is important to emphasize that although the Czech Republic and South Africa are often referred to as emerging donors, both countries are not entirely novices in this game of development partnership, having had development projects under apartheid and communism respectively. That is the subject of the next section.

Development assistance under apartheid and communism

Despite common references to the Czech Republic and South Africa as "emerging development partners" (Lucey and O'Riordan 2014; Sidiropoulos 2012; Walz 2011; Braude 2008), both countries have a long if not stellar history in the politics and business of 'development partnerships'. In the history of both countries, development assistance was tied up with the sordid affairs of both apartheid and communism as tools of foreign policy. Various apartheid administrations used development aid to buy support and win over countries during the country's long period of isolation.

A financial report on waste and corruption that accompanied apartheid South Africa's attempt to buy international friends would be long and repugnant. Various apartheid administrations spent millions on irrecoverable loans and grants to various dictators to spend on extravagant and maleficent projects in order to secure a farthing of goodwill in a hostile environment during the country's long period as a pariah state. A few baleful projects typified this kind of 'development assistance'.

To literally purchase the only state visit during his administration, the Vorster government paid millions to the then dictator of Paraguay Alfredo Stroessner, to refurbish the Palace of Justice in the capital city of Asunción and for the department of agriculture in that country (Sawyer 2000). In the Comores islands, the apartheid government funded extravagant hotel projects developed by the hospitality magnate Sol Kerzner's company in building a tropical resort on the coup-ridden islands (Swayer 2000). To fund these and various other less pernicious projects, the apartheid Department of Foreign Affairs used special financial vehicles under the Economic Cooperation Promotion Loan Fund (1968, amended 1986). This was essentially a slush fund to provide financial assistance to African countries in exchange for political support and votes at the UN (Braude et al. 2008).

The white minority government funded 'development projects' in Malawi and provided technical support for farming projects in Equatorial Guinea, Cote d'Ivoire, Gabon, Swaziland and Lesotho and gave other forms of support to the Central African Republic and the former Zaire (now Democratic

Republic of Congo). All this support was disguised as humanitarian aid even though the obvious purpose was to garner some political support in light of the country's international seclusion. But as Besharanti (2013: 17) argues, the fund contributed to useful development projects in Africa, such as the construction of the Lilongwe airport in 1977, and railway and hydroelectric power development projects in that country.

Similarly, Czechoslovakia had a range of foreign assistance programmes during the Communist period. Like the apartheid programmes, they were used by the Soviet Union to assist friendly countries. These policies consisted mainly of the supply of various equipment, experts and know-how, scholarships and tied credits (Szent-Iványi and Tétényi 2008). Key recipient countries included the so-called 'developing socialist brother' countries, such as Mongolia, North Korea, Vietnam, Laos, Cambodia and Cuba, as well as other developing countries, which oriented themselves towards the Soviet Bloc at one time or another during the Cold War, such as Angola, Ethiopia, Nicaragua and South Yemen (Szent-Iványi and Tétényi 2013: 820). Again, like the apartheid era programmes, these projects were of a political purpose and often had military dimensions.

It is all too easy for current development policy makers and practitioners to simply brush off these experiences as belonging to an ill-fated period in their distant pasts. Yet, these historical examples of the instrumental use of aid of development assistance point to the pitfalls of development that seem intrinsic to such programmes whether undertaken by authoritarian or democratic regimes. Important questions are: should development assistance always be tied? What is the relationship between development assistance and hegemonic desires and impulses? What are the relationships between donor and receiving countries? How do receiving countries perceive the aid? These are important questions, arising from the authoritarian histories of both countries that the Czech Republic and South Africa can take forward as they develop and improve their international development policies and programmes.

Contemporary trends in Czech and South African development assistance

South Africa and the Czech Republic share a number of experiences which they have marshalled to buttress their development assistance programmes. Both countries trade in the international environment on what Horký (2010: 2) calls the "transition experience", to wit, "their relatively successful political and economic reforms have the potential to inform policy-makers in both the post-communist East and the post-colonial South" (2012: 17). However, when both countries seek to add this so-called comparative advantage to their development assistance tools, they need to tread carefully. The transitions of both countries were quite unique and many of their experiences were the result of structural geopolitical changes that are not easy to replicate. They also benefited from unparalleled international goodwill and support that facilitated their transitions.

Additionally, both countries share the experience of having been recipients and donors of aid contemporaneously. This should help them to be sensitive to the concerns of their recipient countries. Immediately following the end of communism, the Czech Republic (then Czechoslovakia) received loans from the World Bank, grants and loans from the European Union, multilateral assistance from UN agencies, and numerous types of bilateral aid from countries such as the USA, Norway, and Canada, among others. For example, the European Bank of Reconstruction and Development funded some 103 projects worth EUR4.7 billion until 2007 (Cabada and Waisová 2011: 91). However, at the same time, the Czech Republic was running its own development assistance programmes in its neighbourhood and in territories as far away as Angola and Zambia. The country's transition to a donor country was first intimated when it moved from recipient to donor of the UNDP in 2001 (Cabada and Waisová 2011: 93) and cemented when it became the first of the new EU members to become an official member of the OECD Development Assistance Committee in 2013 (OECD 2013).

Unlike the Czech Republic, which has graduated to a donor country by virtue of its DAC membership, South Africa continues to receive development assistance. In addition to funds from UN agencies and other multilateral funds, South Africa's largest bilateral donors include the US, the EU, Germany, the UK, France, Netherlands, Belgium, and Nordic countries. Official Development Assistance (ODA) is provided through combinations of budget support, technical co-operation and concessional loans. The majority of development aid goes to health and education sectors, where South Africa still has major deficits and the largest HIV-infected population in the world (DIRCO, 2013). In particular, the US remains a major source of ODA (contributing about $541.681 million annually).

Again, unlike the Czech Republic which now reports its development programmes and spending to DAC, there is no centralised mechanism to account for development financing in South Africa. Still, various estimates stipulate that the country's total spending on development cooperation exceeds the official UN target of 0.7% of gross national income (GNI) (Vickers 2012: 536). If correct, this is a significant mark as it exceeds a few OECD DAC member countries, including the Czech Republic (which has been consistently around 0.12% of GNI since 2005). However, as shown in the table below, both countries have significantly increased their official development assistance figures in the last decade.

Table 1: Net Official Development Assistance (ODA) disbursements in million dollars in CZ, RSA, 2003–2012 (at current prices and exchange rates).

	2003	2004	2005	2006	2007	2008	2009	2010	2011	2012
Czech Republic	91	108	135	161	179	249	215	228	250	219
South Africa	125	100	99	125	120	152	202	246	–	–

Sources: DIRCO, OECD International Development Statistics (database)

According to table 1 above, the Czech Republic has more than doubled its ODA from 2003 to 2012, increasing it by over 140% from US$91 million to US$207 million in 2013 (OECD statistics 2014). According to the Czech Foreign Ministry, in 2013, the Czech Republic funded humanitarian assistance programmes worth about US$3.2 million in 30 countries (as varied as South Sudan, Iraq, Burma, Zimbabwe, and Palestine). By comparison, South Africa's aid flows to Africa increased from about US$1.3 billion in 2002 to US$1.6 billion by 2004 (Vickers 2012: 538). Braude et al. (2008: 13) estimate that by 2007, "actual and pledged transfers to Africa (including Southern Africa Customs Union member states) appear to have increased by 25% to R19 billion or US$2.79 billion." Although data are hard to verify, it is reasonable to estimate that these figures are much higher in 2014 thanks to South Africa's growing engagement with the continent.

Still, both countries are leading countries in development partnership activities and debates in their respective regions. The Czech Republic is a key country among the Central and Eastern European (CEE) and EU new member states, particularly among the so-called Visegrad group countries (the Czech Republic, Poland, Hungary and Slovakia). Although countries such as Nigeria and Egypt play crucial development roles in Africa, their activities are dwarfed by the scope and depth of South Africa's development programmes which make it the largest provider of development assistance on the continent. As Table 2, below shows, this support ranges from "peace-keeping, electoral reform and post-conflict reconstruction to support for strengthening Africa's regional and continental institutions and improving bilateral political and economic relations through dialogue and cooperation" (Vickers 2012: 538).

Table 2: African Renaissance Fund grants for 2012 and 2013 (ZAR' 000).

	2013/12	2012/11
Government of Malawi	229 148	–
Sahel region (South Africa's intervention programme)	135 551	–
Cuba (Economic aid package)	100 000	100 000
Guinea (Rice production, waste management and technical assistance)	73 502	136 383
Democratic Republic of Congo (Observer Mission)	34 900	34 900
Democratic Republic of Congo (South African Police Services to purchase riot equipment)	24 000	24 000
Madagascar (IGM Expansion Project)	14 100	14 100
African Ombudsman Research Centre (AORC)	14 100	–
Mozambique (Operation BAPISA)	13 008	13 008
Saharawi	10 000	10 000
Niger (Humanitarian assistance)	9 336	–
International Diplomatic Training Programme (IDTP)	8 408	12 181
United Nations Mission in Liberia for the Rebuilding of the Liberian National Police	7 141	7 141
Democratic Republic of Congo (DPSA DRC Census)	5 827	–
Guinea Bissau (Presidential elections)	5 735	–
Comoros (Electoral assistance projects)	5 084	5 084
Guinea (Museum project in Kindia)	5 000	5 000
Mali (Timbuktu manuscript project)	2 928	2 928
African Capacity-Building Foundation (ACBF)	2 422	–
University of South Africa (UNISA)	2 023	2 023

Source: African Renaissance Fund, Annual Report, 2013.

Like South Africa, the Czech Republic remains a leader in development partnerships among the post-communist states. Not only does the country provide larger development assistance than other post-communist states in its neighbourhood, it has strategy documents, laws, institutions, and a variety of skilled agencies, organisations, and individuals involved in development programmes. The Czech Republic's bilateral development assistance is concentrated in five programme countries: Afghanistan, Moldova, Mongolia, Bosnia and Herzegovina and Ethiopia. In 2012, these countries received 38% of the Czech Republic's bilateral ODA (OECD 2013).

As it seeks to improve the coordination of development assistance, South Africa can learn a few things from the administration and implementation of Czech development aid. Over the last few years, decision-making about development assistance has been centralised in the Ministry of Foreign Affairs (MFA). This is an ongoing project. In South Africa, development programmes are located in numerous departments and this causes unnecessary conflict and delay. As table 2 below shows, these include DIRCO, the Treasury, the Department of Justice, among many others. Secondly, project implementation of Czech development assistance is centrally located at the Czech Development Agency (CzDA). This has strengthened the relation of development cooperation to foreign policy priorities (Horký 2010: 347). South Africa is well on its way with the formation of the South African Development Partnership Agency (SADPA), which is still in its embryonic stage.

Replacing the African Renaissance Fund, SADPA will be located at DIRCO and is an attempt to solve South Africa's intractable development mechanisms and processes. For too long development assistance programmes were managed by diverse channels and agencies in government leading to political squabbling, difficulties in impact measurement, general reporting, monitoring and evaluation, and transparency. On the latter, there is indeed much to learn from the Czech development programme which has been ranked by NGOs as the sixth most transparent in Europe (Global Campaign for Aid Transparency 2012).

Table 3: Key players in Czech and South African development partnerships.

	Czech Republic	South Africa
Ministries	Ministry of Foreign Affairs (MFA), Ministry of Industry and Trade	DIRCO, National Treasury, Trade and Industry, the Presidency, Department of Defence, Minerals and Energy, Justice and Constitutional Development, Public Service and Administration, Science and Technology, and Agriculture.
Development agencies	Czech Development Agency (CzDA)	South African Development Partnership Agency (SADPA)
Civil society	České fórum pro rozvojovou spolupráci (Czech Forum for Developmental Cooperation-a coalition of over 50 organisations.	Gift of the Givers, Islamic Relief, Rescue SA, and South African Women in Dialogue, have been direct implementers of ARF projects in other parts of Africa.

	Members include, among others, ADRA, ARPOK, Člověk v tísni, Charita Česká republika, Občanské sdružení Development Worldwide, Partners Czech)	
Private companies and state-owned enterprises	Platform of Entrepreneurs for Foreign Development Cooperation (a trade organisation representing the interests of private companies). Members include, inter alia, Svaz průmyslu a dopravy ČR (Confederation of Industry of the Czech Republic, representing 1600 members); Svaz strojírenské technologie (Association of Engineering Technology, with 49 members in the Czech Republic and Slovakia)	Standard Bank, Shoprite, Netcare, SASOL, Eskom, Sasol, Transnet
Other public agencies and organisations	Czech Council on International Development Cooperation	Industrial Development Corporation (IDC), the Independent Electoral Commission, the Human Sciences Research Council, the National Research Foundation and the Public Administration Leadership and Management Academy; Africa Institute of South Africa; African Capacity-Building Foundation; University of South Africa

Sources: DIRCO annual reports 2011, 2012, 2013; Czech Forum; Platform of Entrepreneurs for Foreign Development Cooperation

One of the key differences between the development assistance programmes of the Czech Republic and South Africa is the latter country's
increasing role in trilateral development projects. In simple terms, tripartite
development cooperation involves the use of third party donor funds to
support South Africa's technical expertise in another recipient country. For
example in 2011, DIRCO explored trilateral cooperation arrangements with
15 development agencies and reached in-principle agreements for trilateral
cooperation (DIRCO Annual Report 2013: 47). In the 2012/13 financial year,
the African Renaissance Fund received R125.4 million in trilateral funds for
humanitarian and development countries in other countries. These funds came
from Northern donors such as, among many others, the German Federal
Enterprise for International Cooperation (GIZ), the US Agency for International Development, the Norwegian Agency for Development Cooperation
(NORAD), and UNDP. These agencies recognise South Africa's advantage
in the region and support programmes they see as commensurate with their
own development objectives (such as promoting peace and stability and
democracy).

In addition, South Africa is not only a recipient of third party funding,
it also contributes to similar trilateral structures such as those of IBSA
(India, Brazil, South Africa). In March 2004 in New Delhi, India, Brazil
and South Africa established the IBSA Trust Fund, to which each country
contributes $1 million a year to projects that tackle poverty and hunger to
be managed by the UNDP's South–South Cooperation Unit (Beshranti
2013: 34).

One of the major differences between South Africa and the Czech
Republic is that the developing world constitutes the lynchpin of South
Africa's development programme and foreign policy in general. For the Czech
Republic, it is obviously its relationship with the European Union and
development assistance, and relations with the developing world are not an
integral part of its international relations. In fact, Horký (2010: 348) argues
that "in reality and in spite of the legal and institutional changes, there is no
such thing as a broad, holistic and coherent government policy towards the
South". On the other hand, for South Africa, the African continent constitutes
the marrow of foreign policy as captured by the motto of DIRCO, to wit,
"Creating a better South Africa and contributing to a better and safer Africa
in a better world" (DIRCO 2013: 11). This commitment is extended to the
global South in general as can be witnessed in South Africa's eager participation in IBSA and more recently BRICS. The differences between the two
countries are a result of the different models on which their development
assistance programmes are predicated.

The DAC model versus the Bandung model of development assistance

Although it has not reached the targets of the 2005 European Consensus on Development (net ODA to 0.17 percent of GNI by 2010 and 0.33 percent by 2015), the Czech Republic formally joined the traditional group of donor countries known as DAC. It has thus sought to align its development assistance policies, norms and programmes with those of the EU and traditional donors, to some extent. The contested concept of 'Europeanisation' of development assistance has been used to describe the socialisation of the Czech Republic's development assistance model. There are broader definitions that refer to "domestic adaptation to European regional integration" (Graziano and Vink 2006: 7); and narrower definitions suggesting a "process in which states adopt EU rules" (Horký 2010b: 2). Taking the narrower view, some scholars (Lightfoot and Szent-Iványi 2014; Horký 2010b; Goetz 2005) argue that in the case of the Czech Republic, the application of both formal and informal EU rules in development framework in the Czech Republic has only led to 'shallow Europeanisation'. Lightfoot and Szent-Iványi (2014: 1) cite three possible reasons this weak socialisation of new EU member states, particularly the Visegrad group, namely: "perceptions among the new Member States on the procedural legitimacy of the development *acquis*; low domestic resonance with the development *acquis*; and inconsistencies in the activities of norm entrepreneurs."

Partly because of this reluctant Europeanisation of its model, the Czech model departs from traditional DAC approaches in numerous ways. Thanks to its history and its transition experience, the Czech Republic is critical of the depoliticisation of European policy towards the developing world. There is a strong conviction that positive development programmes will be ineffective without fostering democracy and increasing substantial popular participation in the politics of recipient countries (Czech Ministry of Foreign Affairs 2009). The Act 151 of the Czech Parliament on development cooperation and humanitarian aid (2010: 1) also emphasizes "the promotion of democracy, human rights and good governance in developing countries." Similarly, it is not surprising that the Czech Strategic Document emphasizes the idea of 'partnerships' instead of 'aid'.

Democratic ownership of the development process by the developing countries themselves is a key aspect for the aid effectiveness. The Czech Republic's development policy is based on *partnership* with recipient countries. It is driven by demand from partner countries and by their needs, which are generally defined in national development strategies (e.g. Poverty Reduction Strategy Papers). In the forthcoming period, the Czech Republic

will accentuate, more than ever, the involvement of local people (governments, elected representatives, civil society organisations) at all stages of the
project cycle in order to strengthen ownership, and thus the effectiveness, of
cooperation (Czech Ministry of Foreign Affairs 2009: 7 emphasis in original).

Thus, many activities of Czech development programmes are concerned
with the training of independent media and civil society organisations (Horký
2012: 21). Like other Central and Eastern European countries, the Czech
Republic seeks to strengthen political conditionality and criticises the
European Commission and the 'old' member states for not "enforcing it sufficiently because of other, often commercial interests. In the same vein, the
'new' member states have been very critical of the low conditionality of the
general budget support provided by the EU" (Horký 2012: 22).

Unlike the Czech Republic, South Africa's development assistance seeks
to distinguish itself from the DAC model. To begin with, there is a degree of
discomfiture with the nomenclature of development assistance. For example,
like the Czech Development Cooperation Strategy cited above, the annual
report of the Department of International Relations and Cooperation (DIRCO)
refers to 'partnership' and not 'aid'. In that document, the words partner or
partnership appear 76 times and 'aid' only 6 times (except in the financial
statement where it appears more often as a line item). The speeches and
reports of DIRCO officials are laced with numerous references to partnerships, rather than aid. As Minister of International Relations and Cooperation,
Ms Maite Nkoana-Mashabane told the National Assembly in 2013:

> *We have initiated implementation modalities on the National
> Development Plan. One of these is on South Africa's national
> interests with the view to elaborating a policy and strategy in
> a manner that balances our domestic priorities with equally
> important imperatives of cooperation and partnership as well as
> Pan-Africanism and South-South solidarity* (Nkoana-Mashabane
> 2013).

It was for these reasons that the official name of the department was
changed from Department of Foreign Affairs to the Department of International Relations and Cooperation in 2009 reflecting this orientation.
According to the Minister, the purpose was "to help clarify the mandate of
the Department". The name should reflect the new focus that "our government
wishes to place on partnerships and co-operation for development" (Landsberg 2012: 8). Consequently, in its 2013 strategic plan, DIRCO repeatedly
commits itself not to act singularly in South Africa's national interest alone,
but on behalf of the whole African continent. Key to this is the promotion of
democracy and human rights and harmonising regional economic and trade

arrangements to establish a pan-African economic zone (Lucey and O'Riordan 2014: 2).

By doing this, South Africa joins other Southern countries in what I would call the Bandung Model of development partnership (or what Waiz and Ramachandran (2011) call the 'South-South model'). To name it as such does not mean that the approaches of the countries who subscribe to this model are uniform. In fact, the most prominent of these countries such as China, India and Brazil are motivated by divergent motives and use development assistance to pursue their individual country interest. In short, South-South cooperation in the Bandung model does not mean that these countries always act in concert. However, there are important features that distinguish this model from the traditional DAC model. First, the principle of 'non-interference' is a defining aspect of this model and its genesis can be traced back to the historic Bandung Conference of 1955. The first principles listed in the Bandung Declaration were: 1) respect for fundamental human rights and for the purposes and principles of the charter of the United Nations; 2) respect for the sovereignty and territorial integrity of all nations; 3) recognition of the equality of all races and of the equality of all nations large and small; and 4) abstention from intervention or interference in the internal affairs of another country. More pertinently for development assistance, the final communiqué of Bandung urged developing countries to loosen their economic dependence on the leading industrialised nations by providing technical assistance to each other through developmental projects, expert and technical exchange and the establishment of regional research institutions.

Countries that subscribe to this Bandung model (Brazil, China, India, Venezuela, etc.) are very careful to set their model apart from the DAC version. Some of these countries sometimes give as much as they receive. These countries have fundamentally positively reconfigured the architecture of development assistance in unprecedented ways. Although data on the volume and scale of aid programs from emerging donors are sketchy, estimates range between $10 and $15 billion of aid annually, "or 7–10 percent of global official aid" and their contribution is expected to double in the next five years (Chandy 2013). Other researchers provide even higher estimates. Walz and Ramachandran suggest that total estimates of aid from non-DAC donors could have been as high as $41.7 billion or 31% of global gross ODA from DAC donors (2011: 6). In addition to these amounts, there is strong evidence that DAC funding is now flat and that the volume of funding from emerging non-DAC donors is on the rise and is expected to double in the next five years (Chandy 2013).

For the Bandung model, development assistance is portrayed as a horizontal process in the form of mutually beneficial interactions, sharply diverging from traditional vertical donor-recipient relationships. South Africa's White Paper on Foreign Policy has articulated this normative perspective as the 'diplomacy of *ubuntu*', namely: "the philosophy of *ubuntu* means 'humanity' and is reflected in the idea that we affirm our humanity when we affirm the humanity of others" (DIRCO 2012: 2).

For all its positives, the Bandung model is not without problems. There are inherent challenges and paradoxes in development partnerships. For all their valorisation of horizontal approaches to development, South-South development programmes are also bedevilled by political calculations and ambitions and get used to garner political leverage in the international community. These 'horizontal development relationships' are not immune to power imbalances and regional economic rivalries. Walz and Ramachandran (2011: 16) quote one Indian official as saying:

> *We need Africa not only for oil but for political power too... but we do not have the money of the Chinese or the military might of the Americans. Therefore we have to rely on cooperating with African nations... where we have something to give.*

Similarly, South Africa's own development programmes have been caught in similar paradoxes of national interest and political entanglement. Despite its commitment to this Bandung approach, South Africa, like the Czech Republic, has grounded its foreign policy on a resolute commitment to human rights and promotion of democracy. Yet this commitment sometimes comes to loggerheads with its development partnerships requiring policymakers to walk a tightrope. This harkens back the history of development partnerships in both countries under communism and apartheid.

For example, South Africa is currently balancing its existing partnership with South Sudan, where human rights violations in Jonglei need to be considered along with the need for continued political and policy dialogue that promise a resolution. Zimbabwe has been another thorny issue over the last decade or so. In order to twist Zimbabwe's arm to initiate constitutional, political, and economic reforms in 2005, South Africa was willing to pay half of the debt to retain Zimbabwe's IMF membership, but under strict conditions. A senior member of the African National Congress made it crystal clear that South Africa was not prepared to throw Mugabe an unconditional lifeline: "We will look at how do we ensure that such assistance results in sustainable recovery so that we don't find ourselves in a similar situation in a year's time" (Monare 2005: 3). This cajoling and strong-arm tactics are not well received by African 'partners' and the government has had to defend itself against accusations of sub-imperialism or playing an unwelcome big brother role. A government official was quoted as saying that the government wanted to offer aid "in our terms" and "there is no way anyone can see us as an imperialist force wanting to influence things in a direction that would benefit us" (Ndlangisa 2007: 4).

In other words, the political spirit of Bandung, based on principles of solidarity, does not often translate to economic relations. The South African construction companies, consultancies, NGOs, etc. that are part of the package of South Africa's development 'partnerships' are not always guided by the spirit of pan-Africanism, *ubuntu*, and solidarity that the country's develop-ment partnership model is purportedly based on. Furthermore, unlike the government itself, they are not accountable to anyone else except their shareholders and board members.

Conclusion: Pitfalls of development partnerships

It is uncontroversial to argue that South Africa and the Czech Republic are not confronted by any significant external security threats (Dostál et al. 2012; Landsberg 2012). On the contrary they enjoy enviable international goodwill (thanks to their larger than life founding figures of the new democratic dispensation, their relatively smooth transitions, among other things). Yet, they are both incapacitated by a lack of a clear, grand vision to take advantage of these two factors.

Back to the vignettes cited earlier. When the Czech Foreign Minister justified their humanitarian programme to Iraq in 2003, he was clear that he was also looking out for Czech businesses. Humanitarian assistance was tied to the benefit of Czech companies, even if not directly. South Africa faces similar charges. The flourishing of South Africa businesses across the African continent often leads to accusations of South Africa playing a hegemonic (or sub-imperialist) role in the continent.

Because of the allure of the notion of 'emerging donors', it is easy to forget that in the developing world, aid was born in iniquity. Despite its association with humanitarianism, aid has always been tied. Give and take, if you will. There is often a line, a crooked one, between development aid and profit. The story of development assistance has been the tale of hidden agendas. Behind the veil of increased aid (humanitarian or otherwise), there is an army of private sector actors. Thus, when assessing the intentions and impact of the role of 'emerging donors', we need to tame our enthusiasm.

In the case of South Africa, policy makers should not be naive about their role and the perception thereof on the continent. Thanks to the history of apartheid 'assistance' cited above, and the perception of the country as a regional hegemon, even the best intentions can be viewed negatively. Whether the government uses 'development partnership' instead of 'aid', policy and practice has to adequately take into account historic and economic relationships with its neighbours on the continent. Otherwise development programmes will ironically undermine long-term poverty reduction initiatives on the continent.

In providing these cautionary notes, this chapter rejects a dyad of critiques of development partnerships. One views these emerging donors as 'rogue donors' (Naim 2007) who are only motivated by money, desire for access to raw materials and to improve their political standing in international politics. Their model will only breed a world "that is more corrupt, chaotic and authoritarian" (Naim 2007). In this view, development assistance is the province of the traditional powerful countries and their intentions are always good. These new players crowd out and replace "responsible aid programs out of the market exactly where they are needed most" (Naim 2007). The other view holds that development aid was born in iniquity as a tool of empire and colonial domination (Ortlieb 1978; Alemazung 2010; Desai 2013; Appiah 2014) and thus it follows that countries such as South Africa and the Czech Republic should steer away from such practices. Both positions are based on shaky assumptions.

Despite the differences between Czech and South African approaches, both countries seem to approach development assistance in more sensitive ways than traditional donors. This is attributable to their recent roles as both receivers and givers of development assistance. They are well positioned to guard against the bullying and conditionalities that sometimes plague traditional forms of aid. If both countries are to overcome the pitfalls of development assistance, the language of 'partnership' will have to be more than just window-dressing. They will have to avoid the messianic complex and moral superiority that are at the heart of the development industry. In both countries, policy makers, experts and practitioners will have to subject themselves to the high standards of critique and vigilance that they apply to the more traditional donors.

References

Alemazung, J. A. (2010), Post-Colonial Colonialism: An Analysis of Inter-national Factors and Actors Marring African Socio-Economic and Political Development, in: *Journal of Pan African Studies,* Vol. 3, No.10, pp. 62–84.
Appiah, S. (2014), Development Aid as a control instrument in Africa, *OpEd News,* 27 February 2014, online: http://www.opednews.com/articles/

Development-Aid-as-a-contr-by-Solomon-Appiah-Africans_Beliefs_Democratic_Federal-Agency-CIA-140227-4.html (accessed 2.6.2014).

Baun, M. and D. Marek (2009), Czech Foreign Policy and EU Membership: Europeanization and Domestic Sources, Paper presented at the Eleventh Biennial Conference of the European Studies Association, Los Angeles.

Besharati, N.A. (2013), South African Development Partnership Agency (SADPA): Strategic Aid or Development Packages for Africa? *South African Institute of International Affairs*, Research Report 12.

Braude, W., P. Thandrayan and E. Sidiropoulos (2008), Emerging Donors in International Development Assistance: The South Africa Case, in: *South African Institute of International Affairs*, Research Report. pp. 1–29.

Cabada, L. and Š. Waisová (2011), *Czechoslovakia and the Czech Republic in World Politics*, Lexington Books.

Chandy, L. (2012), New in Town: A Look at the Role of Emerging Donors in an Evolving Aid System, *Monthly Developments Magazine*, Washington: Brookings Institution, April 2012, online: http://www.brookings.edu/research/articles/2012/04/emerging-donors-chandy (accessed 4.10.2014).

Czech Ministry of Foreign Relations (2009), The Development Cooperation Strategy of the Czech Republic 2010–2017, online: http://www.mzv.cz/jnp/en/foreign_relations/development_cooperation_and_humanitarian/general_information/development_cooperation_strategy_of_the.html(accessed 4.10.2014).

Government of South Africa (2013), Department of International Relations and Cooperation (DIRCO), Annual Report.

Desai, M. (2013), *The Paradigm of International Social Development: Ideologies, Development Systems and Policy Approaches*, London: Routledge.

Dostál, V., J. Eberle and T. Karásek (2014), Stagnation in 2012 Czech foreign policy, The *New Presence Magazine,* online: http://www.pritomnost.cz/en/czech-politics/199-stagnation-in-2012-czech-foreign-policy (accessed 12.5.2014).

Dostál, V. (2013).Trends of Czech European Policy: Study of European Policy Elites, in: *Association for International Affairs*, online: http://www.amo.cz/editor/image/produkty1_soubory/amocz-trends-of-czech-european-policy-2013.pdf (accessed 12.5.2014).

Drulák, P. (2006), Between Geopolitics and Anti-Geopolitics: Czech Political Thought, in: *Geopolitics*, Vol. 11, pp. 420–438.

Fürst, R. and G. Pleschová (2010), Czech and Slovak Relations with China: Contenders for China's Favour, *Europe-Asia Studies*, Vol. 62, No. 8, pp. 1363–1381.

Geldenhuys, D. (1990), *Isolated States: A Comparative Analysis*, Cambridge: Cambridge University Press.

Goetz, K.H. (2005), The new member states and the EU: responding to Europe, in: S. Bulmer and C. Lequesne (eds.), *The member states of the European Union*, Oxford: Oxford University Press, pp. 254–280.

Government of the Czech Republic, Development Cooperation and Humanitarian Aid, and Amending Related Laws Act 151 of 21 April 2010.

Government of the Czech Republic (2011), Conceptual Basis of the Foreign Policy of the Czech Republic.

Graziano, P. and P. Maarten (2006) (eds.), *Europeanization: New Research Agenda*, Basingstoke: Palgrave Macmillan.

Hendricks, C. and A. Lucey (2013), South Africa and South Sudan: Lessons for Post-Conflict Development and Peace-building Partnerships, *Institute of Security Studies*, ISS Policy Brief no. 49, December.

Horký, O. (2010a), Development Cooperation in the Czech Foreign Policy, in: M. Kořan (ed.), *Czech Foreign Policy in 2007–2009: Analysis*, Prague: Institute of International Relations, pp. 347–361.

Horký, O. (2010b), The Europeanisation of development policy: acceptance, accommodation and resistance of the Czech Republic, *German Development Institute/Deutsches Institut für Entwicklungspolitik (DIE)*, Discussion Paper, No. 18, online: http://www.die-gdi.de/discussion-paper/article/the-europeani-sation-of-development-policy-acceptance-accommodation-and-resistance-of-the-czech-republic/ (accessed 2.6.2014).

Horký, O. (2010c), The Transfer of the Central and Eastern European 'Transition Experience' to the South: Myth or Reality? in: *Perspectives on European Politics and Society*, Vol. 13, No. 1, pp. 17–32.

Horký, O. (2012), The impact of shallow Europeanization of the new member states on the EU's actorness: what coherence between foreign and development policy?, in: S. Grimm, D. Makhan and S. Gänzle (eds.), *The European Union and Global Development – An Enlightened Superpower in the Making?* London: Palgrave, pp. 17–36.

Hrobský, M. (2003), Humanitarian Aid Priority for Czech Republic in Iraq, *Radio Prague*, online: http://www.radio.cz/en/section/curraffrs/humanitarian-aid-priority-for-czech-republic-in-iraq (accessed 2.6.2014).

Landsberg, C. (2012), Continuity and Change in the Foreign Policies of the Mbeki and Zuma Governments, in: *Africa Insight*, Vol. 41, No. 4, pp. 1–16.

Leys, R. and A. Tostensen (1982), Regional Co-operation in Southern Africa: The Southern African Development Co-Ordination Conference, in: *Review of African Political Economy*, Vol. 23, pp. 52–71.

Lightfoot, S. and B. Szent-Iványi (2014), Reluctant Donors? The Europeanization of International Development Policies in the New Member States, in: *Journal of Common Market Studies*, pp. 1–16.

Lucey, A. and A. O'Riordan (2014), South Africa and Aid Effectiveness: Lessons for SADPA as a Development Partner, *Institute of Security Studies*, Discussion Paper 252, online: http://www.issafrica.org/publications/papers/south-africa-and-aid-effectiveness-lessons-for-sadpa-as-a-development-partner (accessed 14.8.2014).

Monare, M. (2005), Zim Set to Agree to SA's Conditions for Aid after IMF Expulsion Threat, in: *The Star*, 4 August 2005, p. 3.

Naím, M. (2007), Help Not Wanted, in: *New York Times*, February 15, 2007.

Ndlangisa, S. (2007), SA to give aid 'on our own terms', in: *Daily Dispatch*, 2 July 2007, p. 4.

Nkoana-Mashabane, M. (2014), Budget Vote Speech by Minister of International Relations and Cooperation, National Assembly, Cape Town, 30 May 2013, online: http://www.dfa.gov.za/docs/speeches/2013/mash0531.html; (accessed 6.6.2014).

OECD (2014), The OECD DAC welcomes Czech Republic as its 26th member, 13 May 2013, online: http://www.oecd.org/dac/peer-reviews/czech-republic.htm; (accessed 2.6.2014).

Ortlieb, H-D. (1978), *Whither Africa? Racism, Neo-Colonialism, Development Aid* (Trans. E. Orsers), Zurich: Interfrom AG.

Panther, S. (2003), SA Mission to Aid Iraqi Zoo, in: *The Citizen*, 24 April 2003, p.10.

Quadir, F. (2013), Rising Donors and the New Narrative of 'South–South' Cooperation: what prospects for changing the landscape of development assistance programmes? in: *Third World Quarterly*, Vol. 34, No. 2, pp. 321–338.

Rubešková, M., H. Schulzová and M. Šimečka (2013), Two decades on from the break-up of Czechoslovakia: Departures, diversions and destinations CEPS Commentary, *Centre for European Policy Studies*, online: www.ceps.eu (accessed 27.5.2014).

Sawyer, C. (2000), Uncertainty over Apartheid-era Loans, *The Star*, 26 April 2000, p. 6.

Shaw, T.M. (1976), International Organizations and the Politics of Southern Africa: Towards Regional Integration or Liberation? in: *Journal of Southern African Studies*, Vol. 3, No. 1, pp. 1–19.

Sidiropoulos, E. (2012), South Africa: Development, International Cooperation and Soft Power, in: S. Chaturvedi et al. (eds.), *Development Cooperation and Emerging Powers: New Partners or Old Patterns*, Johannesburg: Zed Books.

The Global Campaign for Aid Transparency (2012), Aid Transparency Index. Publish What You Find, online: http://www.publishwhatyoufund.org/ index/2012-index/ (accessed 6.6.2014).

Vickers, B. (2012), Towards a new aid paradigm: South Africa as African development partner, in: *Cambridge Review of International Affairs,* Vol. 25, No. 4, pp. 535–556.

Walz, J. and V. Ramachandran (2011), Brave New World: A Literature Review of Emerging Donors and the Changing Nature of Foreign Assistance, *Center for Global Development, Working Paper* 273.

Wheeler, T. (2012), Implications of SA Foreign Aid: Role as a Developmental Partner Is Not Entirely about Altruism, in: *The New Age,* 4 December 2012, p. 20.

Wheeler, T. (2005), *The History of the South African Department of Foreign Affairs 1927–1993,* Johannesburg: South African Institute of International Affairs.

Wolfaardt, P., T. Wheeler and W. Scholtz (2010), *From Verwoerd to Mandela: South African Diplomats Remember,* Cape Town: Crink.

Regionalism as a response to global economic challenges: Case studies of South Africa and the Czech Republic[1]

Vilém Řehák

Introduction

Despite their geographical remoteness and apparent differences in history and culture, South Africa and the Czech Republic share surprising similarities in their modern history. Both countries were created in the turbulent period of World War I, which led to important changes on the global map. The Union of South Africa was established in 1910, a few years before the outbreak of the war, while Czechoslovakia was formed in 1918 as a direct consequence of the war.

In South Africa, the discovery of gold, diamonds and coal attracted foreign capital and led to rapid industrialisation, increased agricultural production, building of infrastructure, expansion of trade and finance and growth of manufacturing. Unlike other African colonies, South Africa played a major role in the world economy (Marks and Rathbone 1985: 11), although it "remained only a peripheral social formation caught in the imperialist nexus" (Davies et al. 1976: 29) as a supplier of raw materials. In 1932, South Africa departed from the gold standard, and as a result in the next two decades profited from rising prices of gold on the global market and experienced a general economic expansion (Innes and Plaut 1977: 92).

The Czech lands were an industrial-agrarian area and the economic core of the Austria-Hungary with almost 70% of industrial capacity of the empire (Kubů and Pátek 2000: 11). Czech economic growth started in 1880 and lasted until WWI, which caused a complete disintegration of Central Europe. The newly born Czechoslovakia had to cope with many problems: destroyed industry, different levels of economic development in the Czech lands and Slovakia, poor infrastructure, and the disruption of economic ties to defeated Austria and Germany. Despite that, Czechoslovakia was able to achieve rapid political and economic stabilisation due to the custom and monetary separation from Austria, repatriation of capital, land reform, inflow of British and French capital, and high investment in public infrastructure and education. The Great Depression disrupted the country's economic upturn. Czecho-

[1]This study was supported by Charles University in Prague, project GA UK No. 834214 "Trade regimes in sub-saharan Africa".

slovakia did not fully recover from a long and deep recession because of growing threat from Nazi Germany, which in turn caused an outflow of foreign capital and domestic Jewish capital (Kubů and Pátek 2000: 52). Nevertheless, in the interwar period Czechoslovakia was a democratic country with a fully developed capitalist economic system based on a free market, responsible and liberal economic policies, relatively high economic efficiency and a credible currency.

In that period, both South Africa and Czechoslovakia belonged to the Top 20 economies in the world. In their best years, the share of South Africa on global exports exceeded 2.5% and the Czechoslovak share was only slightly below 2% (Kubů and Pátek 2000: 340).

Neither country was able to retain its economic position in the second half of the 20th century. The Czechoslovak communist and South African apartheid regimes had profound economic consequences. Czechoslovakia was isolated from its Western trading partners and subjected to directives from Moscow, while South Africa became a pariah in the international community subjected to economic sanctions.

The Communist regime in Czechoslovakia fell in 1989. In the same year, South Africa commenced the formal process of dismantling the apartheid regime, which culminated in free elections five years later. Both countries came out of their isolation and were confronted with a changed international environment in the globalised world. The new political elite had to deal with the urgent and difficult tasks of political and economic transformation, but it also had to focus on other tasks beyond its borders. Both countries had to (re)define their relations within their respective regions, continents and the whole world.

This chapter deals with the phenomenon of new regionalism as a response of states to globalisation and the deadlock in multilateral trade negotiations. The first part is theoretical and focuses on two main questions. First, what is the history of regionalism in the world economy? How does new regionalism differ from the previous older forms? Second, what is the relationship between growing regionalism and the deadlock in multilateral trade negotiations? The second part is empirical and describes the economic transformation of post-communist Czechoslovakia/Czech Republic and post-apartheid South Africa within the framework of the global economy. The third part investigates the role of regional trade agreements and regionalism in economic transformation of both states. The author argues that although the Czech Republic and South Africa pursued rather different goals, they both used regionalism as their principal strategy in searching for their place in the modern global economy and governance system.

Five waves of regionalism

Two processes characterise contemporary global economy: globalisation and regionalisation. Globalisation is a process of relative shrinking of time and space, mutual linkage of global and local social, cultural, economic and political structures, and increasing mutual interdependence. Since the end of the 19th century, due to technological progress, capitalism, colonialism, liberal trade, and gold standard, the global economy is becoming more and more internationalised. The interwar return to economic nationalism and protectionism was considered a temporary anomaly, which should have been reverted by multilateral trade liberalisation sponsored by the General Agreement on Tariffs and Trade (GATT) from 1947. However, the return from protectionism to liberalism proved to be difficult, especially with the rising number of member states in multilateral trade talks. After initial substantial reduction in trade tariffs for several thousands of industrial goods, negotiations about new areas such as services, capital, intellectual property and agricultural production resulted in the stagnation of liberalisation.

Regionalisation is an objective process of regional delimitation of international economic relations, while regionalism is a strategy of states to influence this process (Kučerová 2006: 68–69). Neither is a new phenomenon. Regionalism evolved from militant regionalism of ancient empires through economic regionalism of colonial powers, interwar malevolent regionalism creating large economic blocs with mainly hostile mutual relations, to hegemonic regionalism during the Cold War. In Europe, strategic and security motivation of regionalism was expressed by economic cooperation. In Africa and Asia, regionalism created multifunctional organisations, which tried to surpass the Cold-War rivalry. Contrary to previous phases, regionalism was much more formalised and institutionalised in the post-WWII period.

At the end of the 1980s, regionalism entered the phase of *new regionalism,* which neglects the geographical dimension of its previous forms. When seeking mutual economic benefits, states do not focus only on their region, but even beyond its borders. Bilateral agreements prevail over the multilateral ones and take form of complex free trade areas. They commonly include trade with goods, but also liberalisation of other sectors including services, investment, labour migration, protection of intellectual property, or environmental standards. Integration is deep, but with weak institutional structure, and strictly intergovernmental.

New regionalism has its economic and political reasons. The main set of reasons are globalisation, growing dependence of states on international trade, legal and institutional standardisation, capital liberalisation and slow pace of multilateral liberalisation negotiations. Regionalism is a political and societal response to expansion of market with all its imperfections (Hettne 2003: 31). A further reason lies in the development of the global economy: the United States lost their dominant position to a united Europe, Japan, and emerging markets. In addition, the formerly united group of developing countries is no longer a monolithic bloc (if it ever was). The third reason is deepening and widening of European integration, which serves as a model for other continents, but also presents a threat of being closed economic bloc for non-members. Other reasons are decentralisation and multipolarity of the post-Cold-War world, regionalisation of security threats, and marginalisation and vulnerability of developing countries.

Globalisation and regionalism: Cooperative, or competitive relationship?

The number of regional trade agreements is rising steadily since the beginning of the 1990s. According to the Regional Trade Agreements Information System (RTA-IS), 583 notifications have been received by GATT or its successor the World Trade Organization (WTO) since 1947. Of these, 377 agreements are in force. This enormous number raises a question: what is the relationship between the processes of globalisation and regionalism?

According to some authors (Lawrence Summers, Fred Bergsten, Richard Baldwin, Robert Lawrence), regional agreements are the *stepping stones* for global liberalisation. They bring positive outcomes and are likely to stimulate further liberalisation on a global scale. They can also develop solutions transferable to the global arena, for example regarding the unification of economic, legal and institutional systems. They reduce the number of parties and they strengthen the bargaining power of small states. If the main goal of regionalism is to create larger markets, the logical final target of all regional integration schemes is to broaden preferential access worldwide and to gain from this unrestricted preferential access to other markets. Another argument is that if regional agreements are notified with the WTO, they cannot violate its rules. However, this argument is rather weak – the WTO members do not share the same interpretation of the regional agreements clause and as there is a consensual decision-making procedure in the WTO, all new regional agreements are notified.

At the beginning of the 1990s, this vision was expressed in the concept of *open regionalism*. The basics of the old regionalism were to broaden import substitution strategies from national level to regional level and to create closed economic blocks. Such trade policy is naturally hostile to global multilateralism. Contrary to that, new regionalism is more open and thus supports involvement of states to global negotiations (Sampson 2003: 9). Regionalism is a part of globalisation. Open regionalism has four features: maximum unilateral liberalisation of trade and investment within the region; commitment to the reduction of trade barriers against non-member states; willingness to liberalise trade with non-members on a reciprocal basis; and right of all countries to reduce trade barriers against non-members unilaterally (Bergsten 1997). Open regionalism does not create closed protected blocks and is not a threat to multilateralism (Baldwin 1997: 884–885).

However, this idea proved to be unduly optimistic and the concept too vague. Failure of the GATT/WTO negotiations in the 1990s led to an expansion and reinforcement of regional agreements all over the world. The developing countries strongly opposed global liberalisation in trade with services and rejected to subsume to any global rules concerning intellectual property, public procurement or environmental standards. On the other hand, the European Union and the US were unwilling to open their agricultural markets and to stop subsidising their farmers. The Doha round of negotiations, which was launched in 2001, has stalled since 2008 and it is not surprising that the strongest economies are trying to reach their goals by different means, including bilateral trade agreements with other major world economies. For example, both Japan and the US have signed 13 bilateral agreements since 2000. The European Union initially belonged to the main proponents of global trade liberalisation. Nevertheless, under pressure from European companies willing to invest outside Union borders, it had to change its trade policy as well. The *Global Europe* strategy from October 2006 confirms European commitments to the WTO, but at the same time, it suggests possible directions for bilateral trade negotiations exceeding the WTO framework. Evidently, the European interest is to get a maximum of trade preferences, especially those that also the US and Japan may be able to negotiate for themselves (Heron and Siles-Brügge 2012). The EU and the US also started negotiating a mutual *Transatlantic Trade and Investment Partnership,* which would be the greatest bilateral trade agreement ever.

Empirical evidence thus matches more with a pessimistic view of the second group of authors (Paul Krugman, Jagdish Bhagwati, Arvind Panagariya), who warned that regional agreements would have a negative impact and would be *stumbling blocks* for global liberalisation. These authors argue that an attempt to maximise benefits from any concrete regional integration inevitably leads to protectionism and competition between regions (*competitive regionalism*). Such regional negotiations also redirect institutional and financial capacities of smaller states away from global negotiations. Further problems arise concerning the different legal and institutional frameworks in different regions, which can be hardly solved on the global level.

According to other authors (Alan Winters, Andreas Dür, Diana Tussie), the problem is not so clear-cut. As both regionalism and multilateralism are in some way results of globalisation, they run in parallel and need not necessarily be mutually harmful. Regionalism does not result in the fall of the global trade system (Winters 1996: 45). Both processes proceed in an interaction and regionalism only reflects the fact that some states prefer faster or deeper liberalisation than global arena can offer (Tussie 2003: 114). The debate "has ended in a standoff. Both the stepping stone and the stumbling block advocates can support their positions with logically consistent arguments and both also can muster at least some evidence to back up their arguments. (…) [N]either of the two metaphors can capture the complexity of the effects of regional agreements for the process of globalisation" (Dür 2007: 195). Relationship between regionalism and multilateralism is not a priori harmonious or contradictory, but also depends on its management by key economic powers (Bergsten 1997). Currently, it seems that world order is based on mutual relationship between regionalism and multilateralism and the most favourable situation is openness of regionalism and cooperation of regions with global regimes on one side, and representative and sustainable coordination of global economic relations on the other side (Cihelková 2010: 303).

Analytical framework

This text seeks to explore regionalist strategies of both countries during their economic transformation. Regionalism can be an active, conscious, politically formulated strategy of government to find a suitable position for itself in the global economy. Regionalism can be also a passive non-strategic reaction to the international environment. However, the active and passive forms are inseparable. See for example approaching of post-communist Central Europe to the EU in the 1990s. The EU membership was an openly formulated political and economic goal, but at the same time, it was an economic necessity caused by changed economic environment and break-up of the Eastern Bloc. To some extent, post-communist countries were forced to formulate their pro-European regionalist strategies by external factors. In the following sections, regionalist strategies of both countries are discussed in more details. After setting the historical context, these strategies are examined in three different subsections: regional strategies, continental strategies, and global/bilateral strategies. The same structure of both case studies enables to compare differences and similarities between the two countries.

Republic of South Africa: Quest for leadership

The institutionalisation of apartheid regime in 1948 had no direct effect on economic development of South Africa (SA). While communist states and emerging Asian and African states showed open hostility towards SA, Western states tried to retain close business and financial contacts despite their reserved diplomatic relations (Barber and Barratt 1990: 46). Situation worsened in 1960 after police killed 69 participants of a peaceful demonstration against racial discrimination in Sharpeville. In 1962, the UN General Assembly denounced apartheid regime as a violation of the UN Charter and SA was expelled from international sport competitions. Economic sanctions followed: voluntary arms embargo (1963), partial oil embargo (1973), mandatory arms embargo (1977), and limited trade and economic sanctions (1985). However, sanctions did not affect main export articles, which inevitably lessened their potential impact. Thus, the international pariah status was rhetoric and symbolic act rather than any real punishment (Strange 2000: 192). What mattered much more was the reaction of Western private companies – growing disinvestment and capital outflow. As SA was extremely dependent on foreign capital, it found itself in a very unfavourable situation considering its permanent search for status and security (Barber and Barratt 1990: 327). Moreover, continued propagation of a racist division of labour became less and less functional to interests of bourgeoisie (Davies 1979: 362). SA was also facing a high external debt because of *import substitution industrialisation* strategy and growing expenditures on bureaucracy and security. Internal and external pressures finally contributed to the fall of apartheid.

After the regime change, SA had to go through double transformation – internal political and economic transformation and regaining trust of international community and investors (Strange 2000: 80). Political transformation culminated in the 1994 elections and economic transformation was set out in the Growth, Employment and Redistribution (GEAR) programme in 1996. GEAR had to deal both with globalisation and expectations of people – economic transformation was based on free market, ending of subsidies, deregulation, privatisation, conservative fiscal and monetary policy, attracting foreign investment and budgetary cuts, but it also had to secure basic infrastructure and housing, start land reform and empower the emerging black middle class (Makgetla 2004: 263–271). The task of regaining international recognition was achieved quickly: shortly after first elections, SA established full diplomatic relations with almost all states; restored full membership in the United Nations; and (re-)entered other international organisations like the Commonwealth.

Regional strategies

SA exercises an undisputed leadership role in the sub-region. The *Southern African Customs Union* (SACU) is the oldest functioning customs union in the world (1910). The rationale lies in the personal economic interest of SA, its control of fiscal, monetary and trade policies of SACU, and economic dependency of other member countries on its bigger neighbour. SACU was not substantially changed either during the apartheid period, or during the post-apartheid transformation.

SA's leadership in the greater region is contested. *Southern African Development Community* (SADC) was established in 1979 to lessen economic dominance of SA in the region. This integration project aimed at promoting functional cooperation between its members, but failed to overcome the constraints of nationalism and conflicts. In reality, the organisation expressed only political attitudes of member countries towards apartheid SA. In 1994, SA joined SADC and the organisation was transformed into standard regional trade agreement. SADC was supposed to become a regional grouping consisting of equal members, but this was only an illusion: SA is the largest investor in the region and by far its greatest producer and exporter. Stakeholders in SA were convinced about the necessity of regional cooperation, but not about its concrete model (Hentz 2005: 5–6). ANC, trade unions and small entrepreneurs supported the model of functional integration with an emphasis on industrial development. Afrikaner businesspersons and bureaucrats of SACU preferred creation of customs union. Big corporations and parastatals preferred a model of ad hoc bilateral trade agreements without any institutional structure. The absence of single vision led to slow progress of integration. Moreover, SADC is facing several other constraints. First, there is a collision of trade liberalisation schemes of SACU, SADC and SA bilateral agreements. Second, undemocratic nature of several regimes in the region and regional tensions concerning security and democracy hinder any deepening of cooperation. Third, democratic transformation in SA is still not consolidated (high number of black people living in poverty, rising unemployment, corruption, criminality, increasing xenophobia…). Fourth, trade patterns in the region are very uneven – SA exports manufactured products to other states and imports materials, which resembles the former colonial core-periphery relations (Haase 2004: 198).

Continental strategies

Internationally, SA soon came to be viewed as the natural leader of the African continent due to its economic and military strength, successful democratisation, and the reputation of President Nelson Mandela. However, SA itself was reluctant to assume leadership because of its apartheid history (Haase 2004: 187). During Mandela's presidency it stressed common African heritage of suffering, resilience and triumph (James Barber cited in Alden and le Pere 2009: 157), and oriented its foreign policy towards promotion of civil liberties, democratisation and active internationalism through multilateral institutions (Alden and le Pere 2004: 284). Nevertheless, in practice, financial, commercial, political and defence interests prevailed over the ethical dimension of foreign policy (Alden and le Pere 2004: 286).

Under Thabo Mbeki, the foreign policy of SA changed. It rested on three pillars: The first pillar was the cultural concept of the *African Renaissance*. Mbeki revived historical Pan-Africanism and combined it with contemporary concerns for accountability, democratic governance and neo-liberal emphasis on open markets and foreign investment (Alden and le Pere 2004: 287). It stressed common African identity and equality of divergent cultural values in different parts of the world. Africans were supposed to be solely responsible for transformation and development of their continent and emancipation in the global arena. However, the concept also contained an economic aspect linking SA economic interests with those of Africa as a whole and stressing global competitiveness, free trade, and capital as a means for African development (Vale and Maseko 1998: 274–283). Due to this ambiguity, the concept failed to gain wider attraction across the continent (Alden and le Pere 2004: 290). The economic part of African Renaissance was further elaborated in the *Millennium Africa Programme*, which was supposed to be a new economy strategy for African economic development. However, when Thabo Mbeki announced it, francophone Africa launched its own *Omega plan*. It took some time to merge both these concepts into the *New Partnership for African Development* (NEPAD) in 2001. However, both NEPAD and African Renaissance were criticised by African civil society groups as an attempt by SA to gain control of the continent. The third pillar was a political project aimed at transforming the defunct Organisation of African Unity into a new and more dynamic African Union, openly inspired by the success of European integration.

By the end of the decade, SA eventually accepted the role of African hegemon. However, despite its efforts, SA is far from being accepted as an African leader, because "ability of the South African government to act decisively in the name of African interests is more accepted in global settings (…) than is always the case within Africa" (Alden and le Pere 2009: 145). While hegemony in the region is contested, hegemony on the continent is fully unrealised. Under Thabo Mbeki, foreign policy became more pragmatic, moderate, and appropriate to country's size and resources. Security and wealth creation became a new leitmotif in foreign policy (Alden and le Pere 2004: 287, 294). The result of this shift is that SA pursues its own interests more consistently and in a more selfish way. "By advocating liberalism as a means to redress structuralism, South Africa is simply safeguarding the realisation of realist objectives" (Haase 2004: 181). SA is not yet able to play the role of an aid provider and a big economic engine even within its own region, let alone the whole continent (Teló 2009: 144). This hinders SA in exercising the leading role. African states fear that SA economic and military strength has negative effects on sustainable and equitable development of Africa. Leadership requires followership (Vale and Maseko 1998: 283), which is not the case of SA in Africa.

Global strategies

It is not surprising that SA is trying to realise its economic interests also on the global scene. Although founding member of the GATT, SA participated little in trade negotiations until late-1990s. Then, under the GEAR programme and its stress on trade liberalisation, it became one of the leaders in the WTO talks. There are two reasons for this intensified SA activity. First, liberalisation of agricultural trade is a key factor for enhancing SA global competitiveness. Second, accepting the role of African leader, SA also accepted its role as a North-South mediator (Taylor 2005: 299–302). SA leaders work actively in multilateral arenas to foster South-South cooperation and to reform the current trade regimes, which are disadvantageous to developing countries (Haase 2004: 194). SA considers the Doha round to be essential for accelerating development and increasing the scope of the developing world to bargain on its key issues. SA is a member of G20 group (major economies of the world), Cairns group (agricultural exporting economies), BRICS group (major emerging markets), and IBSA platform (with India and Brazil). All these groups articulate and defend interests of developing countries and insist on the US and the EU to eliminate subsidies of their domestic agriculture production and export. Until this issue is resolved, developing countries will not allow the WTO to include the investment issues into its agenda. Another controversial issue is the protection of the intellectual property: SA is advocating for better access of developing countries to affordable medicines at the expense of pharmaceutical industry. However, SA activity on the continent is not without criticism. Its positions often run counter to those of the Africa Group. When the SA delegation joined the special secret meetings at the Seattle ministerial conference in 1999, it was criticised of further marginalising Africa in the global trade system (Taylor 2005: 303).

Lastly, SA is currently one of the most outspoken African voices in talks on the future of the *African Growth and Opportunity Act* (AGOA). This system of unilateral US trade preferences for democratic African countries was created in 2000 for a period of fifteen years. As this period is halting to its end, African leaders try to negotiate with the US to prolong these trade preferences. As SA together with Nigeria and Angola count for more than 80% of African export to the US, it is naturally very active in these negotiations.

Bilateral strategies

Though its priority is global trade liberalisation, SA is generally open also to bilateralism. Such agreements may help to achieve the basic principle of opening up markets. SA or SACU has initiated and concluded several bilateral agreements. The most important is *Trade, Development and Co-operation Agreement* with the European Union, which was signed in 1999 and which entered into force in 2004. This agreement has three parts. First, it establishes a free trade area between both parties and provides for the liberalisation of 95% of the EU's imports from South Africa within ten years, and 86% of South Africa's imports from the EU in twelve years. Moreover, TDCA touches also free competition among the EU and SA companies and protection for intellectual property. Second, a development aid granted to SA mainly to address issues of job creation and provision of basic social services. Third, economic and political cooperation and dialogue. In 1999, SA has also signed the *Trade and Investment Framework Agreement* with the US, which aims at expanding trade in goods and services and encouraging private sector investment between the two countries as a means of fostering growth, job creation, and economic development.

SACU as a trading bloc in the southern cone of the continent has also initiated trade negotiations. In 2006, SACU has signed a bilateral trade agreement with the EFTA states (Iceland, Liechtenstein, Norway, and Switzerland). Trade agreements with the EU and India are announced to the WTO as being under negotiation (the so-called early announcement). The US-SACU negotiations started in 2003, however, stalled in 2006 due to lack of institutional capacity of SACU to meet high US expectations, particularly related to the investment issues (Heydon and Woolcock 2009: 157–160).

Czech Republic: Back to Europe

Though Germany was the most important Czechoslovak trading partner in the interwar period, in political and security sphere the country relied on strategic alliance with France and Great Britain. In 1945, these patterns were in decay and Czechoslovakia was insecure in the space between new American and Soviet spheres of influence. This new situation provided an opportunity for transformation of political and economic system. Politically, the idea of President Eduard Beneš, which saw Czechoslovakia as a bridge between the West and the East, proved to be a utopia. Economically, the transformation was originally planned on market principles with strong state interventions, however this conception was forsaken very soon and the Soviet model of a centrally planned economy gained preference (Kubů and Jančík 2010: 385).

After the War, the country was dependent upon economic aid from the Soviet Union and more importantly from the USA under the aegis of the United Nations Relief and Rehabilitation Administration (UNRRA) programme. Czechoslovakia was in a very intricate situation: as one of the most advanced socialist countries, its industry needed technologies obtainable only on Western markets. On the other side, Czechoslovakia had close political ties to Moscow and was forced to reject participation in the Marshall Plan and instead sign a trade agreement with the Soviet Union. After the 1948 communist coup, existing ties to Western markets were cut, Czechoslovakia became fully anchored in the Soviet bloc and had to adjust its economy to Soviet needs. In practice, this led to a massive expansion of heavy industry. Czechoslovakia became the "forge" of the Soviet bloc and its economic structure was heavily damaged (Kubů and Jančík 2010: 391).

The eastern counterpart of the western European integration, *The Council for Mutual Economic Assistance* (COMECON), was nothing more than an expression of Soviet ideological and political leadership (Marek 2006: 45). Mutual relationships between the European Communities (EC) and COMECON were complicated and changing with time. Initially, COMECON rejected the EC as economic imperialism and a threat to peace (read: as a threat to Soviet hegemony). In 1960s, a group of Czechoslovak economists led by Ota Šik proposed a radical reform to resolve stagnation of the economy, backwardness of industrial production and an abrupt decline in living standards. Moscow cautiously allowed its satellites to make contracts with the EC. Between 1958 and 1970, export from Czechoslovakia to the EC tripled (Marek 2006: 48–50). Soviet occupation in 1968 brought these renewed ties to the West to an abrupt end once again. However, global situation had dramatically changed. United Kingdom joined the EC in 1973; Western Europe was in economic crisis; competition from the USA and Japan was growing; Germany approached Soviet leadership with its *Ostpolitik*; East-West dialogue started at the *Conference on Security and Co-operation in Europe* etc. Despite remaining ideological cleavages, Eastern European countries started to negotiate trade agreements with the EC – Czechoslovakia signed agreements for metallurgy (1978), meat (1980), textile (1982) and industrial goods (1988). Economic impact of these agreements was limited and for both parties it was an expression of status quo rather than an expression of will to deepen mutual trade relations (Marek 2006: 83). However, Czechoslovakia secured foreign currency income and import of goods and raw materials necessary to revive collapsing economy (Černoch 2003: 24). After the collapse of the Soviet bloc in 1989, for people in post-communist countries the dismissal of totalitarian regimes was naturally connected with their hope for a return of civil liberties and for a better life in economic prosperity (Černoch 2003: 17).

Regional strategies

In the first months after the revolution, regional dimension was almost neglected. One reason was economic disarray caused by the dissolution of the COMECON and urgent need to find new markets for Czech export. Due to relatively cheap and skilled labour and a long industrial tradition, Czech industries were quite successful in changing orientation towards the EU (Chytil and Sojka 2001: 26–27).

Shortly after taking office, President Václav Havel proclaimed "Return to Europe" as the highest imperative of post-communist political leadership. However, accession negotiations proved to be very difficult. Full membership of Central and Eastern European (CEE) countries was a long-term run. Moreover, separate trade agreements between these countries and the EC had a negative impact on regional trade in Central Europe. Only under these unfavourable circumstances, Czechoslovakia, Poland, and Hungary intensified their regional cooperation. In the political sphere, they established the *Visegrad Group* in 1991. In the economic sphere, they created *Central European Free Trade Area* in 1992. This cooperation did not intend to replace, but to ease full integration of member countries into the European Union (Müller 2004: 22).

In 2004, the Czech Republic (CR), Slovakia, Poland and Hungary all became members of the EU. Thus, regional economic cooperation (CEFTA) came to an end as all countries became a part of the EU internal market. The Visegrad Group still exists and serves the purposes of furthering European integration of member countries and advancing their mutual military, economic, energy, and educational cooperation.

Continental strategies

Generally, the motto "Return to Europe" expressed the will to eliminate artificially created barriers dividing the continent for more than forty years.

The whole political scene except for the communist party agreed on this new foreign policy orientation (Müller 2004: 15). However, exact meaning of this relatively vague motto remained unclear and it meant different things for different groups (Drulák 2012: 254). Petr Drulák distinguishes four periods in ideological transformation of Czech political elite regarding its attitudes towards Europe (Drulák 2012: 251–273).

First was the period of "revolutionary euphoria". Former dissidents who focused on a moral aspect of transformation were the key political figures, and proclaimed "non-political policy" and "victory of truth and love over lies and hatred". For Václav Havel, European integration was a process of extending personal civil liberties, creating an open area for self-realisation and freeing European citizens (Černoch 2003: 62). Havel tried to define supranational, probably European notion of brotherhood but this brotherhood was not transformed in any viable political concept (Drulák 2012: 255). This concept was probably too idealistic for the transformation period, which required rather pragmatic solutions. Dissidents quickly lost the game and, after the 1992 elections, had to vacate their positions to economists around Prime Minister Václav Klaus. Nationalism and economic pragmatism prevailed over philosophy.

Second period of "transformation wanderings" started in 1993. The early 1990s were marked by a high level of euphoria related to the same high level of naivety (Zahradil 2000: 32–33). The first agreement on trade and cooperation between Czechoslovakia and the EC was signed in May 1990 and Czechoslovakia joined the PHARE programme designed to help CEE countries in their reform efforts. This agreement had a very limited economic, but a very profound political impact (Marek 2006: 97). The same year, both sides started to negotiate the association agreement, which was expected to have a more political character in relation to expectations of rapid full membership. The agreement was signed in 1991 and contained asymmetric trade liberalisation in favour of Czechoslovakia, creation of free trade area in ten years, gradual implementation of free flow of capital, goods, people and services, and political and financial cooperation. After the breakup of Czechoslovakia, both successor states negotiated their association agreements in 1993. However, these agreements did not accept membership aspirations as leading automatically and unconditionally to accession. Both the EU and the CEE countries had different priorities, temperament, expectations, and illusions (Kreuter 2004). All CEE countries expected rapid deepening of cooperation and accession to the EU, which they equalled with security safeguards, economic prosperity, political cooperation and modernisation of peripheral regions. On the other side, the European Union had several reasons to hesitate when offering membership to CEE countries. Firstly, there were economic reasons: Central and Eastern Europe was regarded as a space of economic disintegration with obsolete, uncompetitive and mainly agricultural economies, which could threaten European agricultural and structural policies. Secondly, political situation in the region was not clear and definite. Thirdly, geopolitical situation changed radically and potential Russian imperialism was not such a threat for Europe as before. Fourthly, the European Union had many internal problems to solve (German unification, accession negotiations with Scandinavian countries and Austria, institutional reform related to the Maastricht Treaty, debates about deepening and widening of the European integration, crisis of western welfare state and rise of unemployment, creation of common market, etc.). Fifthly, there was also a negative experience from Southern enlargement when states less devoted to European idea and more to following their own interests had joined the EU. It is not surprising therefore, that the EU was willing to offer development aid, limited trade concessions and political dialogue to help transformation efforts, but was not willing to offer full membership and to open its markets to sensitive goods. Czech leaders were asking for the opposite – trade, not aid (Dyba 2004: 84). While CEE countries regarded future membership in the EU as a certainty, the EU itself conditioned membership by fulfilment of the *Copenhagen criteria* adopted in 1993 (stable institutions, democracy, rule of law, functioning market economy, for details see Kučerová 2010: 42).

For the ruling Civic Democratic Party (ODS) return to Europe meant return to capitalism (Drulák 2012: 257). Czech leaders were convinced that their transformation strategy was the best possible and they were afraid that bureaucratic and a stagnating Europe would not share the dynamics of Czech economic transformation and would even thwart it (Černoch 2003: 26). ODS also criticised the growing importance of political aspect over economic and did not favour any deepening of integration process: for Václav Klaus, the EU membership was an economically motivated need, nothing more (Černoch 2003: 61). The initial admiration of the EU was replaced by a more pragmatic view (Zahradil 2000: 33). As a result, the Czech government submitted an official application for membership as the last but one of all CEE countries and for a long time showed the biggest transposition deficit.

New government of the Czech Social Democratic Party (ČSSD) that came out of the 1998 elections was much more pro-European. CR entered into the third phase of "European sobering" with new Prime Minister Miloš Zeman. When the European Commission very critically assessed Czech progress, ČSSD promised to accelerate approximation to the EU law dramatically (Černoch 2003: 77–78). ČSSD took European integration as it was with its economic and political dimensions, stressed social and environmental dimensions and defined rapid implementation of European *acquis communautaire* into Czech legislation as the main goal of its government (Drulák 2012: 263). Social democratic attitude towards the EU was at times too uncritical (Müller 2004: 38), probably because the European Union as a theme did not play any major role in political arena (Machonin 2001: 119).

Accession to the EU was the supreme moment of Czech post-revolutionary development (Drulák 2012: 268), which was later followed by the fourth period of crisis. In 2006, the Civic Democratic Party formed a new government and the Czech attitude towards the EU became more reserved. Moreover, Václav Klaus, one of the biggest Czech 'euro-sceptics', was elected President in 2003. Czech society lacks cohesion in some sort of public interest and the EU agenda is still not of a high enough priority (see for example the postponement of introduction of the Euro, signing *European Stability Mechanism* as the last member state, or initial rejection to sign the *Fiscal Compact*). Another change in government in 2013 altered these patterns once again and CR is attempting to become a more responsible member state.

Global strategies

Czechoslovakia was a founding member of the GATT in 1947. However, it remained inactive for decades. CR was a founding member of the WTO in 1994. As a small export-oriented economy, it showed a great interest in rapid global trade liberalisation. Country was successful to establish liberal and transparent trade regime, which was a key ingredient of its economic transformation from planned economy to a market one. Czech leadership actively participated in the new round of multilateral trade talks. However, active participation was limited by economic size and negotiating strength of the country. When entering the EU, the position of CR changed. Although it remains a member state of the WTO, it formally gave up a right to conduct its own trade policy. As a part of the EU customs union, it is bound by the EU common trade policy and common external tariff. Thus, Czech interests must be formulated on the national level and then enforced on the European level.

Bilateral strategies

CR was very active in negotiating trade agreements with its main trading partners. The main destination for Czech export is Western Europe, which emphasises the role of the EU association agreement. CR also negotiated a free-trade agreement with the EFTA countries. The most important bilateral agreement was a customs union with Slovakia in 1993. This was quite a logical step – in reality, Czechoslovakia was dissolved in political terms, but the two new countries remained one economic space. CR has negotiated two other bilateral agreements in the first half of 1990s, with Slovenia and Romania. In the second half of the decade, number of bilateral trade agreements increased (Estonia, Latvia, Lithuania, Turkey, Israel, Croatia, etc.) and CR negotiated several non-preferential trade agreements, particularly with post-Soviet countries. Since 2004, these agreements are not in force and CR does not negotiate new free trade agreements on its own as it is part of the EU common trade policy.

Different goals, same strategies

Czechoslovakia regarded itself as a bridge between capitalist Western democracies and communist Soviet East. The political reality of the Cold War made this idea unfeasible (Marek 2006: 17). Czechoslovakia was firmly rooted in the Soviet sphere of influence and had one of the most conservative communist regimes. This political orientation had dramatic economic effects: if in 1945 the economic level of Czechoslovakia and Austria was the same, then in 1990 the efficiency of Czechoslovak economy was only half of that of Austria (Dyba 2004: 81). The rapid disintegration of the Eastern bloc led to a certain degree of chaos in Czech trade and the country had to change its export orientation and find new markets elsewhere.

Similarly, South Africa regarded itself in the 1950s as a bridge between the European colonisers and African black majority (Barber and Barratt 1990: 6). This idea proved to be incompatible with decolonisation and growing criticism of apartheid by international community emerged. South Africa retained its economic ties to Western capital, but diplomatically it was becoming more and more isolated. After the end of apartheid regime, SA had to undergo internal and external transformation.

Regional strategies

Cooperation within the region seems to be the first logical step in foreign economic policy of any state. SA joined existing regional organisation in 1994 shortly after first free elections and assumed a very active role in shaping its political and economic framework. Trade liberalisation was formulated as one of the key economic policies in the GEAR programme. Despite some internal rivalries within the ruling African National Congress, particularly between pragmatic sections close to the government and leftist sections close to the trade unions, this economic policy has not been challenged until now. On the regional level, SA stressed the same principles as on the national level. On the other side, Czechoslovakia rather neglected this level. Central Europe as a region almost disappeared from the discourse and leaders put emphasis on Europe as a unified continent. However, because approaching the EU proved to be much more difficult and much lengthier than CEE countries had anticipated, they eventually fostered political and economic ties between themselves. In this initial period, regional cooperation was not a political strategy of member states, but rather a passive reaction to external circumstances. After 1993, situation changed and CR became active in formulating and pursuing its regional strategy (Czech-Slovak customs union, Visegrad Group, CEFTA).

Continental strategies

SA is one of the biggest African states and it creates almost a quarter of African GDP. It is one of two dominant African economies and naturally strives for political dominance on the continent. On a continental level, regionalism was again a conscious, openly formulated strategy based on GEAR principles. SA (co-)formulated the concepts of African Renaissance/ NEPAD/African Union, which aimed at fostering economic and political position of Africa in the world. However, economic interests of SA seem to be at least partially incompatible with interests of less developed African countries. As a result, SA leadership in the region, let alone on the continent is highly contested by other states. For Czech leaders, continental level was of an immense importance. As Karel Dyba correctly notes, accession to the EU was not a process of integration, but of re-integration. It was continuation of inter-war development, which was interrupted forcibly by a communist regime (Dyba 2004: 80). Not only had the aspiration for the EU membership economic reasons, it also incorporated political and symbolical level. Becoming a member of the EU meant ultimate separation from its undemocratic communist history and confirmation of being a liberal democratic country with market economy. However, the famous motto "Return to Europe" was very vague and different political groups had different ideas about its meaning. The main division was between pro-European Czech Social Democratic Party and rather anti-European Civic Democratic Party. This conservative party guarded national sovereignty and accepted only economic dimension of European integration, while social democrats treated political and economic dimensions of European integration as inseparable. This led to relatively dramatic changes in Czech attitudes towards European integration with relation to which party is actually ruling. "Return to Europe" was expressed as a main goal of post-communist transformation. However, Czech leadership was not consistently active in pursuing this goal. In some periods, accession to the EU seemed to be only a passive reaction to global economic changes. It was matter of economic necessity, nothing more. This view was strengthened particularly after the outbreak of global economic crisis in 2008.

Global and bilateral strategies

SA is very active both globally and bilaterally. This relates to the fact that its regional and continental leadership is not free of criticism. Another reason is the difference in economic level, economic size, structure of economy and consequently economic interests between SA and many African countries. Moreover, the African Union is not such an integrated entity as its European counterpart and still does not have a coordinated common trade policy. Thus, it is not surprising that SA joins other leading developing countries and emerging global powers (mainly India, Brazil, and China) to form new powerful negotiating coalitions. Due to the slow progress of multilateral negotiations, SA also pursues the strategy of bilateralism and negotiates free trade agreements with developed and leading developing countries. CR was also very active in global and bilateral strategies. Bilateral strategies aimed at enhancing cooperation with its main trading partners, global strategy aimed at speeding up global trade liberalisation. CR as a small export-oriented country strongly preferred the maximal possible trade liberalisation to increase its exports. Since 2004, global and bilateral strategies of CR are realised within the framework of the EU common trade policy. Currently, global and bilateral strategies are part of the continental strategy being a member of the EU.

Conclusion

The current course of the global economy seems to be geared more towards regionalism than multilateralism. Global economy is changing into a network of different trade agreements. There is hardly any state in the world that is not participating in this network. South Africa and the Czech Republic also participate in this trend. They share a common aspect of their transformation represented by deepening and widening of their regional commitments. Both countries realised that active regionalism could enhance their economic performance. Both have chosen regionalism as a strategy to fulfil their immediate external transformation goal: to become a full member of globalised economy and to utilise all its possibilities for economic development and enhancement of living standards of citizens. However, both countries did it in different way. From the short overview of different trade strategies, it is clear that SA pursues an active type of regionalism at all levels – regional, continental, global, and bilateral as well. SA followed in logical steps, starting with regional integration (mid-1990s) and continental integration (end of 1990s) and shifting quickly to global and bilateral level (since 1999). The main reason for this shift is the rather reluctant attitude of African countries towards SA regional and continental leadership and different economic needs of SA and most of African countries. Moreover, for SA, regionalism was not only economic strategy, but also a political strategy to enhance its global status. The Czech regionalist strategy stressed particularly one level, the European Union. As the progress of accession negotiations was very slow, CR focused more also on other levels, regional, global, and bilateral. However, it became very active on these levels when pursuing its own economic interests. Currently, CR is a member state of the EU and all the four levels merged in one under the EU common trade policy. However, despite the prominence of this level and its articulation as the highest goal of post-communist transformation, Czech leadership was not able and/or willing to pursue actively and positively this chosen path. In some periods, the Czech Republic was rather a free rider in the European integration process. We may find four explanations for this difference in regional strategies of both countries. First, there is a different export structure in both countries – CR is oriented towards Western European markets, which explains the emphasis on the continental level. SA exports are more diversified throughout the world (the US, the EU, Asia, and Africa). Second, there is a very different level of economic and political integration on the respective continents, mainly related to the EU common trade policy. Third, the different size of both economies, which implies different goals and strategies to achieve these goals. Fourth, there is a lack of consensus and vision within the Czech political elite, which creates a barrier to more active regionalism, at least on the European level. However, it is predictable that the global regionalist trend will continue in the coming years and both the Czech Republic (through European common trade policy) and South Africa (through SACU and SADC membership or independently) will further develop their regional trade networks.

References

Alden, C. and G. le Pere (2004), South Africa's Post-apartheid Foreign Policy: From Reconciliation to Ambiguity?, in: *Review of African Political Economy*, Vol. 31, No. 100, pp. 283–297.

Alden, C. and G. le Pere (2009), South Africa in Africa – Bound to Lead?, in: *Politikon: South African Journal of Political Studies*, Vol. 36, No. 1, pp. 145–169.

Baldwin, R. (1997), The Causes of Regionalism, in: *The World Economy*, vol. 20, No. 7, pp. 865–888.

Barber, J. and J. Barratt (1990), *South Africa's Foreign Policy. The Search for Status and Security 1945–1988,* Cambridge: Cambridge University Press.

Bergsten, F. (1997), *Open Regionalism,* Washington: Institute for International Economics, Working Paper 97–3, online: http://www.iie.com/publications/wp/wp.cfm?ResearchID=152 (accessed 3.5.2014).

Chytil, Z. and M. Sojka (2001), Ten Years of Economic Transformation in the Czech Way, in: G. Gorzelak, E. Ehrlich, L. Faltan and M. Illner (eds.), *Central Europe in Transition: Towards EU Membership,* Warsaw: Scholar Publishing House, pp. 14–38.

Cihelková, E. (2010), *Regionalismus a multilateralismus. Základy nového světového obchodního řádu?* [Regionalism and Multilateralism: Basics of New World Trade Order], Praha: C. H. Beck.

Černoch, P. (2003), *Cesta do EU. Východní rozšíření Evropské unie a Česká republika v období 1990–2004* [Way to the EU: Eastern Enlargement of the European Union and the Czech Republic in 1990–2004], Praha: Linde.

Davies, R. (1979), *Capital, State and White Labour in South Africa 1900–1960,* Brighton: The Harvester Press.

Davies, R., D. Kaplan, M. Morris and D. O'Meara (1976), Class Struggle and the Periodisation of the State in South Africa, in: *Review of African Political Economy*, Vol. 3, No. 7, pp. 4–30.

Drulák, P. (2012), *Politika nezájmu: Česko a Západ v krizi* [Policy of Unconcern: Czechia and West in crisis], Praha: SLON.

Dür, A. (2007), Regionalism: Stepping Stone or Stumbling Block for Globalisation?, in: S. Schirm, (ed.), *Globalisation: State of the Art and Perspectives*, London: Routledge, pp. 183–199.

Dyba, K. (2004), Česká republika a Evropská unie 1989–2004: Zapomínaná cesta [Czech Republic and the European Union 1989–2004: A forgotten path], in: H. Fajmon, (ed.), *Cesta České republiky do Evropské unie* [Czech Republic's Path to the European Union], Brno: CDK, pp. 80–90.

Falk, R. (1999), Regionalism and World Order After the Cold War, in: B. Hettne, A. Inotai and O. Sunkel (eds.), *Globalism and the New Regionalism,* London: Macmillan, pp. 228–250.

Fawcett, L. and A. Hurrell (eds.) (2004), *Regionalism in World Politics,* Oxford: Oxford University Press.

Gamble, A. (2009), Regional Blocs, World Order and the New Medievalism, in: Teló, Mario (ed.), *European Union and New Regionalism,* Aldershot: Ashgate, 2nd edition, pp. 21–36.

Haase, N. (2004), *South Africa in the African Political Economy: Benevolent or Selfish Hegemon,* M. A. thesis, University of Johannesburg, online: http://hdl.handle.net/10210/1372 (accessed 26.4.2014).

Hentz, J. (2005), *South Africa and the Logic of Regional Cooperation,* Bloomington: Indiana University Press.

Heron, T. and G. Siles-Brügge (2012), Competitive Liberalization and the "Global Europe" Services and Investment Agenda: Locating the Commercial Drivers of the EU-ACP Economic Partnership Agreements, in: *Journal of Common Market Studies,* Vol. 50, No. 2, pp. 250–266.

Hettne, B. (2003), The New Regionalism Revisited, in: F. Söderbaum and T. Shaw (eds.), *Theories of New Regionalism: A Palgrave Reader,* Houndmills: Palgrave, pp. 22–42.

Heydon, K. and S. Woolcock (2009), *The Rise of Bilateralism: Comparing American, European and Asian Approaches to Preferential Trade Agreements*, Tokyo and New York: United Nations University Press.

Innes, D. and M. Plaut (1977), *Class Struggle and Economic Development in South Africa: the Inter-war Years,* online: http://sas-space.sas.ac.uk/4064/1/Duncan_Innes_and_Martin_Plaut_-_Class_struggle_and_economic_development_in_South_Africa,_the_inter-war_years.pdf (accessed 2.4.2014).

Kreuter, J. (2004), Nedorozumění a zájmy na cestě České republiky do rozšířené Evropské unie [Misunderstanding and Interest on the Czech Way to the Enlarged European Union], in: H. Fajmon (ed.), *Cesta České republiky do Evropské unie* [The Czech Way to the European Union], Brno: CDK, pp. 54–79.

Kubů, E. and D. Jančík (2010), Hospodářská obnova Československa po druhé světové válce [Economic Renewal of Czechoslovakia after the Second World War], in: I. Šedivý, J. Němeček, J. Kocian and O. Tůma (eds.), *Československo a krize demokracie ve střední Evropě ve 30. a 40. letech XX. století* [Czechoslovakia and the Crisis of Democracy in Central Europe in the 1930s and 1940s], Praha: Historický ústav, pp. 375–391.

Kubů, E. and J. Pátek (2000), *Mýtus a realita hospodářské vyspělosti Československa mezi světovými válkami* [Myth and Reality of Economic Maturity of Czechoslovakia between World Wars], Praha: Karolinum.

Kučerová, I. (2006), Nový regionalismus versus geografický regionalismus [New Regionalism versus Geographical Regionalism], in: V. Kotábová, and B. Říchová (eds.), *Institucionalizace a decentralizace v Evropské unii* [Institutionalization and Decentralization in the European Union], Praha: IPS FSV UK, pp. 67–89.

Kučerová, I. (2010), *Hospodářské politiky v kontextu vývoje Evropské unie* [Economic Policies within the Context of the EU Development], Praha: Karolinum.

Langton, D. (2009), U. S. Trade and Investment Relationship with sub-Saharan Africa: The African Growth and Opportunity Act and Beyond, in: K. Geisler, (ed.), *U. S. Trade with Developing Countries: Policy, Programs and Trends*, New York: Nova Science Publishers, pp. 19–45.

Machonin, P. (2001), Socio-political processes in the Czech Republic, in: G. Gorzelak, E. Ehrlich, L. Faltan and M. Illner (eds.), *Central Europe in Transition: Towards EU Membership*, Warsaw: Scholar Publishing House, pp. 104–123.

Makgetla, N. S. (2004), The Post-apartheid Economy, in: *Review of African Political Economy*, Vol. 31, No. 100, pp. 263–281.

Marek, D. (2006), *Od Moskvy k Bruselu* [From Moscow to Brussels], Brno: Barrister & Principal.

Marks, S. and R. Rathbone (eds.) (1985), *Industrialisation and Social Change in South Africa*, 2nd ed., Harlow and White Plains: Longman Group Limited.

Müller, D. (2004), Cesta České republiky do Evropské unie [The Czech Way to the European Union], in: H. Fajmon, (ed.), *Cesta České republiky do Evropské unie* [The Czech Way to the European Union], Brno: CDK, pp. 13–53.

Sampson, G. (2003), Introduction, in: G. Sampson and S. Woolcock (eds.), *Regionalism, Multilateralism and Economic Integration*, Tokyo: United Nations University Press, pp. 3–17.

Strange, S. (2000), *The Retreat of the State*, Cambridge: Cambridge University Press.

Taylor, I. (2005), The Contradictions and Continuities of South Africa Trade Policy, in: D. Kelly and W. Grant (eds.), *The Politics of International Trade in the Twenty-First Century*, Basingstoke: Palgrave Macmillan.

Teló, M. (2009), Between Trade Regionalization and Various Patterns towards Deeper Cooperation, in: M. Teló (ed.), *European Union and New Regionalism*, Aldershot: Ashgate, 2nd ed., pp. 127–152.

Tussie, D. (2003), Regionalism: Providing a Substance to Multilateralism?, in: F. Söderbaum and T. Shaw (eds.), *Theories of New Regionalism: A Palgrave Reader*, Houndmills: Palgrave, pp. 99–116.

Vale, P. and S. Maseko (1998), South Africa and the African Renaissance, in: *International Affairs*, Vol. 74, No. 2, pp. 271–287.

Winters, A. (1996), *Regionalism versus Multilateralism*, Washington: The World Bank, Policy Research Working Paper 1687, online: http://ctrc.sice.oas.org/trc/Articles/Regionalism/Winters96.pdf (accessed 3.5.2014).

World Trade Organization (1996), *Trade Policy Reviews. Czech Republic: March 1996,* online http://www.wto.org/english/tratop_e/tpr_e/tp29_e.htm (accessed 21.9.2014).

Zahradil, J. (2000), *Realismus místo iluzí* [Realism instead of Illusions], Praha: CEP.

New nationalist discourses and practices: the South African and Czech experience[1]

Hana Horáková

Introduction

Nationalist discourses as an inherent part of political rhetoric have not vanished in the modern world despite the fact that most nation-states are increasingly multiethnic and multicultural. There is a widely held assumption that nationalist myths and inventions are crucial for politics of identity especially in times of insecurity and change. No wonder that the arguments about the importance of national belonging and cultural difference have had increased prominence in both the countries that are the target of our inquiry – the Czech Republic (thereof CR) and South Africa (thereof SA) – from the 1990s onwards, in the times of transition from totalitarian/autocratic regimes to democratic social orders. Both CR and SA have attempted to redefine national identities.

While 'new' nationalism based on non-racialism has become the backbone of the ANC's government political project of transformation since the demise of apartheid, Czech nationalist discourse has been more or less latent and became more overt only after the split of Czechoslovakia in 1993 and with the accession of the country to the EU in 2004. In both countries, the first phases of nationalistic discourses were rather inclusive projects, aiming at forging a South African society based on 'unity in diversity', and articulating Czech national interests within the EU respectively.

As building nation-states implies internal homogenisation and differentiation (Verdery 1996b), nationalism entails both the process of inclusion and exclusion. In other words, nation-building is not simply about the creation of national unity around a common political project, it is also about demarcating that unity from the Others (Neocosmos 2010). Current conceptions of nationalism in both countries exhibit symptoms of exclusivist orientation that tend to instigate xenophobic discourse and practice. While the prevalence of xenophobia in postapartheid SA is primarily directed at African migrant labour, Czech xenophobic moods are aimed mostly at the 'unadaptable', that is the Roma people (see Synková's chapter in this volume).

---

[1] I would like to thank Stephanie Rudwick and Tereza Hyánková for reading and commenting on an earlier version of this manuscript.

Both current expressions of nationalisms, Czech and South African, though exerting certain similarities, nevertheless display many differences, due to the specific historical, political and cultural development. When it comes to the issue of national identification, the political terrain in both colonial and apartheid SA, and a 'new' SA is much more complex than in Czechoslovakia/CR. SA is a multicultural and multilingual nation, with the grave legacy of apartheid that had deeply divided the society. The transformation from an identity based on reified racial hierarchies and an ideology of 'separate development' to a common national identity, forged by the current political dispensation, is complicated by the ongoing public and political discourse that revolves round the concepts such as ethnic difference, race, culture etc.[2] (Eaton 2002: 45). Since the aim to create a new South African nation is extremely difficult, fierce struggles for a new national/ethnic/racial identity are still underway. On the other hand, CR hosts a highly homogeneous and monolingual population. Czech state sovereignty resides in a majority ethno-nation, i.e. Czechs who perceive themselves as a dominant nation (Verdery 1996b; Holý 2010). National identity is less contested than in SA, yet national tensions do play a substantial role in Czech post-1989 politics. Post-November nationalist discourses are revolved around a whole host of problems such as the emergence of new significant Others combined with weak national ties.

By focusing in detail on post-November 1989 and postapartheid development, the aim of the chapter is to describe, explain and compare issues of nationalism in postsocialist CR and postapartheid SA, in order to better understand the processes of nation-building in the era of transformation. I want to reveal a deeper meaning of nationalist rhetoric constructed by the dominant political actors – the ANC and the Czech postsocialist political elite, and to find out how competing discourses of nationalism impact political and social transformation. Key research questions are: What endangers and what hinders the creation of a unifying national identity? Which are the major social cleavages and fissures inherited from colonial and apartheid past and socialist past respectively that make the process of national identification difficult? Who are the major significant Others?

As nationalism strongly correlates with ethnocentrism and xenophobia on the one hand, and with anti-democratic authoritarianism on the other (Weiss

---

[2]See the contents of *New South African Keywords* (2008), which makes the idea of a coherent national identity complicated.

2003), the other goal will be to analyse (exemplified particularly by South African postapartheid development) the current forms and displays of chauvinism and xenophobic violence and to reveal the links between the state-led nationalist discourses and practices and ethnic/racial intolerance, and between nationalist identification and democratic orientation. To answer the research question as to what are the fundamental conditions which allow xenophobia to emerge in society, it will be shown that one has to take into account the state politics with reference to nationalist discourses in order to understand the fundamental nature of societal xenophobia.

The chapter is divided into three major parts. The first one will look into the competing, nationalist discourses based on the contrasting images of the Czech past that continue to shape the post-November 1989 politics and public opinion, especially at the encounter with the new significant Others. The second part is devoted to the analysis of the postapartheid nationalist discourses shaped by the dominant political actor, the ANC. Further on, it shows how the top-down process of forging new national identity based on autochthonous notions of 'belonging' provokes and reinforces a culture of xenophobia. The third chapter tries to synthetize the main arguments derived from nationalism as mechanism of inclusion and exclusion; make comparisons between the Czech and South African cases; and elaborate on the impact the new nationalisms may have on South African and Czech democracy.

Czech nationalist discourses and practices

According to the constructivist approach to nationalism, national identity is seen as a product of human agency, it is a creative social act; thus, national identity is always subject to change, permanently transacting and redefining itself (Wessemüller 2005: 26).

As Kuras (1998) claims, most nation's histories are partly embedded in legends and myths, partly based on biased interpretation of historical events, but in particular they reflect a dominant discourse of the collective past in a way which is instrumental in creating a particular model of the future. Czechs have often perceived themselves variously as: the economic backbone of the Austro-Hungarian Empire; exemplary Western-style democrats of great value to the democracies of the West, especially to the 'old' EU countries; a bridge between East and West; the most enterprising and westernised of the postsocialist nations; and "wishy-washy morally bent and corrupt artful dodgers" (Kuras 1998: 11). The ambivalence of the ways Czechs view themselves, reflected in a mixture of positive and negative features, is apparent in their persistent self-perception; they tend to regard themselves as the most inadequate and undeserving lot on the planet and at the same time exceptionally enlightened bearers of state-of –the-art wisdom to the world (Kuras 1998).

From the incomplete above-mentioned list of the ways Czech perceive themselves, two competing, nevertheless intertwined, discourses based on the contrasting images of the Czech past emerge: one side of the current post-socialist image's coin stresses the inherent qualities of Czechs as natural democrats, as highly cultural and educated nation; the second idea presents Czech nation as an innocent victim and martyr. Czech identity is negotiated in these two parallel discourses that compete with each other but at the same time draw inspiration from each other, and, from time to time, intertwine, depending on specific historical conditions.

It is apt to ask which strand of Czech national identity is more powerful in current public and political discourse. Holý (2010) claims that the former view is far more widespread, and in essence is at the core of Czech nationalism. Czechs tend to perceive themselves as culturally superior, looking down upon those who lack 'culture' and 'civilisation'. Despite social, cultural, economic, and political stratification of Czech society, there is a common feeling of national identity based upon the idea of cultural homogeneity that is perpetuated through the public education system, public and political discourse. The same historical awareness creates a platform for shared cultural meanings that allow Czechs to understand the world in which they live.

The implicit awareness of the long existence of strong, independent Czech identity and Czech nation is reinforced by the idea that Czech nationalism is nationalism of a dominant nation that is convinced that, unlike its Slovak counterparts, it has already reached its self-determination (Holý 2010: 14). Therefore, it does not need to be displayed, except for the situations of national crisis, or when the Czech national interests are endangered by others. Czechs construct their national identity as natural, not as a cultural construct. "Cultural construction of nation as naturally constituted entity is reinforced by the fact that a person 'se cítí být Čechem'"[3] (Holý 2010: 163). The concept of Czech nation as a community of people speaking the same language and sharing a common culture becomes obvious when Czechs are asked what it means to be Czech. They usually mention three criteria: 1) be born in Czechia; 2) speak Czech as mother tongue; 3) have Czech parents.[4] Foremost, Czech

---

[3] A person 'feels Czech'.

[4] These criteria have been acknowledged both by Holý (2010) and during the informal conversations with several Czech people over the past three years.

national identity is tied to Czech territory. Only those people who live on the Czech territory and speak Czech are considered to be genuine Czechs (Vlachová and Řeháková 2009: 256). On the contrary, compatriots living abroad, though they speak Czech, are not sometimes perceived as 'real' Czechs as they allegedly do not participate fully in cultural and political life of a nation (ibid.).

The idea of a cultured, democratic and peaceful nation that can deal with conflicts in a civilised manner (Auer 2006), a deeply rooted belief in the existence of Czech nation, and both explicit and implicit identification with it, can manifest a long tradition. On the other hand, this idea of the past constructs Czech history with historical discontinuity, in which nation emerges as a subject in shaping outside historical forces. According to this universalist conception, promoted by Czech historians Palacký and Havlíček, Czech playwright and writer Čapek and first Czechoslovak president Masaryk[5], a Czech 'great' nation has always been an active agent of history. As Holý (2010) and Auer (2006) remind us, it brought about the coherent power that enabled the political mass mobilisation during the Velvet Revolution, among others. In the post-November 1989 period, it is associated with the late president Havel and his appeal that the renewed Czech statehood must have a moral and spiritual measure formulated by 'great Czechs' such as Prince Wenceslas, King Charles IV., or Comenius. The discourse has recently manifested itself in the campaign accompanying the Czech presidency of the EU based on the slogan 'Evropě to osladíme!' (Czechs will show Europe!), which meant, in a slightly pejorative sense, that Czech would make things hot for Europe just because they may teach Europe a lesson in high culture, democracy, etc. National pride as one of the basic grounds and expressions of national identity makes the core of this nationalistic discourse. Czechs have always viewed themselves as cultural and educated nation (Auer 2006; Holý 2010). Various objects of national pride–culture, history, economic success, democracy–are often seen as the grounds and expressions of national identity (e.g., Westle 1995; Csepeli 1989; Weiss 2003). In everyday practice (as well as in professional debates by historians, intellectuals and politicians) a tendency to 'make thick line after history' in the political practice reflects the first perspective of a nation as an object of history. Those who support this idea claim that communism was actively built by all those who did not revolt and instead adapted to 'normalization'. In this logic, the Third resistance (against communist power) is justified by those who see a nation as agency.

---

[5]For the sociologically trained Tomáš Garrigue Masaryk who consistently engaged with the so-called 'Czech question', Hussitism as a pre-modern form of democracy stood at the root of the Czech claim to fame. Masaryk believed in the inherent democratic nature of the Czechs.

On the other side of the current postsocialist situation is the lobby of people who construct the Czech society with historical continuity, in which nation is an object of historical forces outside its control (represented by Czech historians Pekař, Patočka and Pithart). Local historiography represents the Czech nation either as an innocent victim and martyr, or a passive recipient of 'progress' constantly thwarted by others – Germans, Habsburgs, Russians, or Brussels bureaucrats. For Patočka (1992), for instance, Czech 'peace-loving' nature is a historic liability rather than virtue. In the frame of this vision, Czech national character is a consequence of the series of defeating historical moment: the battle of White Mountain in 1620; the Munich Treaty of 1938; the Communist takeover of 1948; the invasion of the Warsaw Pact army of 1968. Ill fortunes in history are presented as a legitimisation tool for this perspective, ranging from several situations in which the Czech nation was on the verge of annihilation: for instance the treason of Western countries at the Munich Treaty of 1938, the Communist regime as the imposition of a foreign power, the Soviet Union in 1948, or the 'normalization' which resulted from the invasion to Czechoslovakia by the Warsaw Pact army in 1968. The persistent idea that Czechs have always surrendered allows for making space for the Other who will bring the expected 'cargo' and thus may be beneficial for a 'little' Czech man (*Čecháček*, a pejorative name for somebody with a passive attitude to his/her own life, low esteem and self-respect). An illustrative example for this is the public debate on the accession of CR to the EU which stressed the cargo cult of Europe bringing law and order to the Czech *Schweinerei* (cf. Kučera 2003). The historiographical construction of national selves as victims by history implies that Czechs tend to blame others for their misfortunes. In harsh times, a scapegoat, usually a minority group becomes the target for all anger and resentment. All charges and grievances are focused on him/her/it. The recent economic crisis has triggered off the anger of some Czechs towards Roma who have become a scapegoat, source of all evils affecting society and responsible for the threat felt by the community. The critique based on stereotypical portrayals of Roma as criminals who deserve punishment became widespread among diverse population groups ranging from educated people to unskilled labourers. Czechs tend to accuse Roma for their bad economic position – they allegedly abuse the social welfare system and they get rich without working. A problematic public discourse stressing their putative laziness and their criminal tendencies obscures the real reasons of their complicated situation– lack of government policy of social housing, a state-sanctioned abuse of social welfare system by the owners of lodgings, joblessness resulting from closing inefficient companies, low level of qualification of Roma, a difficulty to actually get a job because of the prevalent prejudices against Roma, and the state-orchestrated system of 'special' schools (initially provided for mentally and/or physically handicapped pupils) where most of Roma children get basic education irrespective of their real intellectual potential, etc.

In fact, as Holý (2010) argues, Czech national identity is negotiated in these two parallel discourses that compete with each other but at the same time draw inspiration from each other. A case in point was the accession of CR to the EU in 2004 under the slogan 'Return to Europe': universalist European values merged with particularist nationalist feelings and emotions. Czech believed that their highly cultured and educated nation would eventually enrich Europe. The persistent ambivalent attitude to the EU is also modelled along the relationship with the Other: on the one hand, the EU is 'imagined' as an entity where Czechs can flourish and their freedom and democratic values are ensured (positive Other), and, on the other, as an 'oppressor' which portrays democratic deficit, restricts freedom, and threatens Czech national identity (negative Other) (Esparza 2010).

In both perspectives, Czechs are constructed as a small-scale nation in Central Europe, on the crossroads of political, religious and cultural movements. The idea of the Czechs as subjects implies their smallness; the little Czech man shows plebeian and servile attitudes and is essentially parochial (Patočka 1992; Holý 2010). The smallness, however, serves as a springboard for diverse strategies of survival. In fact, Czechs are masters in survival due to: outwitting the state exemplified by a good soldier Švejk[6] pretending loyalty to the Austro-Hungarian Empire, or by Czechs who used diverse strategies to survive under the oppressive communist regime, ranging from stealing from 'the state' (*erár*) to covert or overt collaboration with the State Security Service (StB).

If Czechs are objects of these movements, thus, responsibility for failure rests with the other – Catholics, German, communists, Russians, Slovaks, Brussels, nowadays immigrants and above all, Roma people conceptualised in political and public discourses as the 'unadaptable'.

Post-1989 nationalism in Czech politics: national identity and the Other

National identity is always constructed in the opposition to those that are viewed as the Others. In modern history, Czech national identity was

---

[6]Švejkism is a mixture of collaboration and resistance for the sake of survival (Skalník 2009: 244). It is apt to add that it was the Slovaks who tended to define their identity *vis-á-vis* Czechs, not the other way round. The reason has already been stated above – the existence of Czech dominant nation.

constructed both in contrast to those Germans with whom the Czechs shared a cultural, geographical, political and economic space, and in contrast to Austria and Germany. From 1918 to 1992, Czech national identity was also formed in contrast to the Slovaks and Slovakia.[7] And from 1948 to 1991[8] it was defined in contrast to the Russians and the Soviet Union (Vlachová and Řeháková 2009).

Nationalist ideas have played a vital role since the nineteenth century when national movements constructed Czech nation along ethno-cultural lines. After 1918 a theory of 'Czechoslovakism' – a single Czechoslovak nation was accepted by Czechs, rather than Slovaks (Musil 1993, 2003). The attempt to create a multiple identity, composed of Czech and Slovak ingredients, proved to be an entirely artificial endeavour and its product – Czechoslovak identity – was weakened in the course of history.

In the course of time, ideas about nation became deeply embedded in public and political discourse. As nation-state became a basic element of modern political subjectivity, nation in its ethno-cultural meaning entered firmly into the debate on Czech political and social identities. National consciousness, systematically reinforced during the socialist period (Party rule reified and institutionalized the ethno-national principle, see Verdery 1996a) naturally became the focus of political discourse in postsocialism.

Nationalism seemingly does not play a vital role and does not represent any defining ideology of the governing elite in CR. In the early 1990s, the Communists (KSČM) and the far-right (Sládek's Republican Party) represented the only remaining example of parties that have worked nationalism into their political program. Gradually, the 'protection of Czech national interests', primarily related to Germany and subsequently to the EU, became part of the ideology of the dominant political right – the Civic Democratic Party (ODS). Further on, other political parties and their individual representatives became swayed by nationalism, especially around the issue of displaced Sudeten Germans after the WW2 and possible compensation for them, which remains far from settled: the 'displacement' or 'expulsion' continues to influence the Czech politics, as has been clear from the presidential

---

[7]It is apt to add that it was the Slovaks who tended to define their identity *vis-r̂-vis* Czechs, not the other way round. The reason has already been stated above – the existence of Czech dominant nation.

[8]This date is linked to the displacement of the Soviet troops from the country back to Russia. On 21 June 1991 the last railway transport with Soviet soldiers and their military technology left the territory of Czech and Slovak Federative Republic (ČSFR). Six days later the last Soviet soldier followed suit. Thus, the Soviet army ended its twenty-three-year 'temporary' stay in the country (for further information see www.imilovice.net).

election campaign of 2013 (Jeník 2013). The salience of national sentiment, namely resentment with Sudeten Germany – was used by one of the presidential candidates, former head of Czech Social Democrats, Miloš Zeman who won the election in the direct vote. Zeman's deliberately chosen nationalism card, evoking powerful ideas of Czech nation as an unfortunate object of outside forces, eventually proved its vitality and perseverance among Czechs. His radical utterances fell on the fertile social soil 'cultivated' by Havel's apology to Sudeten Germans for their expulsion by the Czech State after 1945, and Klaus' systematic massage of the public evoking the 'foreign peril' (European – the EU in general, and German in particular) and the putative defence of national interests.

Nationalist and anti-European rhetoric has been largely associated with a) the former political elite who get support from their electorate (predominantly KSČM voters), b) the political right represented by the ODS and other smaller political parties on the right such as the Freedom Party (who even won a seat in the European Parliament in 2014 election), and c) extreme nationalist political parties such as Dělnická strana sociální spravedlnosti (The Workers Party of Social Justice), which use xenophobic, anti-Roma rhetoric and also stir negative public opinion against other nationalities.[9]

In the post-1989 history, there are a few events that brought about the need of Czechs to redefine their national identity and provoked a display of Czech nationalism: 1) the demise of Czechoslovakia in 1989; 2) the division of Czechoslovakia into two states at the end of 1992 and the emergence of the CR as an independent state at the beginning of 1993; and 3) the accession of the CR to the EU in 2004. These events loom over the others, less significant such as expressions of Czech patriotism after the victories of sports matches, etc.

First, the Velvet Revolution of November 1989 brought the fundamental change of regime from state-socialism to liberal democracy, discontinuity of state forms (changes in state sovereignty and dependency) and the subsequent drastic changes in relations with past significant Others, such as the USSR and Russians), gradual changes in national make-up of society, which had a substantial impact on the construction of Czech national identity. Nonetheless, it reinforced the traditional self-perception of Czechs as a cultured, democratic and peaceful nation (Auer 2006). The transformations were accompanied by a temporary strengthening of the idea of 'Moravism', taking pains to renew the autonomy of Moravia and Czech Silesia.

---

[9]One of the most frequent slogans used by this political entity is 'Čechy Čechům' (Czechia for Czechs).

Second, the unintended birth of independent CR in 1993 revealed an uncertainty of a Czech state and Czech nation (Klimek 2001). Symptoms of the national identity crisis were primarily linked to the name of the new state. While in Slovakia the term Slovensko (Slovakia) was natural, in the CR the term Česko (Czechia), at that time, was not internalised and accepted by all because such a name was further related to the Bohemian part of the state, in Czech Čechy, and therefore many Moravians and Silesians did not identify with such a denomination for the whole country. Next, it was linked to the revival of a new version of the mythical 'Czech question'[10] among the Czech intellectuals of the 1990s that raised questions "who are we?" and "where do we want to go?" (Esparza 2010: 418).

Uncertain and weak national ideology was an instrument of influence by Euro-optimistic politicians who tended to equate such concepts as 'nation', 'national interests', 'national identity' and 'patriotism' with chauvinism and xenophobia. Such terms were labelled as undesirable in the course of European integration (Kučerová 2002). The same fate met the traditional contents of Czech patriotism, which was rejected and ridiculed; national identity was equalled with nationalist chauvinism. Weak national identity went hand in hand with a low level of patriotism among Czechs. So far, Czech political representation has not been able to formulate any national ideology. As a result, whenever a politician touches upon the issue of missing national ideology and insufficiently formulated national interests, he/she is immediately branded a nationalist (Plecitá-Vlachová 2011: 48; Plecitá 2012).

Third, the EU has become the most significant Other. In CR, the EU plays a positive or negative role depending on who does the imagining. The tension was epitomised by two influential politicians, the former presidents Václav Havel and Václav Klaus[11] who by representing two radically different views of the Czech mission in Europe and the wider world, equally represent different perspectives of Czech and European identity (Auer 2006: 411). Havel's attitude towards the EU was open, cosmopolitan and active because for him Czech national identity would flourish in the EU. For him, the EU would reinforce Czech democracy, national identity, and the security of the country (Esparza 2010: 416–421). Unlike Havel, Klaus has maintained

---

[10]This concept was popularised by Masaryk in the late nineteenth century. It is formed by a set of philosophical and historical meditations about the Czech nation, when Czechs were living within the structures of the Habsburg monarchy and were without their own state (Esparza 2010).

[11]Václav Havel was the first post-communist Czechoslovak president from 1989 to 1992 and then Czech president until 2003. He died in 2011. Václav Klaus was, *inter alia*, Czech president between 2003 and 2012.

a closed and defensive position towards the EU – closed because he perceives the EU as a threat to Czech national identity, defensive in the sense that his only priority is the defence of Czech national interests. He emphasises the 'EU democratic deficit' and its excessive regulation and bureaucracy. In general, his identification and relationship towards the EU are more negative than positive (Esparza 2010: 422). Zeman's attitude to the EU, in contrast, embodied primarily by the hoisting of the EU flag at the Prague Castle, the seat of President, is largely viewed as an extreme, unconditioned, and un-critical gesture towards the EU.

Given the ambivalent and often entirely oppositional views of the EU on the part of Czech political elite on the one hand, and the absence of the debate on national identity *vis-á-vis* Europe on the other, one can make assumptions about the low level of identification of Czechs with the EU, stemming from their overall weak national identity. This hypothesis is partly acknowledged by different surveys and research projects. In 1995 the ISSP (International Social Survey Programme) carried out the comparative survey National Identity I in 23 countries, including CR. In 2003 similar research (National Identity II) was conducted in 34 countries and its third wave of the survey (National Identity III) was held in 2013. The results from ISSP 2003 survey on national identity, and Sociological research of historical consciousness of Czech citizens of 2010 show that Czechs are not much concerned about their national identity and the level of their national con-sciousness is well below levels in Norway, Austria or Hungary. Czechs do not have a particularly strong national pride. The existing level of national pride that resides in Czechs derives largely from history, literature, art, science, technology and success in sports. On the other hand, social memory, myths, symbols and traditions are of little concern for them. Czechs do not celebrate Independence Day of CR on 1 January, and the celebrations of the now non-existent independent Czechoslovak state on 28 October are rather sheepish (Plecitá-Vlachová 2011: 48). The results show a low level of trust for political institutions and the rule of law and a weak national conscious-ness.

As for their level of identification towards the EU, the data taken from Eurobarometer of the European Parliament (EB 79.5) show the downward trend in the loyalty towards the EU – from 38 percent in 2012 to 34 percent in 2013, as opposed to the upward trend in the average EU number from 48 percent in 2012 to 50 percent in 2013. The Czech membership in the EU is positively endorsed only by 31 percent, likewise, only 25 percent Czechs think that their vote has certain relevance, which is the third lowest figure within the EU member states. Though the issue of national identity now belongs to the 8th Priority of the development of the Czech society within the National Policy of the Research and Development 2009–2015 (Theme 4 Czech identity and the World), the level of national identification with the EU among Czechs remains weak. The data showing the extremely low participation in the Czech EU elections held in May 2014 only confirm the trends. The turnout dropped to a record low 18.2 percent, confirming that Czechs attitude to the EU is largely indifferent and distant.

As for the emic conceptualisation of the process of Europeanisation based on recent anthropological research of local community (see Horáková 2007), the EU is predominantly viewed as an *economic* entity – "where money is sitting, perhaps where it is going": in the former case the idea is how to drain money from the EU and those who are capable of doing that are highly appreciated.[12] Czechs tend to perceive Europe as an economic and political entity, swayed by the problems that may refer either to 'the others in Europe'- such as the recent problems with some of the Eurozone countries, or the issues that may interfere directly with their existing lifestyles – e.g. adapting them-selves to different European norms and regulations that infringe their everyday life. Putative tensions heralded by Czech intellectuals as an echo of disputed political debates (Havel vs. Klaus vs. Zeman) between European cosmo-politanism and nationalist ideology have given way to the perception of the EU as an 'indifferent Other', that is the Other Czechs are largely indifferent to.

Nationalist discourses and practices in South Africa

The issue of South African national identity and nation-building was widely debated both in the academe and public space between 1990 and 1996.[13] The discourses of 'rainbow nation', non-racial unity and the ethos of reconciliation defended by the moral authority of Nelson Mandela helped reinforce the nation-building agenda (Hart 2013: 155). When Thabo Mbeki became presi-dent, the nation-building discourse shifted to the African Renaissance, stressing the need to renew the whole continent of Africa, with SA as a mental leader. In the past fifteen years the nation-building discourse has largely been neglected[14] while new topics have come to the forefront of academic and public debate. Does this neglect imply that South Africans have already

---

[12]This concerns even those who are able to outwit the EU institutions, which can be viewed as one of the reminders of the socialist era and national ideology under socialism when it was a common strategy to fool the state with the aim to ensure a better living standard.
[13]It is beyond the scope of this text to present a comprehensive review of the literature on nation-building in South Africa.
[14]At the expense of the dominant 'intergroup' or 'race' relations paradigm (see Eaton 2002).

reached a sense of unified nationhood, that a South African nation has already been born? Or are there other pressing issues that deviate public and scholarly attention from the topic of national identity? The answer to the former question cannot satisfy those who believed in the fast emergence of a new South African nation. Identity politics still remain vital and contested as the goal to create a single South African society is one of the most difficult endeavours the postapartheid political dispensation has ever outlined.

As to the latter question, Hart (2013) claims that the reason why the nation-building agenda has faded away both from public and political discourse is the adoption of neoliberal macro-economic policies after 1996 which brought about bitter disappointments among the majority of South Africans, especially those who remain impoverished. The legacy of apartheid is still palpable in many realms of social reality. Socio-economic inequality even intensified despite certain efforts of the ruling elite in deracialising of income distribution in the upper layers of South African society (see Natrass and Seekings 2002). Neoliberalism has become the dominant frame for the development of postapartheid SA (despite the fact that the present-day ANC members distance themselves from neoliberalism and declare themselves strongly antineoliberal and pro-poor), thus side-lining the former nationalistic discourse. According to Hart (2013), key markers of postapartheid SA in the new millennium are 1) coercive rule of the postapartheid state; 2) the rise in new social movements representing expressions of popular discontent towards the ANC; and 3) the emergence of so-called service delivery protests.

Though the shift in official discourses and practices is hardly deniable it does not automatically imply the entire eradication of the issues of nationalism and nation-building. Nationalism has not been wished away in postapartheid SA; on the contrary, it remains as complex and contradictory as is often the case of any other society in transition. There are still lively debates on various facets of national identity in the making, as Eaton reminds us: the predicament of Afrikaner identity in the new SA, 'White guilt', Africanisation of South Africa, etc. (Eaton 2002: 45). To understand the major issues postapartheid SA is facing, an insight into the key facets of African nationalism within the ANC is essential. Therefore the following subchapters will try to analyse the development of the postapartheid political discourses of nation-building.

The ANC Nationalist Discourses

There have been multiple state-ANC's efforts to build a new inclusive, non-racial national unity in the past twenty years that reflect the complex nature of African nationalism within the ANC since its origin in the early twentieth century.[15] There are three key ideologies and articulations of the ANC nationalism that have influenced the direction and development of the ANC policies in nation-building from the colonial and apartheid period to the present: 1) liberal-democratic, 2) Africanist, and 3) socialist/communist.

The first ideological strand reminiscent of 'civic' nationalism, represented by Albert Luthuli (who was awarded the Nobel Peace Prize in 1962), Oliver Tambo, or Nelson Mandela, is rooted in Christian values, democracy and universalism, as is evident from the Freedom Charter of 1955, calling for a non-racial democracy in SA. The wording of its preamble ("South Africa belongs to all who live in it, black and white") became the springboard for the ANC symbolic politics after the demise of apartheid and was the key inspiration for the new Constitution adopted in 1996.

The second, Africanist school of thought is associated with a whole host of perspectives and ideas: Garveism; Négritude; Black nationalism; Pan-Africanist ideas; the Black Consciousness Movement. Modelled after Marcus Garvey's exclusivist rhetoric, it was represented in the 1920s for the first time by James Thaele who forged the slogan "Africa for the Africans and Europe for the Europeans" (Frederickson 1995: 162). Garveyite rhetoric and Pan-Africanist ideas had a great impact on the ANC Youth League (ANCYL) launched in 1944, especially on its president Anton Lembede who emphasised the exclusive character of African nationalism in which there is no space for non-Africans, as "no foreigner can ever be a true and genuine leader of the African people because no foreigner can [....] interpret the African spirit which is unique and peculiar to Africans only" (Lembede 1945: 315, cited in Wesemüller 2005: 59). The nationalism Lembede advocated was a racial nationalism, legitimised in cultural terms, stressing the putative sameness of Africans as opposed to materialistic, individualistic Europeans.

In apartheid SA, racial/cultural nationalism within the ANC was surmounted by 'civic' nationalism rooted in cosmopolitanism and universalism. Though there were attempts to return to Africanism under apartheid,[16] non-racial nationalism was far more powerful within the ANC. In postapartheid

---

[15]The ANC, under the name South African Native National Congress (SANNC) was founded in 1912. It aimed at building a common democratic society in which all people living in South Africa would equally take part. In 1923 the name 'African National Congress' was adopted.

[16]One of the most illustrative examples is the formation of the Pan-Africanist Congress which separated from the ANC in 1959, under the leadership of Robert Sobukwe. The PAC criticised the ANC for being too moderate *vis-ŕ-vis* the oppressive apartheid regime. To a certain extent, Steve Biko's Black Consciousness Movement could also be considered as a strand of racial nationalism as it promoted black national awareness, uniting all non-whites in the struggle against racial oppression. Biko's inclusive concept of 'blackness' aimed against multiracial South Africa stressed the self-reliance of Africans and criticised their dependency on white culture.

SA, Africanism has not faded away, as will be shown in the following text. The role of racial struggle was *inter alia* incorporated in the ANC document Strategy and tactics of the National Democratic Revolution (NDR) of 2007 claiming that the "aim of the NDR is liberation of Africans (in general blacks) from political and economic dependency (serfdom), and the improvement of the quality of life of all South Africans, particularly the poor of whom blacks make the majority" (ANCYL political education manual).

The third strand of nationalist ideology derives its thought from socialism and communism. The goal is to achieve socialist economy, class solidarity and non-racialism. Under the slogan "unity of working class overcomes racial divides", it is associated with the South African Communist Party (originated in 1921) and the Congress of South African Trade Unions (COSATU).[17]

These three styles not only account for the existing internal tensions, ideological fragmentation or the emergence of competing factions within the postapartheid ANC, but also explain the broad electoral platform that stands behind the twenty-year-political domination of the ANC. To maintain its power and influence, the ANC uses all three components that draw inspiration both from particularist, ethno-racial discourses, promoting racial exclusion, and universalist non-racial discourses, promoting racial integration and equality before the law. The third ingredient revolving around the socialist/communist ideas enters both the above-mentioned discourses and practices; on the one hand, the appeal to socialism was part and parcel of the universalist-oriented Freedom Charter of 1955; on the other hand, socialist ideology represented by the current populist politics (Julius Malema) is unequivocally embedded in racial nationalism.

The above mentioned typology roughly corresponds with three development phases of the postapartheid ANC politics, under three presidents: 1) Mandela's inclusive discourse of rainbow nation and reconciliation, 2) Mbeki's Africanisation, and (3) Zuma's 'new' nationalism based on nativism and populism.

Rainbowism

In the first multiracial national election of 1994 the ANC ultimately won political power and became the (only) dominant political actor. On an institutional level, the interim ANC-led Government of National Unity (1994–1997) consolidated the new nation-state and adopted the Constitution in 1996 which

---

[17]COSATU originated in 1985 as the key actor in the struggle against apartheid. Today it is part of the governing Tripartite Alliance, with the ANC and SACP.

provided the legal foundation for the existence of the republic whose orientation in the frame of human rights as non-racial and non-sexist arouse admiration of the world community as one of the most liberal constitutions worldwide.

To maintain the dominance, the ANC strove to gain loyalty from the electorate and legitimise its position not only in the political, social and economic realms, but also in the symbolic, ideological sphere. The imperative became the building a new, non-racial nation and new national identity that would overcome the legacy of apartheid – a deeply divided society along racial and class lines. The aim to create a united, non-racial and non-sexist society was not only engraved in the Constitution of 1996, but it also became the backbone of the project of National Democratic Revolution (NDR),[18] which is the basis of the ANC/SACP/COSATU Alliance. The three main principles of the NDR included non-racialism, reconciliation, and a single South African culture. The ethos of non-racialism dwells in the assumption that race as the key factor of social identification under apartheid must be eradicated. The ultimate goal of racial transformation is an internally compact, colour-blind society with race and ethnicity as irrelevant factors. Non-racialism is impossible to achieve without reconciliation between the apartheid victims and their perpetrators and supporters. The idea of a single South African culture based on a collective South Africanness, while asserting the existing plurality of cultural minorities, is construed as a response to the apartheid legacy of division, conflict, polarisation and violence.

The key discursive field that embraces the three components (non-racialism, reconciliation, and single South African culture) is 'rainbowism' (Wesemüller 2005; Baines 2009; Horáková 2010, 2011). The metaphor of the rainbow nation was initially introduced by Anglican Archbishop Desmond Tutu in 1989; then it was used by Nelson Mandela in his State of the Nation address in 1994. This idea represents resistance to the apartheid legacy of deeply divided society while pointing to the ideal of South Africa's common, shared future. It stresses reconciliation and tolerance embodied in the work of the Truth and Reconciliation Commission (TRC).

Critics of the concept point to the inherent tensions between a perceived need for national unity and a national identity on the one hand, and the need to acknowledge cultural diversity and to accommodate group identity on the other hand (Frankental and Sichone 2005: 254). They doubt that the emphasis

---

[18]The origins of the NDR in South Africa date back to 1928. The programme guided by the resolution of the 2nd Congress of the Communist International was adopted by the ANC with the aim to liberate Africans from national oppression and class exploitation.

on multiculturalism and the celebration of cultural diversity can be reconciled with the national political project (Horáková 2010). Challenges revolve around the assumption that multiculturalism, by overstating cultural diffe- rences among diverse 'population groups', undermines, or at least challenges, the possibility of cultural unity across South African society. Furthermore, the concept of the rainbow nation associated with multiculturalism reinforces the deeply entrenched assumption held by South Africans that divisions are not only social and economic but predominantly *cultural*. Thus, even (if) when the (socio-economic) inequalities are reduced, 'rainbowism' will still not lead to reducing polarity and conflicts in society (Horáková 2011).

Mandela's ethos of the rainbow nation found its 'material' response in the Reconstruction and Development Programme (RDP) based on the redistri- bution of existing wealth towards the poorest. Though it improved life of millions of blacks (electricity, access to water, the so-called RDP houses), the programme was not fully successful. It did not stimulate the rise of black middle class that would be able to create jobs and contribute to the national economy. Mandela's unwillingness to support black bourgeoisie was ap- parently motivated by the awareness of infamous predatory, greedy elite in other African postcolonial countries that were instrumental in plunging national economies.

Mandela's idea of the rainbow nation envisaged the rapid growth of a single national identity and culture. However, as this top-down project was a product of social engineering, similar to apartheid, the urge to create South- Africanness was met with a lukewarm response. Kotzé's (1997) research results of 1997 show that only 17 percent of people identified as South Africans. Moreover, it was not clear what the contents of the new South African culture should be. By and large, the preponderance of evidence shows that the vision of the rainbow nation remains a romantic ideal, perpetuated at a symbolic level. In practical life there is little social and racial integration. SA remains a deeply divided society along the lines of race and class. As Hart (2013: 7–8) claims, the inclusive reconciliatory discourses of the 'rainbow nation' and of forgiveness made possible the negotiations to end apartheid; they, however, ceased by the end of the 'Mandela decade'.

Africanism

From 1996 onwards, 'rainbowism' was gradually superseded by Africanism. Thabo Mbeki's 'I am an African' address on the occasion of adopting the new South African Constitution in 1996 gradually directed the ANC party rhetoric towards a more exclusive form of nationalism than the one offered by

Mandela. In the 'South Africa: two nations' address of 1998 Mbeki repudiated Mandela's one-nation legacy by pronouncing that there were two nations, one white and rich, the other black and poor. For the first time, Mbeki made explicit references to a racial connotation of nation when he linked nation to skin colour – he actually equalled 'haves' with whites and 'have-nots' with blacks. The statement is problematic at least for two reasons. First, though it is clear that the majority of the impoverished South Africans are black, it is no longer true that all of the rich are white and all blacks are poor. Second, though maybe unwittingly, Mbeki happened to entrench the now common view of the existence of 'two (race) nations' in postapartheid SA. Even though the ANC was built on non-racialism, Mbeki started playing what is colloquially termed 'the race card', which then strengthened the already entrenched negative assumptions about the Other along racial lines. Again, race has made a determinant of identity. Mbeki's obsession with race and racism, as opposed to Mandela's rainbow nation inclusiveness, is difficult to neglect. He is seen by many public commentators as a racial nationalist working constantly to mobilise blacks against an imagined white threat (Johnson 2009: 59).

By and large, the ANC under Mbeki replaced non-racial politics with a narrow African nationalism, stressing a discourse of indigeneity (Chipkin 2007). Critics (cf. Johnson 2009) claim that the nationalist bourgeoisie in the guise of the ANC (ab)used popular ideas of Africanisation to promote its own class interests. They argue that Africanism resembles Afrikaners' empower-ment under apartheid. The discourse of Africanism allegedly brought about merely cosmetic changes to postapartheid politics – a shift from an Afrikaner elite to a black elite, in both cases with ties to the ruling party (Reddy 2008). The case in point is the project of Black Economic Empowerment (BEE) aimed at empowering black business. Initially planned as a programme of deracialisation, it failed to reduce the inequality gap (which, in fact even increased).[19] Instead, only a tiny layer of 'historically disadvantaged people' got rich, among them predominantly members or former members of the ANC or those with close ties to the movement. Critics labelled the BEE as 'crony capitalism' (Adam et al. 1998). Similar critique is voiced about the affirmative action policies as part of the Employment Equity Act (EEA) of 1996 which aimed at redressing the wrongs of the apartheid past. It argues that by intro-ducing 'racial quotas' in business and public life (to reflect the population

---

[19]The GINI index rose from 0.66 to 0.70 in the past fifteen years, most substantially among the black population. The ever increasing inequality has affected the country's position within the Failed State Index; its 115th position in the 'high warning' category is particularly determined by the high score (7.7) in the uneven economic development indicator (http://ffp.statesindex.org).

make-up) the new political dispensation keeps relying on apartheid racial classification, in the country where non-racialism is even part of the Constitution. Another strand of liberal critique points out that not only affirmative policies tend to reproduce the racial divisions of the past; they also amount to a reverse discrimination and 'reverse racism' associated with government efforts to transform the demographics of South Africa's white-dominated civil service.

The prevailing discourse of racial nationalism launched by Mbeki's two nations' address has had serious implications of the possibility of nation-building. As Maré (2005: 518) noticed, the State, rather than using inclusive factors decided to employ divisive strategies and symbols that threaten to "split the country apart". By promoting racial thoughts, Mbeki's nationalist policies univocally belong to the divisive strategy. The others, such as renaming towns, cities, streets, and removing or erecting statues and monuments, follow suit. As Maré (2005: 509) reminds us these all resemble apartheid practices designed to separate development; thus, they serve as mirror images in which "the old common sense with new content prevails".

ANC's new nationalism, populism and nativism

The third period was triggered by the ANC crisis characterised by manifold internal tensions and conflicts that culminated at the 52nd national conference in Polokwane in 2007, which elected Jacob Zuma as the new president of the ANC, representing a significant defeat for Thabo Mbeki. In the general election of 2009 Zuma became South African president, and he happened to renew his mandate in the general election of 2014. Under his presidency South African politics has entered a new, turbulent phase: the relations between the members of the Tripartite Alliance have worsened; strikes in mining industry and country-wide social protests against poor service delivery have intensified; socio-economic inequality and unemployment have risen. By and large, the public mood has changed. During the first ten years of democracy, political narratives about the rainbow nation exuded optimism that was largely shared with the public. The 'discourse of hope' was also evident in the popular media that introduced diverse marketing campaigns such as "Proudly South African", "Alive with Possibility", and "South Africa: Good News" (Roberts et al. 2010: 1). But as the overall situation had not been improving, especially for the masses of impoverished South Africans, signs of a transition from an age of hope to an age of uncertainty or despair were reported (Roberts et al. 2010). They were associated with concerns about mounting violent crime, increasing unemployment and poverty as well as with widespread corruption in central and provincial governments linked to the misappropriation of resources. The erosion of trust in public institutions and political actors and their disability to deliver on expectations was reported (Kagwanja 2009). The widespread disillusionment with the postapartheid period that has not witnessed any substantial alleviation of inequality manifested itself in the wave of mass protests and violent demonstrations by impoverished people against poor delivery service, food price inflation and the cost of living, as well as the frustration over the ever increasing crime rates, and about the HIV/AIDS pandemic linked to the Mbeki's denialism and reluctance to supply effective anti-retroviral drugs.

The 'bad mood' accompanied by radicalisation of some sectors of South African society found its response in the radical strand of transformation discourse in the ANC designed as transition to socialism. Socialist ideology is not new in the ANC thought, as has already been mentioned. It was part of the key ideological expression, such as the Freedom Charter of 1955, and the National Democratic Revolution (NDR) whose key assumption was that capitalism is a transitory phenomenon that is to be superseded by the second phase, of socialist revolution (Hart 2013: 8). Thought the NDR has over the years been subjected to various interpretations and meanings, its major aim has always been the national liberation movement translated as the "shortest route to socialism" (COSATU 9th Congress Resolution); "dialectical resolution of the class, gender and national contradictions" (the 1969 Morogoro ANC Strategy & Tactics and Political Report); and "non-capitalist or socialist oriented transition in South Africa" (SACP's GS What is the National Democratic Revolution).[20]

The 2007 ANC Strategy and Tactics, which is the basis of the NDR's second postapartheid decade, particularly specifies the goal of *economic* emancipation of Africans, attempting to fulfil the revolutionary dimension emphasised by the SACP and COSATU. The attainment of NDR objectives "forms a basis for a socialist revolution" (ANCYL political education manual). Socialism is therefore linked to the NDR while the NDR is the road to socialism.

However, as a critical scholar argues, irrespective of its emphasis on socialist ideology, the NDR shows no signs of giving way to socialism (Hart 2013: 174). Radical critics within the ANC criticise the movement for betraying the Freedom Charter in favour of large business corporations.

---

[20] The information on diverse interpretations and meanings of the NDR is taken from the ANCYL political education manual on NDR.

The response to the 'bad mood' and radicalisation of society was multiple, proliferating expressions of nationalism, including the 'new' ANC nationalism, as well as a rise of populist politics in SA (Hart 2013: 4).

As for the 'new' ANC nationalism, it is as ambivalent as any other nationalist strands before. On the one hand, there has been a shift from Mbeki's transformation and the narrowly conceived BEE to Mandela's policy of nation-building enriched however by the accent for the poor that saw its concrete shape in the Broad-Based Black Economic Empowerment (BBBEE). On the other hand, a renewing the objectives of the NDR (the deployment of cadres, control and management of all power levels) strives to gain ideological domination in all state organs and society. The ANC's centralisation of power is accompanied by the metamorphosis of nationalism into nativism and populism. The launch of the Native Club in 2006 as a new forum for the black intelligentsia resonated with current crises within the ANC and the Tripartite Alliance and the second decade of South African democracy punctuated with a popular sense of betrayal. The debates revolved around key issues of race, citizenship, inclusion and exclusion, the limits and dangers of neoliberalism, as well as the dangers and limits of populist African nationalism (Ndlovu-Gatsheni 2007). The formation of the Native Club came as a major challenge to those who favoured the spirit of 'rainbowism' (Ndlovu-Gatsheni 2009). The Club was viewed as the 'Third transformation pillar' (Mafolo 2006), with a special emphasis on culture, underlined by the banner 'Where are the Natives?' in reaction to the decline of black intellectuals in postapartheid SA. The main aim was cultural decolonisation of (black) South Africans. The attempt to entirely eradicate apartheid and colonial thinking was accompanied by the promotion of native languages and culture, tradition, music. Ubuntu became a factor in the nation-building moral renewal, with the appeal to the active participation of blacks in the national discourse of socio-economic, political and cultural issues (Ndlovu-Gatsheni 2007).

Populist politics have strengthened in the new millennium (Hart 2013: 189). The embodiment of populism in SA is *'enfant terrible'* Julius Malema, the former president of the ANCYL and now, 'commander in chief' of the Economic Freedom Fighters (EEF). Malema, initially a fierce supporter of Zuma, was expelled from the ANC in 2012 for performing the so-called hate speech in public (singing the pejorative song 'Kill the farmer, kill the Boer') and for his overall disrespect towards the ANC. In June 2013 he founded a new political party (EEC) which is currently the third-largest party in both houses of the South African Parliament, gaining a 6.35 percent share of the vote in the 2014 general election.[21] Malema has successfully managed to

---

[21]http://www.elections.org.za/resultsnpe2014/default.aspx

capture and amplify the revolutionary potential of popular antagonisms (Hart 2013: 197). He is popular among the disillusioned, impatient young blacks, living in townships and rural shanty towns who see no perspective in improving their social and economic positions and are discontent with the prevailing macro-economic politics. His potential electorate includes 50 percent of the unemployed in the age group between 20–24 a majority of whom (86 percent) lacks education and qualification.[22] Economic freedom fighters' motto is that political emancipation without economic empowerment is useless. Thus, economic emancipation translated as nationalisation without compensation is the key factor in national liberation. Malema's radicalism and militancy is directed towards whites (white-owned capital) in general, and the biggest oppositional party Democratic Alliance (DA) and its head Helen Zille in particular, whom he frequently calls colonialist, imperialist, racist, and even cockroach.[23] Likewise, he labels whites as settlers (an infamous term used by Mugabe), members of the Indian community as 'macula', which can be translated as 'coolies'.[24] Malema's "inflammatory and racially tinged populism" (Hart 2013: 208) reasserts a narrow African nationalism. His political style has stirred radicalism, xenophobia and racism, all elements that are already present in some sectors of South African society. In international perspective he contributes to the Western prejudice of the inherent inability of black people to successfully govern an industrial nation (Sparks 2003).

Impact of ANC's new nationalism on South African society: xenophobia in postapartheid South Africa

Populism, nativism and racially inflected Africanist nationalism have far-reaching effects on a fragile postapartheid South African society. Many South Africans, especially Afrikaners, feel unsure and unsafe about their place in the country which they perceive as their homeland. The rise in intolerance, xenophobia and racism is echoed in the emergence of right-wing training camps where young Afrikaners are being trained to fight for their Afrikaner heritage, or in the rise of gated communities and 'homelands' such as Orania or Kleinfontein.[25]

---

[22]http://www.tradingeconomics.com/south-africa/unemployment-rate
[23]http://www.news24.com/SouthAfrica/Politics/Malema-calls-Zille-a-cockroach-20101030
[24]http://africawitness.wordpress.com/2011/10/21/malemas-makula-word-upsets-indians/. The term 'coolie' used in South Africa indicates a contemporary racial slur for people of Asian descent.
[25]An illustrative example is Kommando Korps (see https://afrikanerjournal.wordpress.com/tag/kommando-korps/). For further information on Afrikaner 'homelands' Orania and Kleinfontein, see http://www.orania.co.za, and http://www.kleinfontein.net respectively.

New forms of racism are widely debated in SA, such as reverse racism, or 'black racism' towards whites, and black racism towards the black immigrants. The latter is connected to the opening of the country's borders after 1994. SA, viewed as the most advanced African state, has become a magnet for refugees, economic migrants and so-called 'illegal aliens' from other African countries, partly from South Africa's neighbours, Mozambique and Zimbabwe, partly from Nigeria. Simultaneously, xenophobic practices have been reported as a common feature of life in postapartheid SA (Harris 2001; Neocosmos 2008, 2010).

There have been numerous outbreaks of violence since 1994; the aggressors were always local blacks who blamed their victims for crime, unemployment, the spread of HIV and patronisation of local women. The victims were black 'outsiders' portrayed as *Makwerekwere* (the babblers) meaning those incapable of articulating local languages that epitomise economic success and power (Hart 2013; Neocosmos 2010).

The most pronounced events are connected with a wave of xenophobic violence of May 2008 which started in the Johannesburg township of Alexandria and spread rapidly through the rest of the Gauteng province before communities in KwaZulu-Natal, Limpopo and the Northern and Western Cape embarked on violent riots of their own. Eventually, more than 62 people, mainly citizens from Somalia, Mozambique or Zimbabwe, were killed by mob violence and thousands were left homeless. The violence has been labelled in different ways –criminal, xenophobic, or Afrophobic. Similarly, there are diverse, often competing explanations of these events. Existing explanations of xenophobia in South Africa emerge in terms of economic crisis, political transition, relative deprivation, or as remnants of apartheid (Neocosmos 2010: 105).

Although there is no doubt that racist exclusion as well as economic and political crises may have served as a trigger, the above mentioned accounts cannot explain the xenophobic attacks in its entirety. Hence, the central issue in the attempt to explain xenophobia in SA is to understand it as a political discourse (Erasmus 2005).

Given the current shift of South African nationalistic discourse from the all-inclusive into the exclusivist form, there is a widely held assumption that xenophobia is a product of a nationalist discourse in postapartheid SA based on the politics of belonging and the construction of citizenship. Kersting (2009) argues that the new nationalism focuses on the new political cleavage between autochthony and origin. Citizenship is seen as a key factor. Rights to social welfare, to employment, to land etc. are increasingly denied to newcomers and immigrants. Hence, internal economic inequality can be seen as a trigger for these new trends. Neocosmos (2008) points to the fact that it is not the white foreigners who are targeted, which can be explained by the anti-rural and pro-urban character of South African nationalism. The post-apartheid state simply shifted this rural-urban binary opposition to Africa-South Africa, such that Africa is perceived as rural and backward and South Africa as urban and modern. Thus, xenophobia is associated with African nationalist discourse in SA which is fundamentally of urban, modernist nature, without any rural, that is backward connotations; 'illegal immigrants' in SA are implicitly or explicitly seen as coming from the backward rural areas of the continent, or from 'failed states'. Similarly, Mosselson (2010) shows that the violent exclusion of foreigners is one of the central ways in which the new South African political community is being shaped. Despite the apparent spontaneity of the violent attacks, they were provoked by overtly political actions and by specific social groups. Nyamnjoh (2010), likewise, reveals the roots of the xenophobic violence in the way political agents and public institutions construct the boundary between *Makwerekwere* as 'undeserving outsiders' and South Africans as 'deserving citizens'. The public discourse of government authorities, immigration offi-cials, the media, and the general public suggests that black unskilled migrants are unwelcome. *Makwerekwere* are considered a threat to the physical and moral health of the nation and should therefore be kept out of SA.

All the above mentioned authors claim that xenophobia can be explained in the framework of the politics of postapartheid nationalism – both as a political discourse and practice. The underlying conditions for the existence of xenophobia within South African nationalism are part of xenophobic discourse in SA both on the state level, and in society.

As for the state's role in the culture of xenophobia, narrowly conceived racial nationalism is closely related to the ANC's immigration policies and practices that can be considered as another dimension of the ANC post-apartheid hegemonic project aimed at remaking the nation after apartheid, namely 'Fortress South Africa' (Hart 2013; Crush 1999). This conception deals with control, exclusion and expulsion. National identity is founded on a notion of indigeneity and autochthony, and is essentially exclusive – the state defines citizenship in terms of descent so that right of access to the South African labour market is increasingly defined in restrictive terms towards the 'foreigners' who are conceived as the non-indigenous. The primacy of autochthony (Comaroff and Comaroff 2001) is directly embedded in the immigrant legislation (legal discrimination): South African citizenship is restricted to those who can prove some form of indigenous link with the country (Neocosmos 2010: 107). Xenophobic discourse and practices are equally motivated by exceptionalism of SA, "an exclusionary conception of the nation and citizenship on the African continent" (Neocosmos 2010: xii). According to this perspective, SA resembles more a Southern European, or Latin American country than an African country. Reasons to support this argument are manifold: levels of industrialisation, modernisation, development, the achieved level of democracy and putative reconciliation between 'races'. Africa, namely its sub-Saharan part is viewed as its counterpart, associated with notions of backwardness, primitivism, authoritarianism, poverty, and failed state status. This argument fits well within a constant celebration of South African democracy and its Constitution and contributes to a national sense of superiority (Neocosmos 2010: 151). Foreigners, especially African nationals, are perceived as threatening the unity of the nation, and the fragile democracy. The outcome is a "contradictory mix of nationalist and individual arrogance and entitlement at the expense of the rest of the world, particularly Africa" (Neocosmos 2010: 5).

Not only government legislation but also other political agents are contributing to fashioning xenophobia. Leading politicians called illegal immigrants a threat to the RDP, branding them potential criminals, drug smugglers and murderers (*Mail and Guardian*, 7–13 June 1996). Others use unfounded statistics (there are no data to support the contention) to spread the 'evidence' on the link between foreign persons and fraudulent and criminal behaviour (an infamous statement by the ANC ex-Director General of Home Affairs in 2002 on 90 per cent of foreigners who are in SA with fraudulent documents). Diverse statements from powerful and influential people on migration tend to incite anti-immigrant feelings among the South African public. The dominant perspective constructed by the state and the state politics is reinforced in the media, by xenophobic utterances and anti-immigrant terminology. Regular refrains that migrants "steal jobs" and are "flooding into the country illegally" (*The Star*, 21 July 1997) and reflected in the public space. The xenophobic discourse was evident in cries such as "This country is ours"; "The foreigners must leave or die"; (*Mail and Guardian*, 16 to 22 May 2008).

Czech and South African nationalism compared

In each country, national identity crisis is a result of an abrupt and sudden historical change. In CR the change involved: a) the end of the communist regime and the dissolution of the USSR between 1989 and 1991; (b) a subsequent regime change resulting in the advent of market economy and liberal democracy; (c) a break-up of Czechoslovakia in 1993. These changes gave rise to: i) the sudden disappearance of significant Others like the USSR in 1991; ii) new levels of relationships with the Slovaks, who became external Others after the split of Czechoslovakia; and iii) the formation of new relationships towards the new significant Others, such as the EU.

Czech nationalist discourse is shaped by two competing, yet intertwining ideologies, based on the contrasting images of the Czech past: the first one views Czechs as active agents who as 'natural democrats' can teach the others lessons in democracy and culture. The other image portrays Czechs as passive victims of outside forces. Both these perspectives help shape the post-November 1989 political and public discourse, which is equally ambivalent and contradictory. In fact, there is no one vision of Czech national identity that dominates public debates. Rather, Czech national identity is an ongoing and open-ended contest between different nationalist discourses (Auer 2006: 425). It is obvious that these discourses can be used for further advancement of radically different political projects. The vision of active Czech nation for whom democracy is 'hereditary and inborn' can not only support optimistic, self-congratulatory, liberal-democratic projects but it can also lead to chauvinism and racism against those who 'lack' the necessary civilizational characteristics, such as the internal essential Other – Roma.

In postapartheid SA, despite the dominant position of the ANC (the ANC has won all the national elections since 1994) the Congress is not ideologically united. The demise of apartheid brought new challenges to the ANC nationalism. The old tensions between racial and non-racial concepts play a continuing role, now under the completely different political and socio-economic conditions. Moreover, the changing articulations of African nationalism have to compete with other forms of ethnic and national resurgence in response to the forging of united nation-state after 1994, such as a new wave of Afrikaner nationalism, re-awakening of Zulu ethnicity, strengthening of Indian cultural identity, etc. (see Davies 2009; Maré 1992; Singh 2005). As the goal to build a non-racial society seems more and more distant, the question remains what kind of the ANC nationalist discourse predominates at present – a moderate, pro-democratic and inclusive one as the one represented by Mandela in the early postapartheid period, or the more recently emerging militant, radical and exclusivist discourse represented by Malema, among others, Clearly, both strands continue to be inherent parts of the ANC ideology at present. As I have tried to argue in this chapter, there is an obvious shift from Mandela's vision of rainbow nation and reconciliation, via Mbeki's Africanisation to the new nationalism characterised by political radicalism, nativism and populism under the Zuma presidency. As Ndlovu-Gatsheni (2009) and Desai (2008) argue, African nationalism, that initially assumed the character of developmentalism and a civic conception of the nation, fell into cultural nationalism and nativism as a way to compensate for the contemporary crisis and decline.

What is the impact of this discourse on South Africa society? What are the political implications of the resurrected nationalism for the democratic development of new SA? Nationalism works on the basis of exclusion (superiority over outsiders) and inclusion (equality among insiders). All over the world, fierce struggles over belonging and exclusion of 'strangers' are taking place (cf. Geschiere and Jackson 2006). As has been shown, the exclusivist conception of nation can result in discrimination and political incapacitation. The possible victims of national superiority and xenophobia directed against 'outsiders' are not only refugees and immigrants from the other parts of Africa, but also South African citizens who are simply perceived as non-South African (e.g. Shangaans). Such a public-state nationalist discourse (as a product of a specific relation between state and society) that excludes 'outsiders' in SA helps create conspiratorial enemies and scapegoats and as such is a betrayal of the idea of non-racialism. As Neocosmos noticed, xenophobia in today's SA is a *structural* feature of state nationalistic discourse and practice, not an accidental occurrence (Neocosmos 2010: 108). Its underlying features include 1) the essentialist and primordialist state-centred notion of nation and the concept of citizenship based on indigeneity; 2) animosity and conflict between the urban and rural exacerbated by the decline of migrant labour after the demise of apartheid; 3) South African exceptionalism which views the rest of Africa as economically and politically backward. The relations between postapartheid SA and the rest of Africa have a quasi-colonial undertone intensified by South African economic dominance and its successful, largely peaceful transition to democracy. 'Fortress South Africa' is to be defended against *Makwerekwere* – barbarians who flood the country, take away jobs, and commit crimes. Xenophobia is fostered by milder to extreme chauvinistic statements of leading politicians (largely from the ruling party) that goes largely unchallenged; on the contrary, it is rather reinforced in the public sphere and by the media.

Conclusion

The aim of the chapter was to describe, explain and compare issues of nationalism in postsocialist CR and postapartheid SA. It confirmed the assumption that the urge to forge national unity embedded in dominant nationalistic discourse is apparent especially in times of crises, transitions and transformations, filled with insecurity and change. With the large-scale transformation challenging formerly established institutions and discourses, nationalism and politics of identity start to thrive (Verdery 1996a).

Nationalism has not faded away in either of the two societies in transition. On the contrary, it is being enlivened by diverse actors for complex and often contradictory purposes. Nationalism is a contested idea both in the new SA, and in postsocialist CR. Diverse nationalist sentiments derived both from history and the present conditions contribute to its current discourses and practices.

In both countries, the first phases of politically promulgated nationalistic discourses after the demise of apartheid/state socialism were rather inclusive projects, aiming at forging a single South African society (Mandela's 'rainbowism'), and redefining Czech national identity vis-á-vis Europe respectively (the Czech 'Return to Europe'). Yet, as has been shown in this chapter, even in this period these discourses were far from being ideologically homogeneous. The reason is above all the heterogeneous nature of the discursive field of the ANC nationalism. It is shaped by three key ideologies: liberal-democratic, Africanist, and socialist/communist; all three components draw inspiration both from particularist, ethno-racial discourses, promoting racial exclusion, and universalist non-racial discourses, promoting racial integration. Unlike postapartheid SA, the issue of Czech national conscious-ness based on the existence of a dominant nation became a seemingly indisputable part of post-November 1989 public and political discourse. However, in the course of time, nationalist tensions played a more and more active role in Czech political and public life. The salience of national senti-ment manifested in the issues concerning the 'protection of Czech national interests' after the country accessed the EU, and the attitude of the majority population towards minorities, especially Roma, has swayed public and political discourse in postsocialist CR. In SA, wide-spread disillusionment with the postapartheid period has opened the gate causing a rise in populism, nativism and racially inflected Africanist nationalism, which tend to instigate xenophobic discourse and practice. Thus, xenophobia, primarily directed at African migrant labour, can be explained, *inter alia*, in the framework of the state-led nationalist discourses and practices. In other words, xenophobia in today's SA is a structural feature of state nationalist politics.

What, then, can be the impact of the new nationalisms on South African and Czech democracy? As state resources are diminishing, even the most sensitive among those in power tend to see migrants from Africa as potentially dangerous as the overwhelming perception is one of foreigners as 'takers' rather than as 'contributors' (Neocosmos 2010: 108). Any sort of defence of the powerless and the marginalised constitutes a political suicide for any professional politician. Chipkin (2004) puts it unequivocally: democracy and African nationalism modelled after the slogan "Africa for the native Africans" instead of "Africa for All" are totally antithetical. Racially inflected nationalist politics can destroy the existing extremely fragile social contract and undermine the substantive dimensions of democracy (Gumede 2014).

Nationalist, largely anti-EU discourse, combined with weak national identity, can equally lead to authoritarian, anti-democratic ideas, tendencies and practices already latent in some sectors of Czech society. So far, extreme chauvinism in politics has been largely reserved for extreme political groupings but utterances with racial undertone (on the unadaptable/asocial, i.e. on the Roma how they abuse social welfare system) are heard among the politicians from the 'established' political parties such as the ODS, TOP 09 and ČSSD. Novel forms of national intolerance such as the use of anti-Gypsy images are on increase among the majority of Czechs. In times of economic crises, high unemployment and an ever-decreasing trust in democratic institutions, exclusivist nationalist sentiment can substantially erode the uncertain Czech democracy.

References

Adam, H., F. van Zyl Slabbert and Kogila Moodley (1998), *Comrades in Business: Post-Liberation Politics in South Africa*, Cape Town: Tafelberg.

Africa witness, Malema's 'Makula' word upsets Indians, online: http://africawitness.wordpress.com/2011/10/21/malemas-makula-word-upsets-indians/ (accessed 15. 7. 2014).

ANCYL political education manual, online: www.ancyl.org.za/.../political/.../NDR%20Presentationb(1) (accessed 20. 5. 2014).

Auer, S. (2006), After 1989, Who are the Czechs? in: *Nationalism and Ethnic Politics*, Vol. 12, pp. 411–430.

Baines, G. (2007), The Master Narrative of South Africa's Liberation Struggle: Remembering and Forgetting, in: *The International Journal of African Historical Studies*, Vol. 40, No. 2, pp. 283–302.

Chipkin, I. (2004), Nationalism as Such: Violence during South Africa's Political Transition, in: *Public Culture*, Vol. 16, No. 2, pp. 315–35.

Chipkin, I. (2007), *Do South Africans Exist? Nationalism, Democracy and the Identity of "the people"*, 1st ed., Johannesburg: Wits University Press.

Comaroff, J. and J. L. Comaroff (2001), Naturing the Nation: Aliens, Apocalypse and the Postcolonial State, in: *Journal of Southern African Studies*, Vol. 27, No. 3, pp. 627–651.

Crush, J. (1999), Fortress South Africa and the Deconstruction of the Apartheid Migration Regime, in: *Geoforum*, Vol. 30, pp. 1–11.

Csepeli, G. (1989), *Structures and contents of Hungarian national identity. Results of Political Socialization and Cultivation*, Frankfurt: Peter Lang.

Davies, R. (2009), *Afrikaners in the New South Africa: Identity Politics in a Globalised Economy*, Tauris Academic Studies.

Desai, R. (2008), Conclusion: From Developmental Nationalism to Cultural Nationalisms, in: *Third World Quarterly*, Vol. 29, No. 3, pp. 647–670.

Eaton, L. (2002), South African National Identity: A Research Agenda for Social Psychologists, in: *South African Journal of Psychology*, Vol. 32, pp. 45–53.

Erasmus, Z. (2005), Race and Identity in the Nation, in: J. Daniel, R. Southall and J. Lutchman (eds.), *State of the Nation, South Africa: 2004–2005*, Cape Town: HSRC, pp. 9–33.

Esparza, D. (2010), National identity and the Other: imagining the EU from the Czech Lands, in: *Nationalities Papers*, Vol. 38, No. 3, pp. 413–436.

Eurobarometer of the European Parliament (EB79.5), online: www.europarl.europa.eu/.../eurobarometre/ (accessed 15.6. 2014).

FFP (Fragile State Index 2014), online: http://ffp.statesindex.org (accessed 2.7. 2014).

Frankental, S. and O. B. Sichone (2005), *South Africa's Diverse Peoples: A Reference Sourcebook*, Santa Barbara, Calif.; Denver, Colorado; Oxford, England: ABC-CLIO.

Frederickson, G. M. (1995), *Black Liberation. A Comparative History of Black Ideologies in the United States and South Africa*, Oxford: Oxford University Press.

Geschiere, P. and S. Jackson (2006), Autochtony and the Crisis of Citizenship: Democratization, Decentralization, and the Politics of Belonging, in: *African Studies Review*, Vol. 49, No. 2, pp. 1–14.

Gumede, W. (2014), The DA as an opposition: Lessons from 20yrs of democracy, in: *The Journal of the Helen Suzman Foundation*. Focus 72 – Democracy and its discontents, issue 72, April 2014, pp. 25–33, online: http://hsf.org.za/resource-centre/focus/focus-72-democracy-and-its-discontents/focus-72-democracy-and-its-discontents/view (accessed 15. 5. 2014).

Harris, B. (2001), A Foreign Experience: Violence, Crime and Xenophobia during South Africa's Transition, *Centre for the Study of Violence and Reconciliation*, Violence and Transition Series, Vol. 5, online: http://www.csvr.org.za/index.php/publications/1646-a-foreign-experience-violence-crime-and-xenophobia-during-south-africas-transition.html (accessed 17. 2. 2013).

Hart, G. (2013), *Rethinking the South African Crisis. Nationalism, Populism, Hegemony*, Durban: University of KwaZulu-Natal Press.

Holý, L. (2010), *Malý český člověk a skvělý český národ*. [The Little Czech and the Great Czech Nation], 2nd edition, Praha: SLON.

Horáková, H. (2007), The Local and the Global: In Search of European Identity in the Czech Local Community, in: *The Anthropology of East Europe Review: Central Europe, Eastern Europe and Eurasia*, Vol. 25, No. 1, pp. 112–116.

Horáková, H. (2010), Heritage, Tourism, and Nation-Building in Post-Apartheid South Africa, in: P. Chabal and P. Skalník (eds.), *Africanists on Africa. Current Issues*, Berlin: LIT Verlag, 195–208.

Horáková, H. (2011), Non-racialism and nation-building in the new South Africa, in: *The Annual of Language & Politics and Politics of Identity*, Vol. 5, pp. 109– 124.

Horáková, H. (2012), Social Identification and Nationalist Discourses in Post-Apartheid South Africa, in: V. Fiala (ed.), *Multiple Identities in Post-Colonial Africa*, Olomouc: House Moneta-FM, pp. 122–140.

International Social Survey Programme: National Identity II – ISSP 2003. Online: http://zacat.gesis.org/webview/index.jsp?object=http://zacat.gesis.org/obj/fStudy/ZA3910 (accessed 22. 3. 2014).

Johnson, R. W. (2009), *South Africa's Brave New World*, London: Penguin Books.

Jeník, T. (2003), Just Us. A sociology student looks at post-1989 nationalism in Czech politics, in: *The New Presence. The Prague Journal of Central European Affairs*, pp. 32–34.

Kagwanja, P. (2009), Introduction: Uncertain democracy – elite fragmentation and the disintegration of the 'national consensus' in South Africa, in: P. Kagwanja and K. Kondlo (eds.), *State of the Nation, South Africa 2008*. Cape Town: HSRC Press.

Kersting, N. (2009), New Nationalism and Xenophobia in Africa – A New Inclination?, in: *Africa Spectrum*, Vol. 44, No. 1, pp. 7–18.

Kleinfontein, online: http://www.kleinfontein.net (accessed 2. 7. 2014).

Klimek, A. (2001), Něco málo o české národní identitě. [A bit about Czech national identity], in: *Střední Evropa*, Vol. 106, pp. 121–6.

Kommando Korps, online: https://afrikanerjournal.wordpress.com/tag/kommando-korps/ (accessed 2. 7. 2014).

Kotzé, H. (1997), *Culture, Ethnicity and Religion: South African Perceptions of Social Identity*, Konrad-Adenauer-Stiftung: Occasional Papers.

Kučera, V. (2003), Co jsou Češi zač? Takoví voříšci Evropy, *MF Dnes,* 30 October.

Kučerová, S. (2002), Konec české národní identity [The end of Czech national identity], in: S. Kučerová (ed.), *Česká a slovenská otázka v soudobém světě*, Brno: Konvoj, pp. 220–7.

Kuras, Benjamin (1998), *Czechs and Balances: a nation's survival kit*, Praha: Baronet.

Mafolo, T. (2006), The Third Pillar of Our Transformation, in: *Umrabulo*, No. 26.

Mail and Guardian, 7–13 June 1996.

Mail and Guardian, 16 to 22 May 2008.

Maré, G. (1992), *Ethnicity and Politics in South Africa*, London and New Jersey: Zed Books.

Maré, G. (2005), Race, Nation, Democracy: Questioning Patriotism in the New South Africa, in: *Social Research*, Vol. 72, No. 3, pp. 501–530.

Mosselson, A. (2010), There is no difference between citizens and noncitizens any more: Violent Xenophobia, Citizenship and the Politics of Belonging in Post-Apartheid South Africa, in: *Journal of Southern African Studies*, Vol. 36. No. 3, pp. 641–655.

Musil, J. (1993), Czech and Slovak Society, in: *Czech Sociological Review*, Vol. 1, No. 1, pp. 5–21.

Musil, J. (2003), Emergence and Survival of the Nation-State, in: *New Presence*, pp. 19–21.

Natrass, N. and J. Seekings (2002), Class, Distribution and Redistribution in Post-Apartheid South Africa, in: *Transformation*, Vol. 50, pp. 1–30.

Neocosmos, M. (2008), The Politics of Fear and the Fear of Politics: Reflections on Xenophobic Violence in South Africa, in: *Journal of Asian & African Studies*, Vol. 43, No. 6, pp. 586–594.

Neocosmos, M. (2010), *From "Foreign Natives" to "Native Foreigners": Explaining Xenophobia in Post-apartheid South Africa: Citizenship and Nationalism, Identity and* Politics, 2nd ed., Dakar: CODESRIA.

News 24 (2010), Malema calls Zille a cockroach, online: http://www.news24.com/ SouthAfrica/Politics/Malema-calls-Zille-a-cockroach-20101030 (accessed 15. 7. 2014).

Ndlovu-Gatsheni, S. J. (2007), Tracking the historical roots of post-apartheid citizenship problems: the Native Club, restless natives, panicking settlers and the politics of nativism in South Africa, in: *ASC Working Paper*, Vol. 72, Leiden: African Studies Centre.

Ndlovu-Gatsheni, S. J. (2009), Africa for Africans or Africa for "Natives" Only? "New Nationalism" and Nativism in Zimbabwe and South Africa, in: *Africa Spectrum*, Vol. 44, No. 1, pp. 61–78.

Nyamnjoh, F. B. (2010), Racism, Ethnicity and the Media in Africa: Reflections Inspired by Studies of Xenophobia in Cameroon and South Africa, in: *Africa Spectrum*, Vol. 45, No. 1, pp. 57–93.

Orania, online: http://www.orania.co.za (accessed 2. 7. 2014).

Patočka, J. (1992), Co *jsou Češi? Malý přehled fakt a pokus o vysvětlení.* [What are the Czechs like?], Praha: Panorama.

Plecitá, K. (2012), *Národní identita a vztah k Evropské unii. Česká republika v západo- a středoevropském srovnání*, Praha: Studie Národohospodářského ústavu Josefa Hlávky.

Plecitá-Vlachová, K. (2011), Czech National Identity: Struggling to Survive, in: *Our Modern Identity*, pp. 41–49.

Reddy, T. (2008), The Challenge of African Democracy, in: *African Affairs*, Vol. 107, No. 428, pp. 471–481.

Reddy, T. (2010), ANC Decline, Social Mobilization and Political Society: Understanding South Africa's Evolving Political Culture, in: *Politikon*, Vol. 37, No. 2–3, pp. 185–206.

Roberts, B., M. wa Kivilu and Y. D. Davids (2010), Introduction: Reflections on the Age of Hope, in: R. Benjamin, M. wa Kivilu and Y. D. Davids (eds.), *South African Social Attitudes*, Cape Town: HSRC Press, pp. 1–16.

Shepherd, N. and S. Robin (2008), *New South African Keywords*, Johannesburg: Jacana.

Singh, A. (2005), *Indians in Post Apartheid South Africa*, Concept Publishing Co.

Skalník, P. (ed.) (2009), *Transition to Democracy. Czech Republic and South Africa Compared*, Praha: Set Out.

South Africa Unemployment Rate, online: http://www.tradingeconomics.com/south-africa/unemployment-rate (accessed 2. 7. 2014).

Sparks, A. (2003), *Beyond the Miracle. Inside the New South Africa*, Chicago: The University of Chicago.

The Star, 21 July 1997.

van Gelder, E. (2011), *Survival of the whitest: inside an Afrikaner boot camp*, online: http://www.telegraph.co.uk/news/worldnews/africaandindianocean/southafrica/8891519/Survival-of-the-whitest-inside-an-Afrikaner-boot-camp.html (accessed 20. 3. 2014).

Verdery, K. (1996a), Nationalism, Postsocialism, and Space in Eastern Europe, in: *Social Research*, Vol. 63, No. 1, pp. 77–95.

Verdery, K. (1996b), *What Was Socialism, and What Comes Next?* Princeton University Press.

Vlachová, K. and B. Řeháková (2009), Identity of non-self-evident nation: Czech national identity after the break-up of Czechoslovakia and before accession to the European Union, in: *Nations and Nationalism*, Vol.15, No. 2, pp. 254–279.

Weiss, H. (2003), A Cross-National Comparison of Nationalism in Austria, the Czech and Slovak Republics, Hungary, and Poland, in: *Political Psychology*, Vol. 24, No. 2, pp. 377–401.

Wesemüller, E. (2005), *African Nationalism from Apartheid to Post-Apartheid South Africa: A Critical Analysis of ANC Party Political Discourse*, Stuttgart: ibidem-Verlag.

Westle, B. (1995), Nationale Identität und Nationalismus, in: U. Hoffmann-Lange (ed.), *Jugend und Demokratie in Deutschland*, Opladen: Leske and Budrich, pp. 195–243.

20. výročí odchodu sovětských vojsk a ukončení vojenské okupace Československa, 2012, *Milovice Net*, online: http://www.imilovice.net/index.php/historie-mesta/8-20-vyroi-odchodu-sovtskych-vojsk-a-ukoneni-vojenske-okupace-eskoslovenska (accessed 15. 6. 2014).

2014 National and provincial election results, online: http://www.elections.org.za/resultsnpe2014/default.aspx (accessed 2. 7. 2014).

Czech racism towards Roma and colonised social services

Hana Synková

Introduction

Ways of thinking that appear after the change of political regimes can redefine boundaries of the state citizenship and shift the mechanisms of inclusion and exclusion. It seemed for a short time during and after the Velvet Revolution, that Roma people would become an integral and accepted part of the Czecho-slovak population longing for a democratic society. Romani leader Emil Ščuka spoke at the 25. 11. 1989 demonstration:

> *We, Roma, also belong to you, citizens and patriots. We were born in this homeland and we would like to live here. We are here not on contract as foreign workers. We will live here and want to live here in such a way that we would not be ashamed and you would not be ashamed of us. In such a way that your and our children would be like brothers and sisters. We support Civic Forum!* [1]

He was acclaimed by 800,000 strong crowd (Romea 2009). Ščuka and other activists founded a political party Romani Civic Initiative, which entered into the coalition with Civic Forum (and its Slovak counterpart) and thanks to this coalition gained 6 seats in 1990 parliament (Guy 2001: 294, 316). In 1992, the Charter of Fundamental Rights and Liberties was adopted by the Czechoslovak Parliament. It stated that "everyone has the right of free decision about his/her nationality" (Listina 1992). Such right was practiced already in 1991 census, where 32, 903 people claimed Romani nationality (Czech Statistical Office 2012). The estimates, however, put the number of the Roma between 150,000 and 300,000, which is between 1.2–2.7 percent of the total population (Sobotka 2007: 152). The explanations for non-acknowledgment of nationality are multiple; from fear through low need to express it in state documents to weak nationalist movement. The small number of potential electorate led later on to the failure of ethnic parties (Vermeersch 2005: 459). The current situation could not be further from the hopes of 1989 not only in terms of political representation. Roma are systematically excluded from the imagined body of the Czech nation.

This chapter will focus on the situation of Roma which I have monitored for several years in anthropological research (on segregation of Roma or on

---

[1] The revolutionary movement and political party.

NGOs working with Roma[2]) and more recently, in the last three years, also through my involvement with the Office of the Government Agency for Social Inclusion, where I coordinate applied research.[3] The comparisons made with South Africa will be rather cautious; however I will be showing that theories of colonisation, which have so far not been massively used for this topic, can be useful for thinking about the context in which Czech and Slovak Roma are living. Such 'colonisations' enable the persistence of racism, especially in its subtle forms, which will be explained through the notion of cultural racism.

Spectres of racism

Similar to 'African people', as shown in Ngcoya's contribution in this volume, 'Roma' people were always theorised from the perspective of the power centre. Be it the Romantic image of 'nomads' that roamed the country and filled the sexualised and savage imaginary of the 19th century bourgeoisie or the rationalist ideas of Enlightenment Austro-Hungarian rulers, who wanted to create a controllable and sedentarised body of 'new Hungarians' and 'civilise' them. The Romanticism values the simple and rural ways of life and projects the idea of 'poor, but happy' people into the image of the 'Gypsy', the last free 'noble wild man' (Baumgartner and Kovács 2007: 17). It considers the loss of tradition a threat to the authenticity of a Romani identity; integrated Roma are no longer 'the true Roma'. Romantic artistic image of Roma resulted in hundreds of paintings of nomadic Roma or images of seductive Romani women in the literature and drama (like the motif of Carmen). Roma presented an opposition to suppressed morals of the bourgeoisie, served as evocation of free life and certain mystique. The image of Roma entered Western symbolic literary canon and excluded Roma from nationalist mythologies (Trumpener 1995). The image of Roma was, however, always constructed against the unspoken image of non-Roma, and was in some ways central to that creation through representing the 'Other'.

The idea of an enlightened state has been to create a unitary state based on principle of equality, 'utility' and strong administration (Willems 1997: 33–34). Rulers Maria Theresa (1717–1780) and Joseph II (1741–1790) thus started the compulsory school attendance, targeted the power of the Catholic Church, allowed the existence of protestant churches and tried to unify different sub-groups of the society into one population of citizen, which

---

[2]See e.g. Synková 2010.
[3]This government body is focused mainly on the support of municipalities that have bigger share of poor population, composed mainly of Roma segregated in special parts of the municipality.

resulted in assimilationist politics. The state forced Jews to adopt German names and speak German or nomadic Roma to settle, stop 'wasting time on music', stop wearing 'outlandish' clothes and become 'productive' (and tax-paying) citizens. Ideally, Roma should be re-educated as agrarians and labourers. As part of this re-education, Romani children could be forcibly removed and brought up by non-Roma (Guy 2001: 287). The Enlightenment does not celebrate Romani authenticity and tradition as Romanticism does, but tries to reduce the civilizational 'backwardness' of Roma (see also Ries 2008). Both images correspond to the Orientalist approach towards Romani populations. Paradoxically, these two approaches could coexist quite well as in terms of power relations; they are two sides of the same coin.

State policies towards 'ethnic groups' are often a mix of these two approaches, oscillating over the time towards the first or the second extreme. The first policy is connected to recognising the 'difference' of the group, be it the 'savage' difference of the people who are considered to be in close connection to nature or a difference that shows itself in distinct ethnic traits. Such policy promotes an isolation or preservation of the group due to its 'savage' status or/and its distinct cultural heritage. What is considered to be valuable on the cultures of others is often determined by the state institutions. The 'Enlightenment' approach tends rather to unify the citizenry into one membership category and to 'modernise' the 'others'. Such modernity again tends to be imagined largely by the group, which is in power, and has strong assimilationist undertones. The domination of the more powerful group is legitimated by the natural superiority of one group in educational domain, scientific achievements or healthy lifestyles. The poverty and underdevelopment of others, give the group the right to act. The Czech Republic and states that preceded it, never completely abandoned assimilationist policies, despite going through several episodes, when it was officially possible or even slightly encouraged to organise on the basis of ethnicity, like at the end of the 1960s or after the 1989[4]. The stereotypical tendencies that appear in the case of Czech and Slovak territories are comparable to those about Africans in South Africa in the beginning of the twentieth century. As the South African military representative and politician Jan Smuts noted:

> *The African is the only happy human I have come across... The African easily forgets past troubles and does not anticipate future troubles... and there is complete absorption in the present... wine,*

---

[4]In the case of Roma in the Czech Republic we cannot speak about organising on a certain 'territory', as the Romani population is spread in many regions and represents small percentages of inhabitants of the cities.

*women and song in their African forms remain the great
consolation of life... These children of nature have not the inner
toughness and persistence of the European, not those social and
moral incentives to progress which have built up European
civilization in a comparatively short period* (Smuts 1929: 75–76
in Eze 2010: 38).

One could well replace 'Africans' with 'Roma' in the above quotation, as
these images of timeless presentism, celebration and on the other hand innate
deprivation would be completely credible as describing stereotypes about
Roma in the past as well as now.

In the case of Roma on the territory of the former Czechoslovakia,[5] there
are several groups of Roma, the main group being the population of Slovak
Roma, then the population of Hungarian Roma from Slovakia, both coming
to the Czech lands after the WWII (Hübschmannová 1994: 18–25). These
groups do not lend themselves to easy romantic stereotyping, both of them
were sedentarised already during the Austro-Hungarian Empire in 18th and
19th century and most of the population has been living ever since in impoverished segregated settlements at the edge of the Slovak villages or even
several kilometres away from them. These places emerged gradually through
the concentration and crowding of Romani population usually at the worst
land in the village, through intentional displacement by the authorities,
aggravated during the WWII. Then there is a group of Vlach Roma, partly
nomadic till the 1958, when the travelling was banned by the law inspired by
the Soviet administration (Ministry of Interior 1958; Zapletal 2012). The issue
of land tenure is important, as many of the settlements were built illegally,
but it cannot be automatically equated to the former indigenous land tenures
in South Africa. The land has been already owned by local nobility and
farmers prior to the settlement of Roma and their economic and social interconnection with local agricultural system. During the war the Slovak Republic
was an independent clerofascist state that severely limited Romani movement
through laws and edicts (Roma had to live further from the main roads, had
limited amount of hours, when they could visit the towns, travelling and horse
dealing was forbidden, men had to work in work camps, travelling in public
transport was forbidden etc.; see Jurová 2009). Roma were targeted by
pogroms perpetrated by the local Slovak militia or German troops or by
displacement to work camps and concentration camps. In the Czech lands,
where part of the country became a direct territory of Nazi Germany and

---

[5]The situation in both countries is largely interconnected; Czechoslovakia was only divided in
1993.

inland a protectorate, Roma (sedentary Moravian Roma and largely nomadic Czech Roma) were almost totally exterminated. At that time the laws openly targeted Roma by naming them as the target population of segregationist (or extermination) policies and thus were remotely comparable to apartheid measures. Discriminatory measures towards certain groups were directly legitimated by the state.

It does not mean however that other periods were without the state discrimination; the state historically often targeted common activities of Roma, like nomadism or mendacity, or invented categories, which replaced the name of Roma in the texts of regulations, but were mostly considered to mean Roma. Czech and Slovak lands often did not use racial categories as the legal basis of their policy, but made discrimination function rather through exclusionary discourses and discriminatory interpretations of measures and practices by officials or common people. Racism thus had rather more subtle overtones and talking about 'race' or 'colour' has been mostly considered politically incorrect, despite of the use of such discourse by some politicians. People thus have to do a certain work of translation of what is being said or written, but some expressions and signs have became so commonsensical, that their meaning is obvious, like the expression 'unadaptable people', which recently returned to the public discourse after having been used already during socialism.

South Africa has in this respect a different history, as open racial categorising was considered 'the norm' for large part of its history. The ideology of slavery has been built on the idea of racial inferiority of the colonial subjects and its abolition (first in 1834 in the Cape Colony of South Africa) did not mean that the society de-racialised. In his overview of the racial politics in South Africa, Paul Maylam (2001) shows that informal racial discriminatory practice has continued throughout the South African history, formalising in some periods into a distinct 'racial policy' in the laws that preceded the apartheid era (one of the significant laws being Natives Land Act, 1913 depriving the most of the 'native' black population of the right to own land) and in the apartheid itself. We can however also find laws targeting different groups of populations indirectly like the Franchise and Ballot Act (1892) in the Cape, which raised the amount of property needed to vote and thus excluded mostly non-white voters, but also some poor white voters. Currently the discourse is again much less overt – according to Maylam (2001: 243) it is "more implicit racial discourse centred on crime, corruption and incompetence".

Discourse analyst Theun van Dijk (2000: 33–34) distinguishes two kinds of racism – the first one is the 'old' racism, based on considering people racially inferior, publicly denouncing them and running official measures of extermination and segregation against them. Such original form of racism would be more common for slavery regimes, apartheid and colonial histories. The new racism is more subtle. Its proponents want to be seen as democratic and respectable, so they firstly deny there is any racism in their discourse. They do not consider people racially inferior, just different, but this difference is often imagined in a negative way. Van Dijk (2000: 34) describes that the targeted group is considered to have: "a different culture, although in many respects there are deficiencies, such as single-parent families, drug abuse, lacking achievement values, and dependence on welfare and affirmative action pathologies that need to be corrected of course". For this type of racism, we could also use the term of 'cultural racism' (Blaut 1992). Very often it is the culture of the group itself, which is considered to be a problem, hindering the development of the group (in the case of Roma 'large families requiring reciprocity' or 'living in the present and inability to plan'). Unequal position of the group is thus explained not by exclusionary mechanisms, but by its 'inner' cultural deficiencies. Such explanation legitimates the low position of the group in the social hierarchy. If the situation should be improved, the culture has to be changed and the 'way of life' of such people somehow 'corrected'. The dominant group usually holds such power over media and public life, that it can normalise this discourse to the extent that people do not detect its ideological background. The official discourse and its variants thus largely colonise the public life. Throughout history, nuances of naming Roma and describing their 'incorrect' ways of life fit mainly into the 'cultural racism' form.

Needless to say, the effects of such forms of racism towards people are not necessarily less degrading than the effects of the 'old racism'. The everyday experiences of people suggest that there is still a systemic discrimination, it is just not called a racial discrimination, but a treatment, which is based on the fact, that the person is imagined or feared to have a certain culturally influenced 'character' or presumed to behave in some way. James Blaut (1992: 289–290) notes that many Western countries ended up with 'racism without racists' or racism that thrives well even under the (scientific) denial that something like the category of 'race' is a valid concept. Blaut distinguishes racism as practice and racism as theory. Racism as practice (and experience) does not change too much over the years, people are constantly discriminated against and suffering. There are however changing discourses and theories that explain racism over time (racism as theory). Explanatory frameworks for Czech racism have been changing, but they were mostly close to a cultural racism model.

Everyday visual categorising stays important for 'activation' of racist attitudes and Roma that are lighter-skinned can pass more easily. Czechs however tend to categorise the skin colour dichotomically and are able to categorise anyone a bit visibly darker as black and suspect his or her Romani origin (South African people of colour would be considered black). In this respect they are closer to the United States practice of 'one drop rule' (Eriksen 2002: 83).

Socialist 'development'

After the post-war expulsion of the German population mostly from the Czech border areas, these areas were populated by the migrants from the Czech hinterland but also from Slovakia. As part of this migration, large numbers of the Romani population have come to work in industrial centres and some worked in agriculture. Today then the Czech Republic is populated by the third or fourth generation of these post-war Romani inner state migrants. The socialist Czechoslovakia (after 1948) considered 'the Gypsy question' (*cikánská otázka*) mainly a social and economic one, created by the capitalist regime. The answer was the employment and removal of poverty (Law 2012: 44–45). The policies of socialist Czechoslovakia were strongly assimilationist, organising schemes of re-education of Romani citizens in health and schooling, destroying some settlements in Slovakia, trying to channel their Romani inhabitants to certain Czech cities and quarters, abolishing nomadism and controlling families' standards of living through social workers, etc. The discourse accompanying these policies was based on elevating the 'backward' Roma towards the ideal of a socialist citizen, meaning usually a politically active manual worker living in good material conditions. Law (2012) calls this ideal a 'racial proletarianisation'.

Socialism and its discourse had largely 'enlightened' and 'modernist' background. It had proposed the healthy and modern living environments for masses, which materialised in the new districts of panel block of flats, destroyed the peasant families and created big agricultural cooperatives with 'scientific' ways of land cultivation and breeding. Furthermore, the socialist ideology attempted to change gender relationships (see Ahari's chapter in this volume) through high rates of employment among women and mothers. Blaut (1992: 293–296) considers 'modernisation' theory a new cultural-racist theory that enabled holding old structures of colonial dominance in place.

The socialist state definitely did not question the structures of dominance that were in place, it tried rather to erase the group distinction and thus the need to recognise the dominance. The term *cikánský způsob života* (Gypsy way of life) was used to describe the backward way of living connected to stereotypes like work shyness, unsupportive attitude to schooling or irrational believes. Roma were mostly referred to as *občané cikánského původu* (citizens of Gypsy origin) that should take part in modernisation. The above mentioned enforced 1958 settlement of all nomadic people served also to control Roma who migrated from the Slovak settlements. Those people that got to the police register were not allowed to move without permission.

Another measure that followed was called *řízený rozptyl* (controlled or organised dispersal) decided by The Central Committee of the Communist Party in 1961. Under this policy, 40,000 of Slovak Roma from the settlements were supposed to be moved to different Czech cities (Pavelčíková 2004: 83). The settlements were supposed to be destroyed. Roma were categorised into three 'levels of integration'. The first category were people that already lived 'as majority', meaning they worked, sent children to school and lived among non-Roma. These were not targeted by the dispersal, 'only' by further assimilation policies. In the second category were those people who work, but fluctuate, do not have perfect hygiene and live with other Roma. They were candidates for the dispersion and had to be controlled. The third were the most 'backward', who live 'in a typically Gypsy way of life', thieves, handicapped, living in unhealthy conditions. They were rigorously targeted and children from these families were supposed to be taken to orphanages (Pavelčíková 2004: 88–89). Slovak and Czech cities and villages were 'paired' together, but often the Czech cities did not want to accommodate migrants and give them work and the migration did not materialise. People sometimes migrated back to Slovakia or to other Czech cities and the policy partly failed. The organised migration from 1966 to 1968 amounted to 494 families, but the non-organised one was estimated at 2,250 families (Pavelčíková 2004: 92–93). Romani migrants in general were often given the worst housing in the Czech cities (in Prague these were often semi-basements[6]) and many cities even illegally refused to give them a permanent stay permit, so people crowded in the apartments of their relatives or lived in the accommodation, which belonged to their employers (Guy 2001: 293).

Ethnic differentiation was not supported and was present only through some folklorist events. The only short period, when the state allowed establishing a separate ethnic-based organisation, was after the period of the Prague Spring between 1969 and 1973. The organisation was thus the result of the more liberal atmosphere during the Prague Spring, when the previous

---

[6]Information obtained in meetings with Roma witnesses as part of the research in the project *Prague Shared and Divided*, Multicultural Centre Prague 14. 5. 2014.

politics towards Roma started to be revised. The organisation was dismantled a few years later due to the strengthening 'normalisation' of the regime, which revoked previous reforms. The organisation's political agenda was not huge, but it created some networking possibilities and started to portray Romani culture as a positive force and value (it attempted, for instance, to employ Roma in some traditional crafts), however stereotypical that portrayal might have been. In 1968 the Romani agenda also migrated from the Ministry of Interior to the Ministry of Labour and Social Affairs and an assimilation approach was replaced by a so-called 'integration' approach (Davidová 1995: 203).

Apart from direct state policies targeted to 'citizens of Gypsy origin', the state ran several policies which had segregationist and even ethnocidal effects. These policies did not overtly address Roma, i.e. there was no mention of Roma in the text; nonetheless some of them were applied largely or almost exclusively to Roma. Some municipalities also used the above-mentioned state scale to classify local Romani families. In 1970 in the mining town of Most, Roma that were classified into the first group, became candidates for integration and could get housing inside the city. The 'second' and 'third' group were moved to the large and distant housing project. Soma non-Roma people, who also ended up in there and some Roma who could afford it left the district soon and the situation worsened, which gradually created one of the big ghettoes of the Czech North.

In South Africa the housing segregation has been at first regulated by different city councils (Port Elizabeth and East London established segregated areas already in 1850s; see Maylam 1995: 22–23). Later there was legislation also on the state level. Orange Free State in 1890s allowed segregated areas in cities, Union of South Africa created Natives (Urban Areas) Act of 1923 that regulated the access of Black community to White areas and pushed the Black community out of towns. The Group Areas Act of 1950 assigned different residential areas to different races. Those measures have been differently interpreted by researchers; famous is Maynard Swanson's (1977) explanation of fear of diseases legitimating residential segregation, but researchers like Maylam (1995) point rather to the broader economic interests of the power elites in land ownership and industrial development.

We can see that in Czechoslovakia policy measures also supported the residential control (the police created a register of nomadic or migrating Roma, these had to settle and could not travel or move without permission), but the state policy, sometimes contrary to the local administration policies, first focused on dispersal, because the Communist Party believed in assimilation. The segregated areas were created mostly as a result of municipal decisions and through directed or accidental concentration of Roma in the worst available housing, such as dilapidated old houses in the city centres. These locations became lucrative after 1989, which started a large gentrification process of displacement of Roma to ever more peripheral locations. The economic reasons for segregation are thus stronger than ever also in the Czech Republic.

A further discriminatory strategy by the Czech government was a gradual schooling segregation of a large part of Romani children to special schools for mentally handicapped children. It concerned up to 40 percent of Romani children already in the 1960s (Pavelčíková 2004: 82). There was no need of using the ethnic category to segregate them, there were 'objective' psychological tests given to children that they often could not pass, due to the different early education setting and impoverished environments. The tests have been set to the standards of the middle class Czech child, whose early education included language and motor development through picture books and different educational toys. The system of tests has not been massively reformed and the Czech Republic lost the case against the group of former students of special schools at the European Court of Human Rights in 2007 (detailed analysis of tests can be found in Lábusová et al. 2010).

An even more serious measure was sterilisation (mostly) of Romani women, which was allowed by the 1971 Sterilisation Directive. Socialist countries had developed pro-natalist policies by supporting young families, but around the 1970s, there were efforts to bring this support of population growth to a new level. There were eugenics ideas about the need to support not any family, but mainly 'quality families' and 'quality genes'. The documents spoke about families with 'multiple children', about 'unfit parenthood' and 'socially unadjusted citizens' (Sokolová 2005: 87). Ordinary social workers and doctors were jointly responsible for interpreting these labels ethnically. It was estimated that there were hundreds of Romani women sterilised mostly without informed consent in birth clinics or hospitals and pushed towards sterilisation by the pressure of their social workers.[7] Similarly, reports from South Africa documented that the state family planning programme initiated in 1974 had to face accusations of forced sterilisation, coerced contraception and genocidal goals (Kaufman 1997: 3). Carol Kauf-

---

[7]The dissident movement Charter 77 did a survey of 156 women in 1989 and found that 70 percent of them were sterilised. Another number has been provided by a Czech ombudsman, who surveyed 87 complaints by women that were collected by NGOs between September 2004 and December 2005. The research in Slovakia between August and October 2002 by Center for Reproductive Rights and *Poradňa pre občianske a ľudské práva* found 140 women sterilised, 110 of them even after the fall of communism (Klepárník 2008).

man investigates why such politically compromised program was still successful and sought after by women. She argues that "the vigorous but politically compromised family planning program facilitated women's control over their fertility in the context of that uncertainty" (Kaufman 1997:6). In her research Sokolová cites also from one research interview, showing that not all women were unaware of what they were doing and that they also used the sterilisation as an exercise of control over their bodies in the situation of economic difficulties and gender subordination (Sokolová 2005: 93). South African regime however also planned a eugenic sterilisation policy through developing immunological approach to control fertility of black women. This project was prepared by the Chemical and Biological Warfare program, but fortunately it was not finished. Some information concerning the programme was released during the 1998 Truth and Reconciliation Commission hearings (Rothscum 2010).

Several professions worked with Roma during socialism. After the assimilation approach changed into an 'integrationist' one in the 1970s, social workers, apart from engaged teachers, became one of the contact points to the 'state'. There was even a special category of workers created at the district level in 1974 – social curators[8] for Gypsy population. For Roma (as for any other client), social workers were an ambiguous profession. Under socialism, some were feared, because they had the power to take children to an institutional care, which happened to many families, who were considered too poor or 'disorderly'. The bad treatment of the child was not the only reason for taking children away, families could be targeted when they did not have enough material resources and functional (meaning 'tidy') households. Socialism thus largely contributed to the 'institutionalisation of Romani lives' and it happened that some parents had to regularly part with their children who were sent to orphanages. Apart from schooling and orphanages there was imprisonment, army service or social work interventions. The criteria of assessment of the families were not clear and depended on the interpretation of a social worker.[9] On the other hand these social workers could be approached for help with paper work and economic problems and were able

---

[8]'A kind of' social worker and mediator, but also a person, who was instructed to 'control' the Romani population. Social curator is otherwise a term describing people, who work with former prisoners.

[9]During one of my first research visits to Slovak Romani households about ten years after the regime change, women tended to open their wardrobes showing me their neatly arranged clothes. I did not understand why, until I figured out they considered me to be a certain kind of social worker, because these people were one of the few non-Roma, that ever visited the households (Synková 2004).

to pressure the municipality to get the families into the waiting lists for apartments and sometimes negotiate a quicker allocation of housing. The position of curators was abolished after the regime change, but the Czech state still approaches Roma through 'the caring and controlling profession' of social worker.[10]

We might imagine a social worker partly as a colonial actor – it can access very intimate spaces of households, it has influence on the composition of the families (now the process of 'taking children away' is not so easy, but still, he or she can recommend division of families in order to access gender segregated asylum houses, etc.; Agency for Social Inclusion 2012). Some social workers became very powerful figures with strong paternalist networks built around them. At the same time, some social workers were so affected by the experience of human suffering, that they seriously searched for innovative and more empowering ways in which the state can approach Romani population.

Becoming developed by Europe

The stories of the hardships during the war and migration or stories about the social and economic mobility in the new place are not part of the general Czech discourse about Roma. Also the stories about brute socio-economic decline of families after the Velvet Revolution of 1989 stay enclosed inside the families. Even though it has become possible to express opinions openly after the regime change, these stories have not found the audience or much media support. The change of regime enabled the possibility to officially claim Romani nationality. This largely symbolic gesture made organising on the basis of ethnicity possible and some civic organisations were founded. The recognition of Romani nationality, however, did not mean that Roma would be automatically recognised as citizens of the Czech Republic. That showed itself seriously during the 1993 division of Czechoslovakia, when the Czech Republic set up such criteria of admission for citizenship for Slovaks that half of Roma had not qualified. They had problems with proving 2 years of permanent residence despite living in the Czech Republic for most/all of their lives, and no criminal record for 5 years (Guy 2001: 297). The covert purpose was to send Roma back to Slovakia or at least to exclude them from the possibility of receiving state support.

The apartheid regime could implement similar measures openly. In The Bantu Homelands Citizenship Act of 1970 it forced all black people to

---

[10]Care and control are the two ambiguous roles that the society requires from the social worker. In some periods helping is more important than controlling, but both are present to some extent. Controlling role of the social worker prevailed during socialism (see e.g. Šveřepa 2008).

become citizens of the land of their ethnic origin (of one of the ten self-governing territories) and removed their South African citizenship. It therefore exoticised them as tribal and 'ethnic', converted them to foreigners, who could work in South Africa as unprotected 'guest workers' end excluded them to the financially dependent and impoverished territories, which served as a reserve of cheap labour (King 2007).

Roma are also still largely perceived as foreigners, rather than citizens in the Czech Republic. In different surveys, Czech population tends to name Roma automatically, when asked about their relationships towards foreigners. Racist discourse is often connected to the idea of 'sending them back' either to Slovakia or even to India, or at least 'sending them away' (to an imagined Romani Bantustan). Housing segregation is more extreme than ever and apartments on the 'open market' become unavailable for Romani families, while public housing was largely privatised. Open market and the possibility to choose where people will live, to whom they rent their apartment, where they will be studying (already at the level of elementary schools, which was not previously possible), or the rise of unemployment only exacerbated the existing inequalities. Many Roma thus consider 'the democracy' as a kind of disaster for their livelihoods and families.

The Czech Republic in the 1990s imagined itself as one of the most modern and democratic countries of the East, which was nourished by the tradition of the Velvet Revolution and dissident movement, having less chaotic economic transformation than in some other countries. In our common discussion, this was described as Czech 'exceptionalism'. 'Catching-up with Europe' became a primal goal of the governments, which was cemented by the 1999 admission to NATO and the EU accession process (accomplished in 2004). The image of functioning democracy was however slightly delegitimised by the critique that the European Commission directed to the Czech Republic and other countries of Central and Eastern Europe concerning their non-transparency and their discriminatory approach towards its minorities, especially Roma.

The change to a certain 'second class country', which now has to be developed by Western European states, and adopt certain obligatory measures, has been bitterly perceived by many politicians. Some, like the former president Václav Klaus and co-author of the Czech privatisation project, tried to deny (e.g. in BBC Hardtalk in 2003) that Roma in the Czech Republic face serious problems. Others, like the first post-89 president and former dissident Václav Havel on the other hand pointed to the fact that the position of minorities is essential for a functioning civil society – he named Roma a 'litmus test of civil society' and indicated that creating democratic institutions is in itself not enough, but people in general have to change their behaviour

(Kamm 1993). The ten years span between these interviews illustrates well the shift of the general discourse towards the greater denial.

It became clear that Western European countries sometimes do not apply minority protection measures that they themselves ask candidate countries to apply. The concept of ethnic minority support is virtually nonexistent in France; Great Britain and Spain had unresolved conflicts with their Basque, Catalan or Irish population and Roma in many Western European countries did not have sufficient protection either. The interest of these countries in applying minority protection measures is also motivated by the fear of migration from the East. Roma and other minorities have even been considered a kind of 'security threat', Western European states were worried that the regime change releases massive Romani migration (Guglielmo and Waters 2005). The state of Romani minorities in Central and Eastern Europe has been regularly monitored by the Organization for Security and Cooperation in Europe. There is the perception of Western European countries, that the East is somehow 'more ethnic' and that it cannot manage well its ethnic conflicts. At the same time Central and Eastern Europeans have their own discourses of modernity and Europeanness and consider any Eastern neighbour more ethnic and underdeveloped. Bakić-Hayden (1995) calls these pushes of the 'East' to the East 'nesting orientalisms'. In the Czech Republic, when the term 'ethnic group' is used, it often means Roma or some other minority groups no one would say that the division of the Czechoslovakia was an 'ethnic conflict'.

The unpopular European minority measures were applied rather leniently and despite the continuous criticism from the European Commission, it finally showed that the accession countries would be accepted despite still showing serious problems in the treatment of minorities. During the 1990s, the state usually funded cultural events and activities and not many funds went to social issues. It concentrated on legal and symbolic recognition of the minorities. A small number of Romani NGOs was founded, which also focused on the propagation of 'Romani culture' usually in the form of various local music events and celebrations and some NGOs started to organise activities for Romani youth. Critics of this 'culturalist' approach noted that the state mainly wanted to support stereotypical 'dancing Roma', but did not care about Romani employment and other issues. Such approach seemed lacking, because at that time many Roma lost their work in industry and other parts of the privatising job market and the neo-Nazi movement became stronger committing even racially motivated murders.

The neo-Nazi movement grew largely from the subcultural group of skinheads, which formed already during the 1980s, but in the 1990s it gained wider support and popularity especially through a popular and legitimate music band Orlík (Eaglet). The movement has been composed mainly of younger men and part of the movement created links to extreme right parties (Smolík 2010: 144–149). Recently it has established several political parties, from which Workers Party has been the strongest (after it was banned in 2010, it has been re-created under a slightly different name). The movement has contacts to German and Austrian neo-Nazi movements and organises anti-Roma demonstrations. In some localities it attracts public and electoral support, but in national elections it gets only around 1 percent of votes. Xenophobic discourse and language, however, are also regularly used by mainstream political party members.[11] The media contributes to the negative image of Roma; according to the latest research, media sources still refer to Roma as 61.9 percent in connection to crime. In 80 percent of these crime-related sources they are portrayed as perpetrators. A significant number of media publications describe problems in coexistence between Roma and 'majority' population and identifies Roma as a source of these problems (Křížková 2013).

After the end of apartheid, openly xenophobic parties had much less chance to win public support. South African neo-Nazi movements were connected primarily to two parties (Afrikaner Resistance Movement and White Liberation Movement), which peaked in activity during the campaigns against the dissolution of apartheid at the end of 1980s and beginning of 1990s. Their specificity in comparison to the Czech case is the base in Afrikaner background,[12] which draws historical connections to the Boer wars for independent Afrikaner/White state. For the Afrikaner Resistance Movement it is also its specific connection to Protestantism and legitimation of the difference and separation of races in religious terms. While being marginalised, this movement tries to rejuvenate its base through organising bootcamps for youth, where the racist language is reproduced together with the discourse of Afrikaner freedom and the need to defend itself (see Channel 4 News 2013). The discourse of fear can be seen as well in the more mainstream Freedom Front Plus election manifesto, which criticises land reform and affirmative action discriminating 'against whites and other minorities' (FF+ 2014). While the comparison with the Czech Republic is difficult here,

---

[11]Like The Dawn of Direct Democracy (6.88 percent votes in 2013) or Civic Democratic Party (7.72 percent in 2013). Municipal elections usually bring more xenophobic incidents than national elections. These incidents are connected to a broad spectrum of parties.

[12]Apart from the existence of small Romani and Moravian (Eastern part of the Czech Republic) parties, the parties usually do not target separate ethnic allegiances. If there is nationalism, parties are stressing the general Czech nationalism against strangers, foreigners and EU.

the need to defend itself (against the Romani criminality, etc.) is evoked even in the Czech situation with completely different majority/minority ethnic ratios.

The beginning of the 1990s was the time when Romani leaders tried to enter the Czech political life and established wider contacts with the international Romani movement. Roma Civic Initiative, however, has never found enough electorate to come close to the 5 percent threshold needed for entering the Parliament. Roma are not only a 'minority in terms of power', but also a 'numerical minority', which needs different political strategies than in South Africa. Romani political leaders rather concentrated on running NGOs as a parallel way to influence public opinion and promote the national-building agenda, some Roma also joined mainstream parties. Romani NGOs also started to run media – an internet radio, information sites and magazines, partly also in Romani language; however their public has not been large to compete with the mainstream and change the above mentioned general discourse, which remains largely stereotypical.

The culturalist state approach has slowly changed with the media promoted asylum emigration of Czech Roma to Canada and Great Britain in 1997. Many officials claimed that Roma did not have any reason to leave and ask for asylum, did not face 'serious' discrimination and that they were economic migrants. In 1997 a special body that had to survey the 'state of the Romani community' was set up at the Office of the Government and this body also formed a civic commission composed of Romani activists. The function of a 'Romani advisor' at the districts was created. In a way this position resembled former social curators and advisors mediated between authorities and local Roma, dealing mostly with social issues. This time however there was an aim to employ Roma themselves to do the advisory work, thus making them a kind of 'specialists' on their own groups. Advisors were abolished in 2003 together with the abolition of the districts and the responsibility shifted to superior regional governments with only one position devoted to the task. Another 'ethnic specific' function has been a function of Romani pedagogical assistant at schools, which started to be tested in 1990s and was recommended by the Ministry of Education in 2000.

During the 'cultural' and at the beginning of this 'social turn', the Roma were targeted as an ethnic group, requiring not only the 'cultural support' as any other recognised national minority, but also a specific approach given by their cultural specificity (which was still often described as lacking, compared to the non-Romani ways of life). Because of this specificity, it was proposed, Romani workers should work with Roma. These 'Romani jobs and institutions' were however not in any powerful system position. The government body was only a consultative one, the position of school assistants was precarious and not well paid, and advisors were often ignored, becoming 'token Roma' dealing with Romani issues that could be then ignored by other parts of the administration. This approach came under serious critique in the next phase.

Contested ethnicity in social work

Since 2000, there has been a return to integration policy and rhetoric and series of official Romani integration conceptions has been started. Pre-accession funds like Phare[13] and later on European Social Fund are being used, however with mixed results (for the critique and evaluation see e.g. Guy 2009). European funding changed the social work possibilities profoundly. The opportunity to get bigger amounts of money lead to a continuing professionalisation of many social work NGOs. The former volunteers became full-time employees and NGOs started to recruit professional social workers. Issues concerning Romani people, which have never been a priority for the state, become one of NGOs' domains (together with the care about homeless people, prostitutes and people who suffered drug addiction). NGO funding through grants and the general 'projectisation' of the sector has very similar effects all over the world – it is the sphere with shorter-term initiatives, precarious jobs, a lot of administration, a need for professionals who would be able to process this administration, and a sphere, which cares about the issues outsourced or not favoured by the state. According to Ferguson (1990) and others, NGOs were much criticised of being the neoliberal (and neo-colonial) actors. Such actors are restricted by the donor policies, which favour depoliticised development or social work over anti-racist movement support or other more critical activities. The discourses and practices of international development have been close to the Czech social work milieu. The biggest organisation that now runs the largest network of social work projects targeting 'socially excluded localities', People in Need, is at the same time the biggest Czech development organisation. It opened its first 'Romani programme' after the end of the 1990s asylum migration.

Seeing the ineffectiveness of the previous systems of care, the practice of 'terrain social work' (Nedělníková et al. 2007) has been promoted by NGOs from the beginning of the new millennium. The terrain social worker should not be sitting in the office, but should be visiting people in places where they live. Such practice is used mainly with Romani clients, people suffering drug

---

[13]This programme is financed by the EU to assist countries of CEE, who wish to join the EU and helps them to move 'closer to EU'.

addiction or homeless people. Terrain social work was later officially re-cognised by the Social Services Law of 2006. This type of work is provided to the people living in localities, which were at first called 'socially excluded Romani localities' (GAC 2006: 10–11). The concept of 'social exclusion/ integration' and later 'social inclusion' became a new discursive device to approach Romani issues. Roma were largely renamed as 'socially excluded populations'. The critique was raised against the 'ethnic approach' as it was considered too essentialist (Moravec 2006). The reason for exclusion, this critique claims, is not present in the 'Romani culture', but in the mechanisms of exclusion from the job market, housing, education, etc. Such exclusion is faced also by other groups of people and not all Roma are excluded, so the general professional social work should be able to provide to all of these groups. Ethnicity is not a sufficient qualification to work with other people of the same group (or any group) and being Roma does not mean that one has good connection to grassroots. The rise of the required qualifications and administration demands prompted some Roma from the first small 'wave' of Romani workers to leave the job and they were replaced by non-Romani graduates (Synková 2010). There are still some Roma left in this terrain social work 'job niche' and a few young Romani people are studying their BA levels in social work (the percentage of higher educated Roma is usually estimated to be very low, accurate data is not available[14]). The job of such workers is however very demanding and low paid.

The critique was largely supported and nourished by some academics and social workers, who have seen the ethnicisation of the issue as stereotypical and one of the reasons of policy failure (e.g. Moravec 2006). Ethnicisation has been also considered to block many efforts on local level, where authorities did not want to apply measures that would be targeted only on Roma, but prefer to target 'all poor population'. Affirmative action program-mes are thus almost nonexistent (apart from a small programme that supports Romani secondary school students). The discourse has been gradually de-ethnicised – Romani programmes were renamed by a more neutral name, Romani assistants became assistants of pedagogue and social excluded Romani localities became social excluded localities. Romani NGOs were disappointed by this process, which makes Roma invisible, and also became losers in direct competitors for funding with top mainstream NGOs (Synková 2011).

---

[14]Disparate research recorded 3 percent of people with secondary education and 18 percent with vocational training in the 12 socially excluded localities (World Bank 2008). The 2001–2002 research of Masaryk University, which surveyed 1000 Roma in 10 cities, found that there were 24.4 percent people with vocational training and 6.4 percent had more than vocational training (Navrátil 2002).

With such policy and discourse development, it is hard to present exclusive claim to support Romani population and it can be easily delegitimised. Strong affirmative action seems to be so far off-limit. It makes it also hard for activists, media, NGOs and politicians to talk about the discrimination of Roma or racism. First, the fact of Romani discrimination has not been broadly accepted even by the political elites, suffering was not publically discussed and institutions that archive the narratives about it are marginal even in the academia – like the Romani Studies Seminar at the Institute of South and Central Asia of Charles University.[15] The 'average Czech person' also harvests many stereotypical feelings towards Roma which contributes further to their negative image and discrimination. In recent study, only 11 percent of 1070 respondents would accept Roma as a neighbour (Czech News Agency 2014). Collecting data about nationality is prohibited by the state that worries about its misuse (as it was during the World War II), so any antidiscrimination fact-finding has to be very carefully argued. Schools often refuse to answer questions about the number of their Romani pupils, especially when the question is directed to special schools. Despite the de-racialisation movement in South Africa, there is no such taboo on collecting ethnic or racial data. These data are on the contrary key for the movement's success, so we can find statistics about percentage of different 'races' working in social work profession (Earle 2008) as well as critical assessments of welfare service provision in terms of race, class and gender of its workers and board members (Gathiram and Hemson 2002), that would be envied by some Czech social scientists. Being post-racial often means that the anti-racist movement loses its focus (Lentin 2011).

Social exclusion discourse has been described as one of the neoliberal Euro-discourses (Bourdieu and Wacquant 2001), which are able to form basis of policies, but are not very effective in changing the structures of inequality. Another culturalist discourse has been suggested by some academics (Novák 2003) as a replacement for ethnic approach. It proposed that it is a 'culture of poverty', which contributes to the bad situation of people, and which also did not help to focus attention on systemic deficiencies. The same critique has been directed to individual social work, which is the main model of approach to the client (or in today's marketised language 'the user of services') in the Czech Republic. There are some community centres, which provide at least some space for Romani youth and points of contact, but activities that would be successful in bringing Roma people to the direct discussion with local authorities or bringing together diverse neighbourhood communities are very

---

[15]This institute got also its deal of critique of orientalism and essentialism for being ethnically focused.

hard to find. The financing structure makes NGOs dependent on many other actors and also direct confrontation with municipalities is usually avoided, as the organisations would lose their carefully built lobbying networks, through which they try to influence local policies.

The language of current South African social work, as indicated in the founding White Paper for Social Welfare (1997), is much more radical and supportive of community involvement and participation of the target groups in decision on welfare provision. Even though we can find slogans like 'war on poverty' in this paper (p. 13), the focus on inequality is still strong and the official documents speak about people in more dignified way than the materials produced by the Czech Ministry of Labour (2002), which describes some clients as *'people that survive through socially unacceptable behaviour'*. Leading figures in South African social work are aware that professionalisation and standardisation of social work presents risks connected to its neoliberalisation and de-radicalisation as can be seen from the talk of Professor Vishanthie Sewpaul (Sewpaul 2014).

The careful and 'depoliticised' approach of Czech social services has been recently criticised by the group of left-leaning academics and activists connected to anarchist movement. This movement tried to defend Romani tenants from eviction in two cities. These cases were media promoted and contributed to the general discussion about the non-existing provision of social housing by the state. Local NGOs were criticised by activists for being ineffective in finding quality housing, activists were criticised by NGOs for being disruptive and ignorant of local situation, taking people hostage on the basis of their own ideological background. Despite the isolation of these cases and their incomparability to the movements in Spain or the United States, these cases allowed for some direct contact between Romani and non-Romani activists and local Roma on people-to-people basis and brought some young Roma from these houses around to the idea of establishing self-defence networks across the Czech Republic. At this stage it is hard to say, if similar activities could challenge the status quo, but they have been at least first signs of thinking differently about the issue, creating uncomfortable disruptions. On the level of community organising and protest, grassroots networking or creating home-grown theories for change, South Africa could serve as a vast source of intellectual inspiration for Czech and Romani activism.

Conclusion

This exercise of comparison brought many challenges connected to the different historical and political situations of respective countries, but it also revealed that some mechanisms and discourses of discrimination are similar, notably the Orientalist imagery, hygienic or security discourses or vast exclusion of people of colour from their citizenship rights. In both countries the practice of 'cultural racism', which points to the deficiencies in the group behaviour, is currently more frequent than the biological explanations of inferiority. The situation in South Africa now seems more hopeful, as there has been considerable restructuring of access to power and broadening of citizenship rights. The possibility of participation of Roma in positions of decision makers is minimal. In both countries access to 'full' citizenship is still severely limited by the economic landscape. Anthropologist Jean Comaroff (Bangstad et al. 2012: 129) points to the fact that the regime change was preceded by the liberalisation of the economy and contributed to its collapse: "the seeming triumph of global capitalism and the global deregulation of production were making racial capitalism in the old South African style a less profitable anachronism". She identifies a challenge valid for both countries – how to think about redistribution of resources in the context of a neo-liberal economy that both countries embraced with such little critique. The issue of economic pressures, class and their interdependencies with 'race' present an important topic both for future research and for practical political organising.

References

Agency for Social Inclusion (2012), *Rodina a sociálně-právní ochrana dítěte* [Family and the Socio-legal Protection of a Child], online: http://www.socialni-zaclenovani.cz/rodina-a-socialne-pravni-ochrana-ditete (accessed 21.9. 2014).

Bakić-Hayden, M. (1995), Nesting Orientalisms: The Case of Former Yugoslavia, in: *Slavic Review*, Vol. 54, No. 4, pp. 917–931.

Bangstad, S, T. H. Eriksen, J. L. Comaroff and J. Comaroff (2012), 'Anthropologists Are Talking': About Anthropology and Post-Apartheid South Africa, in: *Ethnos. Journal of Anthropology*, Vol. 77, No. 1, pp. 115–136.

Baumgartner, G. and É. Kovács (2007), Roma und Sinti im Blickfeld der Aufklärung und der bürgerlichen Gesellschaft [The Gaze of Bourgeois Society and Enlightenment on the Roma and Sinti], in: G. Baumgartner and T. Belgin (eds.), *Roma & Sinti – 'Zigeuner-Darstellungen' der Moderne*, Krems: Catalogue of the exhibition of the same name in Kunsthalle Krems, pp. 15–23.

Blaut, J. M. (1992), The Theory of Cultural Racism, in: *Antipode*, Vol. 23, 289–299.

Bourdieu, P. and L. Wacquant (2001), Neoliberal Newspeak: Notes on the New Planetary Vulgate, in: *Radical Philosophy*, January 2001: 108.

Channel 4 News (2013), *South Africa's Far-right*, online: https://www.you-tube.com/watch?v=9BpANbql3tc (accessed 21.9.2014).

Czech News Agency (2014), Romové mají špatnou pověst. Drtivá většina Čechů je nechce za sousedy [Roma have Bad Reputation. The Vast Majority of Czechs does not want them as Neighbors], online: http://www.romea.cz/cz/zpravodajstvi/domaci/romove-maji-spatnou-povest-drtiva-vetsina-cechu-je-nechce-za-sousedy (accessed 18.9.2014).

Czech Statistical Office (2012), Tab. 37, *Vybrané základní ukazatele v dlouhodobém vývoji – Česká republika.* [Chosen Basic Indicators in the Long-term Development – Czech Republic], online: http://www.czso.cz/csu/2012edicniplan.nsf/t/03002EA010/$File/ZVCR037.pdf (accessed 21.9.2014).

Davidová, E. (1995), *Romano drom – Cesty Romů 1945–1990* [Ways of Roma 1945–1990], Olomouc: Vydavatelství Univerzity Palackého.

Department of Welfare and Population Development (1997), *White Paper for Social Welfare*, Pretoria: Government Printers.

Eriksen, T. H. (2002), *Ethnicity and Nationalism: Anthropological Perspectives*, London: Pluto Press.

Eze, M. O. (2010), *Politics of History in Contemporary Africa,* New York: Palgrave-Macmillan.

Ferguson, J. (1990), *The Anti-Politics Machine: "Development," Depoliticization and Bureaucratic Power in Lesotho,* Minneapolis and London: University of Minnesota Press.

Freedom Front Plus (2014), *Manifesto of the FF Plus for the Election of 2014*, online: http://www.vfplus.org.za/2014-election-manifesto (accessed 19.9.2014).

GAC spol. s. r. o. (2006), *Analýza sociálně vyloučených romských lokalit a absorpční kapacity subjektů působících v této oblasti* [Analysis of Socially Excluded Roma Localities and Communities and the Absorption Capacity of Subjects Operating in the Field], Prague: Ministry of Labour and Social Affairs.

Gathiram, N. and D. Hemson (2002), Transformation of Welfare? Race, Class, and Gender in the Management of Welfare Agencies in South Africa, in: *Community Development Journal,* Vol. 3, 209–219.

Guglielmo, R. and T. W. Waters (2005), Migrating towards Minority Status: Shifting European Policy towards Roma, in: *Journal of Common Market Studies*, Vol. 43, No. 4, pp. 763–785.

Guy, W. (2001), The Czech lands and Slovakia: Another False Dawn? in: W. Guy (ed.) *Between Past and Future: the Roma of Central and Eastern Europe*, Hatfield: University of Hertfordshire Press, pp. 285–332.

Guy, W. (2010), EU Initiatives on Roma: Limitations and Ways Forward, in: N. Trehan and N. Sigona (eds), *Romani Politics in Contemporary Europe: Poverty, Ethnic Mobilisation, and the Neo-liberal Order*, Basingstoke: Palgrave/Macmillan, pp. 23–50.

Hübschmannová, M. (1994), *Šaj pes dovakeras – Můžeme se domluvit* [We can make ourselves understood], Olomouc: Pedagogická fakulta Univerzity Palackého.

Jurová, A. (2008), Historický vývoj rómskych osád na Slovensku a problematika vlastníckych vzťahov k pôde ("nelegálne osady") [Historical development of Romani settlements in Slovakia and problematic of land property relationships ("illegal settlements")], in: M. Jakoubek and T. Hirt (eds.), *Rómske osady na východnom Slovensku z hladiska terénneho antropologického výskumu*, Bratislava: Open Society Foundation, pp. 131–175.

Kamm, H. (10.12.1993), Havel Calls the Gypsies 'Litmus Test', *The New York Times*, online: http://www.nytimes.com/1993/12/10/world/havel-calls-the-gypsies-litmus-test.html (accessed 13.8.2014).

Kaufman, C. E. (1997), *Reproductive Control in South Africa*, Policy Research Division Working Paper Series, no. 97, New York: Population Council.

King, B. H. (2007), Environment and Development in the former South African Bantustans, in: *Geographical Journal*, Vol. 173, No. 1, pp. 6–12.

Klepárník, V. (2008), Role lidskoprávních organizací na řešení problematiky protiprávních sterilizací romských žen v České republice [The role of NGOs in the problematic of illegal sterilizations of Romani women in the Czech Republic], *Econnect*, online: http://www.ecn.cz/index.stm?apc=zm2071392vx1 — (accessed 10.9.2014).

Křížková, M. (2013), Analýza mediálního zobrazení Romů v českých médiích od začátku července 2011 do konce května 2012 [Analysis of image of Roma in Czech media from July 2001 to May 2012], Prague: Agency for Social Inclusion.

Lábusová, A., T. Nikolai, S. Pekárková and M. Rendl (2010), *Nemoc bezmocných: lehká mentální retardace. Analýza inteligenčního testu SON-R* [The Illness of the Powerless: Light Mental Disorder. Analysis of the test of intelligence SON-R], Prague: Člověk v tísni, o.p.s.

Law, I. (2012), *Red Racisms: Racism in Communist and Post-Communist Contexts*, Basingstoke: Palgrave Macmillan.

Lentin, A. (2011), What Happens to Anti-Racism When We Are Post Race? in: *Feminist Legal Studies*, Vol. 19, No. 2, pp. 159–168.

Listina základních práv a svobod [Charter of Fundamental Rights and Liberties] Online: http://www.czso.cz/csu/2012edicniplan.nsf/t/03002EA010/$File/ZVCR037.pdf (accessed 13.9. 2014).

Maylam, P. (2001), *South Africa's Racial Past: The History and Historiography of Racism, Segregation and Apartheid*, Aldershot: Ashgate.

Maylam, P. (1995), Explaining the Apartheid City: Ten Years of South African Urban Historiography, in: *Journal of Southern African Studies,* Vol. 21, No. 1, pp. 19–38.

Ministry of Interior of the Czech Republic (1958), *Zákon o trvalém usídlení kočujících osob* [Law on the Permanent Settlement of Nomadic People], Law No. 74.

Ministry of Labour and Social Affairs (2002), *Zavádění standardů kvality sociálních služeb do praxe. Průvodce poskytovatele* [Implementation of Standards of Quality of Social Services into Practice. A Guide to a Provider], Prague: MPSV.

Moravec, Š. (2006), Nástin problému sociálního vyloučení romských populací [Outline of a Problem of Social Exclusion of Romani Populations], in T. Hirt and M. Jakoubek (eds.), *„Romové" v osidlech sociálního vyloučení* ['Roma' in the Trap of Social Exclusion], Plzeň: Vydavatelství a nakladatelství Aleš Čeněk, pp. 11–69.

Navrátil, P. (2002), *Výzkum interetnických vztahů* [Research of Interethnic Relationships], Brno: Phare.

Nedělníková, D. (ed.) (2007), *Metodická příručka pro výkon terénní sociální práce* [Methodics for Delivery of Terrain Social Work], Ostrava: MPSV.

Novák, K. A. (2003), Romská osada – tradice versus regres [Romani settlement – tradition versus regres], in: M. Jakoubek and O. Poduška (eds.), *Romské osady v kulturologické perspektivě,* Brno: Doplněk, pp. 31–40.

Pavelčíková, N. (2004), *Romové v českých zemích v letech 1945–1989* [Roma in the Czech lands from 1945 to 1989], Prague: Úřad dokumentace a vyšetřování zločinů komunismu.

Ries, J. (2008), Writing (Different) Roma/Gypsies – Romani/Gypsy studies and the Scientific Construction of Roma/Gypsies, in: J. Ries and F. Jacobs (eds.), *Roma-/Zigeunerkulturen in neuen Perspektiven. Romani/Gypsy Cultures in New Perspectives*, Leipzig: Leipziger Universitätsverlag, pp. 297–291.

Romea (2009), Exkluzivní VIDEO: Emil Ščuka a Jan Rusenko v roce 1989 na Letné [Exclusive VIDEO: Emil Ščuka and Jan Rusenko at Letná in 1989], online: http: //www.romea.cz/cz/zpravy/exkluzivni-video-emil-scuka-a-jan-rusenko-v-roce-1989-na-letne (accessed 1.5.2014).

Rothscum, D. (2010). *South African Apartheid government planned to commit genocide through vaccines*, online: http://www.godlikeproductions.com/forum1/message1287361/pg1?regp=bm9fMTQxMTMzNTI1NA== (accessed 5.9.2014).

Rozhovor prezidenta Václava Klause pro BBC World – *HardTalk* [The Interview of the President Václav Klaus for BBC World – HardTalk], online: http://www.klaus.cz/clanky/1026 (accessed 13.8.2014).

Sewpaul, V. (2014), *Professionalization of Social Work in South Africa*, online: https://www.youtube.com/watch?v=hDQcfTDy2QM (accessed 13.8. 2014).

Smolík, J. (2010), Subkultury mládeže: Uvedení do problematiky [Youth Subcultures: Introduction to Problematic], Prague: Grada Publishing.

Smuts, J. (1929), *Africa and Some World Problems, Including the Rhodes Memorial Lectures Delivered in Michaelmas Term, 1929*, Oxford: Clarendon Press.

Sobotka, E. (2007), Human Rights and Roma Policy Formation in the Czech Republic, Slovakia and Poland, in: R. Stauber and R. Vago (eds.), *The Roma: A Minority in Europe: Historical, Political and Social Perspectives*, Budapest, New York: Central European University Press, pp. 135–162.

Sokolová, V. (2005), Planned Parenthood Behind the Curtain: Population Policy and Sterilization of Romani Women in Communist Czechoslovakia, 1972–1989, in: *The Antropology of East Europe Review*, Vol. 23, No. 1, pp. 79–98.

Swanson, M. (1977), The Sanitation Syndrome: Bubonic Plague and Urban Native Policy in the Cape Colony, 1900–1909, *Journal of African History*, Vol. 18, No. 3, pp. 387–410.

Synková, H. (2011), *Legitimation and Professionalization of a Romani NGO in the Czech Republic*, PhD. Dissertation, Prague: Charles University.

Synková, H. (2010), Claiming legitimacy in/of a Romani NGO, in: M. Stewart (ed.), *Multi-disciplinary Approaches to Romany Studies*, Budapest: Central European University Press, pp. 280–291.

Synková, H. (2004), *Čeští a slovenští Romové. Hranice a migrace* [Czech and Slovak Roma. Borders and Migration], PhD. theses, Prague: Charles University.

Šveřepa, M. (2008) Reforma sociálního systému v kontextu pomoci a kontroly [Reform of the Social System in context of Help and Control], in R. Janebová, M. Kappl and M. Smutek (eds.), Sborník konference *Sociální práce mezi pomocí a kontrolou*, Hradec Králové: Gaudeamus.

Trumpener, K. (1995), The Time of the Gypsies: A 'People Without History' in the Narratives of the West, in: K. A. Appiah and H. L. Gates Jr. (eds.), *Identities*, Chicago and London: University of Chicago Press, pp. 338–380.

Van Dijk, T. A. (2000), New(s) Racism: A Discourse Analytical Approach, in: S. Cottle (ed.), *Ethnic Minorities and the Media*, Milton Keynes, UK: Open University Press, pp. 33–49.

Vermeersch, P. (2005), Marginality, Advocacy, and the Ambiguities of Multiculturalism: Notes on Romani Activism in Central Europe, in: *Identities: Global Studies in Culture and Power*, Vol. 12, pp. 451–478.

Willems, W. (1997), *In Search of the True Gypsy: From Enlightenment to Final Solution*, London and Portland, OR: Frank Cass.

World Bank (2008), *Czech Republic: Improving Employment Chances of the Roma*, Report No. 46120 CZ.

Zapletal, T. (2012), Přístup totalitního státu a jeho bezpečnostních složek k romské menšině v Československu [Approach of the totalitarian state and its security services to the Romani minority in Czechoslovakia], *Sborník Archivu bezpečnostních složek*, Vol. 10, pp. 13–83.

Ethno-linguistic dynamics in the two young democracies: A comparison of language stigmas

Stephanie Rudwick

Introduction

The point of departure for this chapter is the premise that any language can obtain the status or stigma of a 'language of the oppressor', provided particular power-relations and socio-political circumstances. The reason behind such a stigma is not of linguistic but of socio-political nature and hence the subject must be located within the Sociology or Politics of Language and it draws from language ideological frameworks and theories. In what follows I aim to compare two languages in two different regions in the world: Russian in the Czech Republic (thereof CR) and Afrikaans in the Republic of South Africa (thereof RSA) through a broad socio-historical and socio-political perspective. My argument is based on the premise that these two languages were spoken by the group of people who were considered 'oppressors' during a particular period of time (apartheid RSA and socialist CSSR) and as a result the two languages acquired – to some extent – the status of a 'language of the oppressor' at that point in history, at least among a segment of the population. In this chapter, I examine the socio-historical construction of these language stigmas, I explore whether they are representative for the attitudes towards the speakers of these languages and I further deliberate about whether the negative attitudes persist today.

Importantly, the label 'language of the oppressor' must be understood in a post-modern and post-structural framework here, where 'oppressor' is not a fixed and stable category but socio-historically and situationally constructed. Dependent on the perspective of the participant or observer, the term/label 'language of the oppressor' must be seen as an alterable category that varies over time and space. The very changeable and malleable nature of attitudes *per se* also makes language attitudes a rather unstable subject of study. Nonetheless, in apartheid South Africa, Afrikaans has quite consistently been portrayed as a 'language of the oppressor' *par excellence* because the entire apartheid apparatus was practically run in Afrikaans and largely by Afrikaners. In socialist Czechoslovakia, the status of Russian as 'language of the oppressor' was much less clear-cut, far more latent and covert, but as I would like to argue here, nonetheless existed.

Negative attitudes towards languages are located within ideological processes in language policy situations, as languages *per se* obviously have no agency 'to do' anything, let alone to oppress anyone. Just as the German language was not responsible for Nazi ideology, the Holocaust and other atrocities perpetrated by the National Socialists in Germany who spoke and promoted German, so was Afrikaans not responsible for apartheid in South Africa and Russian not for Soviet-style communism in Czechoslovakia. However, language dynamics are of socio-cultural and political nature and in many instances language attitudes are constitutive for attitudes about the speakers of this language (Ferguson 1994). It is hence not so likely that someone voluntarily acquires a language spoken by people he experiences as 'oppressive' in his/her environment unless s/he has a concrete purpose in mind. On one hand, the oppressed may well find ways to give expression to the oppression and possibly even reach liberation through the 'language of the oppressor'.[1] It is widely known that the late Nelson Mandela learned Afrikaans while being imprisoned on Robben Island, and one can safely assume that he did not go through this effort because he 'liked' Afrikaans and the people who spoke this language. Mandela knew it was important to learn the language of his enemies in order to understand their thinking and to find out their weaknesses through knowing their mother tongue. There is little doubt that Mandela's proficiency in Afrikaans assisted on a social-emotional level during negotiations with Afrikaner National Party members after 1992.

In this chapter, I primarily explore whether and in how far the stigmas the two above-mentioned languages acquired during the oppressive regimes have lost their negative statuses in the democratic republics and what implications these language attitudes have, by extension, for attitudes towards their speakers. Both the Czech Republic and South Africa are not yet 'robust' democracies and the political fragility may well affect social and linguistic attitudes in the two countries. In the first part of this chapter I discuss relevant sociolinguistic ideologies for the case studies at hand and then exemplify two other languages that acquired negative connotations, namely, English and German. In the next section, I provide the socio-historical background to the study before I move to the comparative perspective of the two young democracies by discussing, albeit merely at an exploratory rather than argumentative level, the current status of Russian in CR and Afrikaans in RSA. While I rely primarily on a literature review in this study, I also include anecdotal details, national and international journalistic work, selected interviews, in/formal conversations and some observational data from both

---

[1]See for instance, Daniels' (2001) seminal study on the 'voices of the oppressed in the language of the oppressor'.

countries.[2] In concluding the chapter I attempt to provide a preliminary prognosis of the status and development of the two languages on focus.

Language ideologies and the 'one language, one nation' fallacy

The topic of language stigmas or specifically the stigmas as 'language of the oppressor' and 'language of oppression' are located within language politics and closely linked to studies of ideology. Language ideology frameworks (Blommaert 1999; Hobsbawn 1990; Woolard and Schieffelin 1994; Wollard 2010) can shed light on how certain languages and linguistic practices become to be seen negatively under particular socio-economic circumstances. Although there exists an extensive literature on language ideologies, few comprehensive studies have sufficiently explored how and why any particular language acquires a negative status or stigma among a certain group of people and how these stigmas may persist. It is clear, of course, that a language and its associated values and discourse conventions affect the relation between the speakers of this language and others. In many language policy situations there are those that are in power and those that are dis-empowered, depending on the status of their language.

Several works, both academic and non-academic, have examined how oppressive and totalitarian regimes have followed particular language policies. Totalitarian regimes use totalitarian language for the creation of an easily controllable mass society and as a tool for keeping power by spreading the dominant ideology (Váňa 2012: 14), such as George Orwell's Newspeak. There are no inherent linguistic characteristics in any language – let alone in Russian or in Afrikaans – that would make them be seen in a negative light. Oppressive and dehumanising words and phrases can be used in any linguistic variety. Arguably, the most comprehensive study of this is by Bosmajian (1983) whose research on the 'language of oppression' began in the 1960s when he examined the rhetoric of the Nazis (Hitler in particular), before and during National Socialism. This study explores how specific words and terminology in several different languages lead to dehumanisation and degradation of human beings; for instance, Hitler's 'Final Solution' labelled Jewish people as 'sub-humans' and 'parasites'. Clearly, language is "never value or politically neutral and was and always will be a reflection of the specific political and social environment in which it is used" (Váňa 2012: 17). In the Czech context Fidelius (1983) discusses in *Jazyk a moc* how Orwellian style Newspeak was coined in the Czech language during the Soviet regime.

---

[2]The author is closely familiar with both countries on focus: she lived eight years in South Africa and during the time of writing completed her fifth year residence in the Czech Republic.

This politicised Czech Newspeak created alienation and purposeful politi-cisation and decolonisation. The neutral Czech term '*lid*' ('volk', people), for example, was misused by the communist regime to (falsely) express what was the *vox populi*. Contrarily to how the term was used, most Czech people at the time did not consider themselves part of this very '*lid*' the government propagated. Similarly, in apartheid South Africa the government also created versions of English and Afrikaans Newspeak. The term 'urban relocation' promoted by the apartheid racists replaced the more appropriate but politically incorrect term 'forced removals' used initially. The term 'urban relocation' could be considered a neutral phrase, if it did not, in reality, trivialise brutal political actions that robbed black people of their humanity by destroying and bulldozing their homes.

Fasold (1984: 148) argued that the "attitudes toward language are often the reflection of attitudes towards members of the ethnic group". Numerous sociological and linguistic researchers have investigated language attitudes in the context of motives for group identification and ethnicity (Fishman 1983; Panther 1994; Ehret 1997). Language attitudes generally reveal a multitude of information about individuals' perceptions towards themselves and others, and are thus inextricably linked to perceptions of identity. Before I turn to the specific cases of Afrikaans in South Africa and Russian in the Czech Republic and examine in how far these languages may have acquired and maintained a stigma, I briefly explore how other European[3] languages, i.e. English and German, have also been seen as a 'language of the oppressor' at a certain place during a certain period of time. Within this topic it is highly important to always consider time and context as language statuses are variable. I refer to the two European languages as examples in order to substantiate my basic argument that practically any language spoken by a group of people who colonised, can more or less easily acquire a stigma or be seen as a 'language of the oppressor'.[4]

Klímova (2007), among others, discussed how the English language represented a 'language of oppression/the oppressor' among Caribbean writers of the former British Empire. The history of the Caribbean region and the English colonisation of its local population fostered negative attitudes

---

[3] I focus on European languages because the speakers of these languages were the prime perpetrators of colonisation. While Japanese, for instance, can also be explored in terms of its negative status in Taiwan or Korea, but to include these geographical areas is beyond the scope of this work.

[4] In fact one and the same language can also have the status of 'language of the oppressor' and 'language of the oppressed' throughout time and space, as Tanaka (2006) has shown in reference to Japanese.

towards British English. Creole and other local dialects in the Caribbean were neglected and disdained for a long time while English was elevated as high-status language. English is, even today, in several regions of the world, attached with the stigma of a 'language of the oppressor'.[5] In Africa, however, it has more recently cleansed itself of some negativity. Spichtinger (2003: 22) argues that English is "no longer perceived as a tongue of the oppressor [in Nigeria] but as performing a useful function in a multilingual society". This is true, to some extent, also in South Africa, although even recent research suggests that for some African people English still remains, among other labels, a "language of the colonizer and oppressor" (De Klerk and Gough 2002; Rudwick 2004, 2008).[6]

German is also a rather good example for a language that acquired a seriously negative status and was regarded as a 'language of the oppressor' in the past, most notably obviously during National Socialism. Clyne (1995: 6), for instance, writes that German started to be seen as a "language of the oppressor subjectively in the eyes and ears of the oppressed, but objectively through the use of German by the occupation forces in the execution of oppression and genocide" during the holocaust and Nazi Germany. German is also not perceived in a positive light by some Czech people today, as the atrocities committed, for instance, in the well-known village of Lidice, serves as a reminder of the cruelties of the Nazi regime.[7] Clyne (ibid.) argues that for German "the situation in Eastern and Central Europe was somewhat different in so far as there had been a more recent occupying power or dominating force using another language, Russian, as an instrument of oppression and dominance". In an interview with a young Russian woman who runs a language school in Prague, she wondered: "I just do not get it. Why have they [Czech people] forgiven the Germans but not us?" The answer to this question is probably complex, but Clyne's suggestion concerning the more recent character of the occupation by the Soviet regime is one – of possibly many – plausible responses.

---

[5]Philippson, who could be regarded the primary critic of the spread of the English language in the world, developed the term 'linguistic imperialism' (1992) to emphasize that English was an agent of imperialism.

[6]The status of English in RSA is one that is highly ambiguous. Africans have been described to have a 'love-hate' relationship with the language (De Klerk and Gough 2002: 370) and labels range from 'language of colonisation', 'language of liberation', 'language of communication' and others. Compared to Afrikaans, however, English is always seen as more positive among Africans.

[7]To support this point I offer a personal anecdote: Speaking German with a friend in the Prague metro, I was once silenced by an elderly lady with the following words *"wir wollen diese Sprache hier nicht hören!"* ["We do not want to hear this language here!"].

Socio-historical perspective

As previously mentioned unequal power relations are the prerequisite for a language to acquire a stigma. Although the Afrikaans-speaking population in apartheid South Africa was considerable while the presence of Russians (mainly just soldiers) in Czechoslovakia was rather small, I would like to argue that their influence – as the ruling and ultimately 'oppressive' powers – was nonetheless quite overwhelming in both places. Russian and Afrikaans politicians imposed their discriminatory political agendas, i.e. Soviet-style communism and Afrikaner-style apartheid, which virtually controlled all aspects of public life for the Czechoslovak and Black South African population. In the next section I will look at each language group in isolation from a socio-historical and present perspective before I attempt a more comparative perspective in the discussion section.

The Russian language, Russians and Soviet politics in Czechoslovakia

After World War II, the communists gained power in Czechoslovakia and the 1948 *coup d'etat* installed Soviet-style communism which included the end of freedom of expression, censored press as well as the prohibition of any kind of 'anti-governmental' activity. Already during this time, all Czech and Slovak children and students had to learn Russian as the first foreign language in schools. In 1968, the Soviet led invasion to Czechoslovakia crushed the 'Prague Spring' reform movement led by Alexander Dubček that had allowed certain socio-political freedoms as well as some 'critical' artistic expressions. The Soviet invasion claimed many lives among the Czech and Slovak population and essentially turned Czechoslovakia into a hard-line regime behind the Iron Curtain.

The status of the Russian language during the Communist regime from 1948 to 1989 was a peculiar one. Officially, it was the Nr.1 language of 'international communication' and the 'Number 1' foreign language taught mandatory at all schools in Czechoslovakia starting already in elementary school and continuing till the end of secondary education (Hnízdo 2011). Russian was also a compulsory subject for all Czech university students, irrespective of whether they were studying a language related discipline or natural science with no link to language study as such. Despite these rather forceful language-in-education policies, there was no organized revolt against Russian and the influence of the language in Czechoslovakia was rather marginal, if compared to the power of Afrikaans during apartheid South Africa, especially on a grassroots level. It was not the Russian language that was spoken to political offenders of the Soviet-State, as was the case with

Afrikaans in apartheid South Africa. Rather, it was the Czech communist Newspeak. Furthermore, the presence of Russians in Czechoslovakia was limited to, on the one hand, roughly 100,000 Soviet soldiers who were kept virtually in isolation from the Czech population and, on the other hand, very few Russian tourists (Hnízdo 2001). Nonetheless, between 1968 and the 1990s the "reluctance to speak Russian was a way to express one's opinion about the political situation in Czechoslovakia" (Hnízdo 2003: 10). Conversely, in socialist Czechoslovakia, to show disrespect toward Russian as a language, for instance during Russian lessons in school or at university, could easily and perhaps 'dangerously' be perceived as 'anti-Soviet' behaviour which ultimately could get one into very deep trouble. Russian, as much I dare to say with reasonable certainty, was not a language that the overwhelming majority of the Czech people embraced to speak. Griest (2006), an American writer fluent in Russian, described an instance, where she upset a young Czech woman by speaking in Russian to her, until she finally exclaimed "stop talking to me in that awful language" (ibid. 88). This, the author writes, made her aware that "people do not like to speak in the language of their motherland's oppressor".

In 1989, the Velvet Revolution led by Václav Havel and his contemporaries brought the Soviet regime to back up and communism to an end. Already from 1990, Russian was no longer a mandatory subject and its study on all school levels decreased drastically in the 1990s (Hnízdo 2011). Throughout the 1990s the number of Czech people who voluntarily studied the language was rather marginal but there appears to be a slight increase since 2000 again.[8] Something, Russian in CSSR and Afrikaans in RSA certainly have in common is the drastic decline of people acquiring these languages in the two countries, simply because there no longer exist any mandatory language lessons in school. Below I describe some of the developments of Afrikaans in education.

Afrikaans, the Afrikaner and apartheid

The Afrikaans language originally stems from Dutch and developed independently only during the 18th century in the Cape region of South Africa. In 1925, Afrikaans gained official status in the Republic of South Africa (next to English). Initially termed 'kitchen Dutch' in a derogatory way in its early days, it was turned into a high status/domain language within only a few decades, through tremendous efforts of corpus development and language engineering. If one strolls through the libraries at the historically Afrikaans universities, i.e. Potchefstroom or Stellenbosch, one cannot help being amazed

---

[8]Personal communication with a lecturer at the Russian department at Charles University.

by the number of scientific work published in the language. Although Afrikaans has Indo-European roots it did emerge as a full-flown language in Africa, and this is the reason why today many Afrikaans-speakers fight to have it accepted as an 'African' language.[9]

Afrikaans has been portrayed in the South African sociolinguistic literature as *the* language of oppression *par excellence*, but to the best of my knowledge, no comprehensive study ever explored the resilience of this stigma in the post-apartheid state. During apartheid, Afrikaans was almost always the medium "used when white policemen arrested black pass offenders" (Giliomee 2003a: 14). After 1948, virtually all agents and ground workers of apartheid were Afrikaans speakers. Furthermore, the vast majority of school children growing up during this time had to learn Afrikaans, apart from very few black township or rural schools were African principals took things into their own hands and promoted only English.[10] Although English was also a 'language of colonisation', the African National Congress (ANC) adopted English as medium to improve internal communication and in order to have an international voice. Afrikaner politicians were well aware of the preference for English among black South Africans and in the mid-70s the Department of Bantu Administration enforced a 50/50 percent rule for Afrikaans and English as languages of instruction in black schools (Hartshorne 1992). Black teachers, students and parents protested and on 16 June 1976 more than fifteen thousand schoolchildren in the Soweto township marched in protest against the language decree with placards bearing slogans such as "Down with Afrikaans" (Giliomee 2003a, b) or "Blacks are not dustbins – Afrikaans stinks" (Ndlovu 1998). The protest and demonstrations spread all over the country and within a few months more than 600 people died, many of whom were school children. These events, documented as the Soweto Uprising, firmly established Afrikaans as 'the language of the oppressor' and most black people refused to learn it.

Today in South Africa, mother-tongue Afrikaans speakers make up about 13.5 per cent of the population, not an insignificant number. But it needs to be remembered that the Afrikaans population is composed of a very heterogeneous group of people and the so-called 'coloured' people form with 54 per cent the majority of Afrikaans speakers, and this group of people certainly

---

[9]This, of course, is a rather contested topic as many black people find it difficult to accept Afrikaans as an African language. It has also been a topic of debate among language specialists and linguists in the country.

[10]Also the situation in current KwaZulu-Natal, then Zululand and Natal, was somewhat different as many isiZulu-speaking children in Natal were taught in their L1 from 1885 (Hartshorne 1995: 308).

would not identify themselves as Afrikaner, the previous 'oppressors'. As one can deduce from the above brief, the socio-historical and demographic position of Afrikaans is drastically different to that of Russian in Czecho-slovakia which practically never had any native speakers, other than soldiers. Also, there was virtually no history of open or organised protest against Russian as a language subject in school or university in Czechoslovakia. Nonetheless, I would like to argue that some parallels between the situations exist and I therefore compare and contrast the two ethno-linguistic dynamics.

Comparative discussion on the current dynamics

In the following section I aim to discuss the current status of Afrikaans in South Africa and the current position of Russian in the Czech Republic. The compare and contrast format of this section aims to unravel similarities as well as differences in the status of the two languages in the two young democracies today.

In South Africa, the situation is fairly clear-cut as several academic studies have made reference to the continued negative attitudes among black people towards Afrikaans.[11] However, there is no comprehensive study focusing solely on the prevalent stigma of Afrikaans in the country. Nonetheless, it could be considered something like 'common knowledge' in South Africa that African people deeply 'dislike' the language. It is safe to say that many black people who were old enough to understand the atrocities of apartheid, roughly 40 years old+, continue to have negative associations with Afrikaans. The language remains, even in current South Africa, and despite some efforts to revise this,[12] one of the primary markers of Afrikaner ethnicity (Blaser 2007; Bosch 2000; Engel 1997; Kriel 2003; Webb and Kriel 2000) and it has convincingly been argued that it does not constitute a flexible variable in a construction of 'Afrikanerdom'. To show disrespect toward Afrikaans was and to some extent still is today perceived as displaying disrespect towards Afrikaners.

Afrikaans is inextricably associated with the apartheid regime and the Soweto Uprising can be seen as watershed moment in which Afrikaans established itself firmly as the 'language of the oppressor'. To some extent, this stigma remains today as many black people in South Africa continue to

---

[11]See, for instance, Vorster and Proctor (1976), Giliomee (2003a, b), or Dyers (2004).
[12]Some Afrikaans-speaking scholars (see, for instance Van der Waal 2008 and Webb 2002) have expound the problem that Afrikaans promotion has often been linked to essentialised ideas about culture, language and identity (Afrikanerdom) and often includes ethno-national and purist ideas of language development.

see Afrikaans as the "language of the [previous] oppressor" (Giliomee 2003b).[13] Also recently, the resentment against Afrikaans and Afrikaners among many black South Africans was accentuated by members of the African National Congress (ANC) Youth League singing a song called 'shoot the Boer' – meaning shoot white Afrikaans speaking people.[14] Today, speaking in Afrikaans in particular situations is often a socio-political statement that can trigger provocation and conflict among black people in contemporary RSA. In contemporary Czech Republic, speaking Russian in particular situations can be an act of mockery or irony.

While non-academic, I would like to mention that in October 2010, a Facebook page was created with the title "We hate Afrikaans". The description of the page says: "To every person out there who thinks Afrikaans is one of the most bull shit languages … we unite and tell the world... Fuck Afrikaans!!!" While the page has only been given 85 likes at the time of writing which admittedly is a rather negligible number in an internet forum such as Facebook, I would nonetheless argue that it is noteworthy that such a page exists. Also considering that I did not find a similar page for any other language. Furthermore, Brad Cibane (2003), who writes regular blogs for the Mail&Guardian *ThoughtLeader* questions in a March 2003 article whether there should be room for Afrikaners and Afrikaans at all in the new South Africa. In the blog, he emphasizes that many young black South Africans continue to refuse speaking Afrikaans due to its negative associations. Although many 'non-whites' speak Afrikaans, the language continues to be strongly linked to Afrikanerdom and by extension 'white' racism.

In comparing the language statuses of Afrikaans and Russian, I rely largely on anecdotal evidence as regards Russian. There is, to the best of my knowledge, no academic study that has examined the status of Russian in the contemporary Czech Republic. It must be assumed that Russian is not equally stigmatised in the contemporary CR as Afrikaans is in contemporary RSA, but it does seem to carry some negative connotation to this day. As two Czech sociolinguists put it: in the post-communist state, "studying it [Russian] served as a symbol of a wish to return to the Soviet dominated society" (Neustupný a Nekvapil 2003: 320). In a less academic source, it is claimed that because of the memories of the Soviet oppression that Russian brings, "many Czechs refuse to speak the language to this day" (Nollen 1997: 18). As a Czech female

---

[13]Several other sources suggest the same: http://medienportal.univie.ac.at/uniview/detail/artikel/the-image-of-afrikaans-in-south-africa-part-2/

[14]Condemned as hate speech by the South African High Court, this song is often translated from its vernacular form into English so as to be understandable and to convey a clear statement against Afrikaners and Afrikaans.

academic self-reflectively proclaimed: "I just cannot speak Russian to Russians. I can only speak Russian to perhaps Ukrainians or other Russian speakers. I don't know what it is, a mental block perhaps?" Russians who live in Czech Republic today do not always feel 'welcome' and have experienced a certain level of hostility among (especially the middle and older generation) Czech people, sometimes only on the basis of their language usage (Sládek 2010). Although Ukrainians and many other people from ex-Soviet countries speak Russian, the language is often sufficient to (mistakenly) label people socio-politically as Russians. The 1994 to 2010 period represented a new era of Russian immigration in the country and the number of Russian people grew from 3,000 to 32,000. From this total, about 18 to 20,000 have permanent or long-term residency. The majority of Russian people live in the capital Prague, but another centre of Russian residence continues to be Karlovy Vary.[15] While the number of Russian people is not that large, there are about 150,000 Russian speakers in the country.

From a linguistic perspective, it is also rather noteworthy that despite the presence of the Russian language during communist and post-communist Czech area there are only very few loan words that have been adopted from Russian into Czech (Danes 1997). After 1989, Russian loanwords that captured Soviet life and its habits were "relegated to the lexicon of historiography" (Neustupný and Nekvapil 2003: 232). While attitudes towards Russian in the Czech Republic are probably not as negative as those towards Afrikaans in South Africa, it nonetheless cannot be denied that the language often triggers negative associations due to the element of Russophobia in Czech society.[16] Bilefsky (2010), quotes a female 50-years old interviewee who has an art business in Karlovy Vary as saying: "The Russians invaded us before and they are invading us again" and concludes that such "sentiments reflect the growing concerns of many Czechs about Russia's motives … in a region where history is never far from the surface". It can be assumed that the individual quoted above may not have positive things to say about excessive usage of Russian in her neighbourhood.

Also, consider the following three anecdotes based on participant observation:

1. August 2013: An elderly (68years) Czech lady (A) is walking in a public park in Prague with her 3-year old female grandchild. Another elderly (60years+) lady (B) walks in near distance on a park trail. While A sits on

---

[15]From: http://www.themoscowtimes.com/news/article/in-czech-republic-russians-are-back-and-thriving/439773.html.

[16]See for instance a recent article by the respected Czech journalist Jan Macháček who writes for RESPEKT magazine: http://respekt.ihned.cz/c1-61674830-rusofobuv-stihomam.

a park bench the little girl starts picking flowers from a cultivated flower field. B approaches the scene and reprimands (in fluent Czech albeit with strong Russian accent) the little girl for picking the flowers. A immediately storms towards B saying: *"Tady, to je náš park. Maja si může trhat co chce. Běžte si řídit park k vám domů!"* [This is our park and Maja can pick here whatever she wants. You (polite form) go and stir [the rules] of your parks at home!]"

2. May 2013: In a 4 star-hotel in Prague, a male (40 years+) employee (A) is sitting at the reception: An evidently wealthy, male (35years+) Russian tourist (B) approaches the receptionist in Russian and complains loudly about the lack of service in the hotel bar while other customers stand aside. The receptionist patiently looks at the young man, seemingly listening, but then very calmly but slightly patronising responds in immaculate English: *"Excuse me Sir, in English or German please. Our establishment is an international hotel"*.

3. February 2014: A 45+-years old Czech man (A) and his foreign girlfriend are meeting a young male estate agent (B) to look at a flat for sale in Prague. As B starts talking in Czech with a strong Russian accent the girlfriend notices how A starts showing little enthusiasm about the flat although it has all important criteria they are looking for. After the couple parts with B the woman confronts her boyfriend (A) asking him why he felt so negative and was rude to the estate agent. He responds: *"I just cannot believe 'this Russian' wants to show me <u>my</u> neighbourhood"*.

Of course there is no clear evidence that any other foreign language spoken in the above-described situations may not have triggered similar responses. In analysing and trying to interpret the above three anecdotes I underlined three terms which express ownership of some kind. In 1) and 2) there appears to be a fear of appropriation by Russians and in 2) there is the inherent claim that Russian is not an *international* language (which is a counter-narrative to the communist propaganda where Russian was supposed to be the quasi-international language). What – as I would like to argue – the above anecdotes have in common is an unwillingness to 'neutrally' engage with the Russian language and/or person. While neither of the individuals (A) in the three episodes is necessarily a Russophobe, it seems that the Russian language, inter alia, triggered some kind of negative feeling in each one of the individuals.[17] It appears that Czech people do not like to be told what to do

---

[17]The Czech person in case 1) and 2) was interviewed retrospectively and questioned about their negative response. In case 1) the essential claim of the individual was: "I really dislike like it when Russian tell us what to do", and in case 2) the main response was that "Russians have no right to feel at home here".

by Russians and it is quite safe to say that among the current generation of people that are 40 years and older there are still many who harvest negative and perhaps even hostile attitudes towards Russian people and some in that age cohort also continue to despise the language. The irony, however, is that at times, the Russian language or the speaking of Czech with a Russian accent can trigger negative feelings towards someone who is, in fact, from Ukraine, Belarus or Kazakhstan and may have also suffered under the Soviet regime.

It has been noted that in the Czech Republic the young generation, unaffected by communism is likely to have a less strong negative attitude towards Russian (Hnízdo 2011). Similarly, in South Africa, black people who were not yet attending school during the time of the Soweto Uprising and especially those born after 1994, the so-called 'born-frees' must also be assumed to have a less negative attitude. However, even many young black Africans refuse to speak the language because of its burdened past (Cibane 2013). Although there is practically no empirical evidence available I would like to suggest that there is a notable generational differences in attitudes towards those two languages in both countries. People above the age of about forty years who have personally experienced oppression through Soviet-style communism or apartheid can be assumed to harvest stronger and more negative feelings towards Russian and Afrikaans than those who were 'born free'.

Conclusion and attempt of a prognosis

In this chapter I have argued that there are some notable parallels in the persistence of the stigma of Afrikaans in RSA and Russian in CR although the latter is far more latent. In South Africa, an attitude change towards more positive perceptions of Afrikaans may occur through 'progressive' Afrikaners who reject the language-culture-identity model and distance themselves of the negative apartheid association of Afrikanerdom and speakers of Afrikaans who are not white and not Afrikaners, such as the members of the coloured community of the Western Cape. While there is a slight shift in attitudes towards Afrikaans among the 'born-frees' towards more neutral-ness or indifference, there is also "knowledge in the blood" (Jansen 2004). By this phrase Jansen captured the power of upbringing and blood linkages in the Afrikaner community in South Africa, but this 'blood knowledge' obviously also exists in other South African communities. There are a number of reasons why Afrikaans has not been cleansed of its stigma. First, the wounds of the past are not and perhaps can never be entirely healed. Afrikaners have caused too much suffering during apartheid in order for black people to be able to entirely forgive. Second, the continuous socio-economic privilege of most (white) Afrikaans-speakers persists even in the post-apartheid state and socio-economic inequality obviously contributes to socio-political and racial friction. And lastly, it has to be admitted that the most vehement racist attacks continue to be committed by Afrikaners[18].

In the absence of solid empirical data on current attitudes towards Russian among Czechs and in the Czech Republic, one can only take educated guesses about its status in the young democracy. I argue that attitudes towards the Russian language among Czechs today are complex but also that it is quite safe to say that a part of the people in the generation 40 years and older continue to see the language in a negative light and associate previous oppression with it. As is evident in one of the citation in this chapter, there is a sense of 'neo' invasion by Russians among some Czech people, as they see ('too many' or 'too wealthy') Russians visit or even immigrate to the Czech Republic. Russia continues to be seen as the greatest socio-political threat (Nedomova and Kostelecky 1997; Škodová 2008). However, "it may be anticipated that the attitude of the younger generations, which did not experience the Communist regime, will be less negative than that of older generations, and will be more inclined to accept the fact that an officially recognized Russian community may indeed exist in the CR" (Hnízdo 2011: 12).

I would like to suggest that 'language(s) of oppression' in Bosmajian's (1983) sense can fairly easily cleanse themselves of their stigma through the change from a totalitarian system to more democratic politics. After all, in the Czech Republic a kind of communist Newspeak, which could be considered a 'language of oppression', was spoken until the late 1980s. Nonetheless, Czech as a language is obviously free of stigma and a treasured mother tongue in the population. However, a 'language of the oppressor' (i.e. a specific language a group people has negative associations with due to previous oppression, for instance during apartheid or communism) is more resilient in its stigma. Although Afrikaners (in RSA) and Russians (in CR) have practically lost political power more than two decades ago, Afrikaans certainly continues to be stigmatised in South Africa, and Russian continues to be seen by many Czech people in a negative light. Metaphorically spoken, the "ghost of the past" still lingers. Once a language has acquired a stigma as a 'language of the oppressor' as Afrikaans did during apartheid and Russian during communism, it does not easily cleanse itself of this negative status

---

[18]See for example, racist student attacks among Afrikaner students at the University of the Free State: http://www.news24.com/SouthAfrica/News/Another-alleged-racist-attack-at-UFS-20140220.

within one and the same generation, i.e. the generation(s) that experienced the oppression. It must also be assumed that the current status of Russian and Russians in the Czech Republic has assumed further negative connotation due to the Ukrainian crisis and the more recent role of Russia under Putin as aggressor. However, such an analysis is beyond the scope of this paper and will hopefully find attention elsewhere.

References

Angogo, R. (1978), Language and Politics in South Africa, *Studies in African Linguistics* Vol. 9, No. 2, pp. 211–221.

Bibo, D. (1998), *History and Czech*, online: http://linguistics.byu.edu/classes/ling450ch/reports/czech.html (accessed 17.2.2014).

Bilefsky, D. (2010), *In Eastern Europe, Pact with Russians Raises Old Specters*, online: http://www.nytimes.com/2010/04/07/world/europe/07iht-czech.html?pagewanted=all&_r=2& (accessed 17.2.2014).

Blaser, T. (2007), *Afrikaner Identity after Nationalism: Young Afrikaners and the 'new' South Africa*, Unpublished Doctoral thesis. Submitted at University of the Witwatersrand, Johannesburg.

Blommaert, J. (ed.) (1999), *Language Ideological Debates.* Berlin: Walter de Gruyter.

Bosch, B. (2000), Ethnicity markers in Afrikaans, in: *International Journal of the Sociology of Language*, Vol. 144, pp. 51–68.

Bosmajian, H. A. (1983), *Language of Oppression*, University Press of America: Laham.

Cibane, B. (2013), Any room for Afrikaners in the new South Africa? in: *ThoughtLeader Mail & Guardian Online*, http://www.thoughtleader.co.za/bradcibane/2013/03/08/any-room-for-afrikaners-in-the-new-south-africa/ (accessed 22.2.2014).

Clyne, M. (1995), *The German language in a changing Europe,* Cambridge: Cambridge University Press.

Daniels, P. L. (2001), *The Voice of the Oppressed in the Language of the Oppressor,* New York/London: Routledge.

De Klerk V. and D. Gough (2002), Black South African English, in: R. Mesthrie (ed.), *Language in South Africa,* Cambridge: Cambridge University Press, 356–378.

Dyers, C. (2004), Ten years of democracy: attitudes and identity among some South African school children, in: *Per Linguam*, Vol. 20, No. 1, pp. 22–35.

Ehret, R. (1997), Language attitudes and the linguistic construction of ethnic identity: the case of Krio in Sierra Leone, in: M. Pütz (ed.), *Languages*

Choices. Conditions, Constraints and Consequences, Amsterdam/Philadelphia: John Benjamins, pp. 327–337.

Engel, U. (1997), Ethnische Konflikte und politischer Neubeginn in Südafrika, in: *Afrika Spectrum*, Vol. 32, No. 1, 25–47.

Fasold, R. (1984), *The Sociolinguistics of Society*, Oxford and Cambridge, MA: Blackwell.

Ferguson, C. (1994), Dialect, Register, and Genre: Working Assumptions about Conventionalization, in: D. Biber and E. Finegan (eds.), *Sociolinguistic Perspectives on Register*, New York: Oxford University Press, pp. 15–31.

Fidelius, P. (1998), *Řeč komunistické moci*, Praha: Triada.

Fishman, J. A. (1983), Language and ethnicity in bilingual education, in: W.C. McCready (ed.), *Culture, Ethnicity, and Identity. Current Issues in Research*, New York: Academic Press.

Giliomee, H. (2003a), *The Rise and Possible Demise of Afrikaans as a Public Language*, Cape Town: Praesa.

Giliomee, H. (2003b), *The Afrikaner. Biography of a People*, Charlottesville: University of Virginia Press.

Griest, S. E. (2006), Soviet No More, in: D. Farley and J. Sholl (eds.), *Traveller's Tales and the Czech Republic, Prague*, Berkley: Publishers Group, pp. 88–95.

Hartshorne, K. B. (1992), *Crisis and Challenge. Black Education 1910–1990*, Cape Town: Oxford University Press.

Hartshorne, K. B. (1995), Language policy in African education, a background to the future, in: R. Mesthrie (ed.), *Language and Social History: Studies in South African Sociolinguistics*, Cape Town: David Philip, pp. 306–318.

Hnízdo, B. (2011), Changing roles of minority languages in the Czech Republic, in: *The Annual of Language & Politics and Politics of Identity*, Vol. 5, pp. 5–22.

Hobsbawn, E. (1990), *Nations and Nationalism since 1970*, Cambridge: Cambridge University Press.

Jansen, J. (2002), *Knowledge in the Blood*, Standford University Press.

Klímova, Z. (2007), *English as a language of oppression*, unpublished MA thesis, Brno: Masaryk University.

Kriel, M. (2003), Approaches to multilingualism in language planning and identity politics: a critique, in: *Society in Transition*, Vol. 34, No. 1, pp. 159–177.

Marjorie, J. (1982), Language Policy and Oppression in South Africa, online: http://www.culturalsurvival.org/publications/cultural-survival-quarterly/south-africa/language-policy-and-oppression-south-africa (accessed 17.2.2014).

Ndlovu, S. F. (1998), *The Soweto uprising: Counter-memories of June 1976*, Randburg: Ravan Press.

Nedomova, A. and T. Kostelecky (1997), The Czech National Identity, *in: Czech Sociological Review,* Vol. 5, No. 1, pp. 79–92.

Neustupný, J. V. a J. Nekvapil (2003), Language Management in the Czech Republic, in: *Current Issues in Language Planning,* Vol. 4, No. 3&4, pp. 181–366.

Nollen, T. (1997), *Culture shock! A Guide to Customs and Etiquette,* Oregon: Graphic Arts Center Publisher.

Orwell, G. (1949), *1984,* London: Penguin Publishers.

Panther, E. (1994), Language attitudes and multilingualism: classroom-based action research, in: *ELTIC Reporter*, Vol. 18, No. 1/2, pp. 32–38.

Phillipson, R. (1992), *Linguistic Imperialism*, Oxford: Oxford University Press.

Škodová, M. (2008), *Vztah Čechů k vybraným národnostem*, Praha: Sociologický ústav AV ČR. Centrum pro výzkum veřejného mínění.

Sládek, K. (2010), *Ruská diaspora v České republice: sociální, politická a religiozní variabilita ruské migrace,* Praha: Pavel Mervart.

Spichtinger, D. (2003), *The Spread of English and its Appropriation*. MA thesis submitted at the Faculty of Philosophy, Vienna, Austria, online: http://spichtinger.net/Uni/sp-dipl3.pdf (accessed 20.2.2014).

Tanaka, H. (2006) Corporate Language Change: the Trajectory of Management Discourse in Japan, the oppressed or the oppressor, in: *Quaderns de Filologia. Estudis Lingüistics,* Vol. 11, pp. 279–288.

The Associated Press (2011), in: *Czech Republic, Russians Are Back and Thriving,* online:http://www.themoscowtimes.com/news/article/in-czech-republic-russians-are-back-and-thriving/439773.html (accessed 17.2.2014).

Van der Waal, C. S. (2008), Essentialism in a South African discussion of language and culture, in: A. Hadland et al. (eds.), *Power, Politics and Identity in South African Media*, Cape Town: HSRC Press, pp. 52–72.

Váňa T. (2012), Language power potential, in: *The Annual of Language & Politics and Politics of Identity,* Vol. 5.

Vorster, J. and L. Proctor (1976), Black attitudes to 'white' languages in South Africa: A pilot study, in: *The Journal of Psychology,* Vol. 92, No. 1, pp. 103–108.

Webb, V. (2002), *Language in South Africa. The Role of Language in National Transformation, Reconstruction & Development*, Amsterdam: John Benjamins.

Webb, V. and M. Kriel (2000), Afrikaans and Afrikaner nationalism, in: *International Journal of the Sociology of Language,* Vol. 144, pp. 19–50.

Woolard, K. A. (2010). Language ideologies: Issues and approaches, in: *Pragmatics*, Vol. 2, No. 3, pp. 235–249.

Woolard, K. A. and B. B. Schieffelin (1994), Language Ideology, in: *Annual Review of Anthropology,* Vol. 23, pp. 55– 82.

Facing the past: Truth, accountability and victims' compensation in South Africa and the Czech Republic

Kateřina Werkman

Introduction

Governments and populations in countries that have overcome oppressive authoritarian or totalitarian rule direct their efforts and hopes towards a better future. Yet, the past is not over with the demise of the previous regime and an election of a new democratic government. Its legacy is evident in many areas, from the institutions of the state and the socio-economic order to people's minds and hearts. Dealing with the past is a long-term and complex process in which such legacy ought to be addressed at all these different but inter-connected levels.

The efforts at dealing with the crimes committed under the former regimes belong to the most challenging. In recent decades, they came to be labelled as transitional justice, commonly defined as a "set of practices, mechanisms, and concerns that are aimed at confronting and dealing with the legacies of past violations of human rights and humanitarian law" (Roht-Arriaza 2009: vii). But there is nothing like a prescribed or even widely accepted set of goals, policies or tools that a country ought to pursue in order to address the legacy of authoritarian rule. In the diverse literature on the topic, authors identify at least three broad sets of processes at the core of transitional justice: first, the justice process to assign responsibility for the crimes committed and decide on the punishment for the perpetrators of gross human rights violations; second, the truth-seeking process through which society strives to establish the truth about what happened and who did what to whom; and third, the reparation process designed to acknowledge and redress victims' suffering (Sandoval 2010; cf. Crocker 1998, 2003; Minow 1998; Bloomfield et al. 2003). There is, however, little agreement on the precise meaning of the leading concepts such as 'justice' and 'truth' and how they relate to one another – are they mutually supportive or are they competing objectives? Further, no consensus exists about what these processes entail and what instruments or mechanisms are best equipped to achieve them.

In recent years, a kind of 'toolbox' has grown out of transitional justice practice across diverse countries worldwide. It consists of some form of criminal prosecutions by either national or international courts, truth (and reconciliation) commissions, reparations or compensations to victims, some form of lustrations or vetting programmes, amnesty procedures, formal apologies or establishing monuments or remembrance days. While all countries in transition are expected to adopt one or more of transitional justice mechanisms as this is seen as "a key to the emergence of a new, more just as well as peaceful social order" (Roht-Arriaza 2009: vii), the actual choice of the institutions considered as best suited for their 'own' transition lies with the government and ideally also with the wider population of the particular country.

Indeed, it is one of the most prominent features of the transitional justice processes that they are highly dependent on the local context. They are also inherently political processes in that they reflect the new regime's present need to legitimise itself and 'protect' the gains of transition just as much as the concerns about addressing the legacy of the past. Comparing the processes across different countries is therefore a tricky and challenging endeavour. In academic writing on the subject, we find comparative studies that focus either on a specific tool across different contexts or on countries with significantly similar transitional processes (cf. Hayner 2011; Nedelsky 2003; Stan 2008). In order to overcome the lack of available frameworks for comparing countries like South Africa and the Czech Republic where historical, socio-political, institutional and cultural factors account for the many differences in their approach towards reckoning with the past, this chapter attempts to assess their efforts against three of the broad aims of transitional justice – truth-telling and truth-finding, accountability and punishment, and victims' compensation. How were these key issues conceptualised and addressed in these countries? What were the main controversies? Can we identify any common patterns?

Several limitations must be acknowledged. Firstly, this chapter focuses only on the top-down processes, more specifically on the official instruments and legislation adopted by the new governments for the purpose of addressing gross human rights violations in the past. It leaves out other policies designed to address the legacy of the past as well as activities at other than state level. Secondly, such a framework does not aspire to be exhaustive by any measure. There are other important aims of transitional justice next to truth, accountability and reparations that are beyond the scope of the present analysis. Indeed, the official mechanisms under study set out to achieve other goals too. One of the most important pursuits of the South African Truth and Reconciliation Commission was reconciliation. The lustration laws in the Czech Republic fulfilled a national security and public safety function as well as a role in institutional reform. This chapter does not aim at evaluating these mechanisms in the full scope of their purposes and mandates but only through their contribution to the key transitional justice processes as defined above.

In the first part, we will briefly introduce the main goals of transitional justice. Such introduction cannot do justice to all the debates both among practitioners and academics that characterise the transitional justice field. The aim here is to identify the key challenges within each of these goals in order to prepare a framework for the analysis of the responses in South Africa and the Czech Republic. The second part describes the legislation and institutions designed in both countries to deal with the legacy of the past, while the third part analyses them against the broad goals of transitional justice. The chapter concludes with a brief comparative evaluation.

Goals for dealing with the past

Truth

Establishing the truth about what happened in the past has often been proposed as one of the preconditions to successful transition in post-authoritarian and post-totalitarian countries as well as to achieving sustainable peace in post-conflict settings. Rotberg and Thompson (2000: 3) suggest that:

> *if societies are to prevent recurrences of past atrocities and to cleanse themselves of the corrosive enduring effects of massive injuries to individuals and whole groups, societies must understand – at the deepest possible level – what occurred and why. In order to come fully to terms with their brutal pasts, they must uncover, in precise detail, who did what to whom, and why, and under whose orders.*

But truth is not easily defined: what kind of truth are we looking for? Is it to be understood only as the "accumulation of forensically-proven facts" or does it require "a more complex and multi-faceted narrative" (Sarkin 2008: 14)? In any case, can one 'truth' about the past be established at all? As Clark (2008: 203) points out with regard to the South and Central American truth commissions, attempts to construct an 'official version' of truth are problematic as "individuals' and groups' recollections of the past often clash, and may be expressed for a variety of well-intentioned or cynically instrumental reasons". In this sense, truth-seeking is an inherently political process. Mamdani (2000a: 178) therefore urges for an acknowledgement of 'truth' in the plural, rather than in the singular. But this is not the same as saying that all interpretations of the past are to be accepted – truth-finding processes also aim at reducing the number of lies that can be publically told unchallenged (Ignatieff 1996: 113).

Justice, accountability and punishment

Ascribing responsibility to individuals and groups for the crimes and human rights violations committed in the past and meting out adequate sanctions has been one of the most difficult tasks facing post-authoritarian as well as post-conflict societies.

One set of dilemmas concerns responsibility: who should be held accountable? Crocker (2003: 48) asks: "How should we understand the degrees and kinds of responsibility with respect to the authorisation, planning, 'middle management', execution, provision of material support for, and concealment of, atrocities"? Those who were directly involved in the commission of crimes are usually easier to hold accountable than those who gave orders and formulated the policies that made violence a permissible or even a recommended way of political struggles (Nerlich 2008: 96).

Further, for which crimes should people be held accountable? "Most regimes in transition attempt to normalize the succession by integrating their response within the existing legal system" (Teitel 2000: 39 cited in Nerlich 2008: 93). But what about cases where the system was 'intrinsically' unjust, even labelled a crime against humanity like the apartheid system, at what cost can its laws be used for reckoning with the past wrongs? (Nerlich 2008: 93).

Yet another one involves the question of what types of sanctions are adequate or appropriate for what type of crimes? Justice in transitional contexts is most commonly understood in terms of criminal prosecution of the perpetrators of violence. While a strong 'prosecution preference' is indeed presently discernible, there is however a growing body of empirical studies from diverse countries that problematize the assumption that punishment is always the preferred option among the population (Weinstein et al. 2010; Longman et al. 2004; Lambourne 2009). Clark (2008) distinguishes three broad models of justice as responses to crime – retributive, deterrent and restorative. The key difference between these three models lies in what they identify as the purpose of punishing the perpetrators and, related to this, what form it should take. In the retributive and deterrent justice models, punishment of the perpetrator is understood as the central aim. In the restorative justice model, punishment is not the primary aim. The emphasis here is on restoring relationships – between perpetrators, victims and the broader community.

Compensation to victims

It is generally accepted that during the process of dealing with the past, society ought to fulfil the duty to "repair the past" – but there are a number of theoretical and practical problems (du Bois 2008: 117). What compensations should be considered? Monetary reparations are sometimes believed to be the most obvious need of victims, yet putting a value on "losses from torture and murder strains the moral imagination" (Minow 1998: 104). Other options such as restitutions of property taken from the rightful owner, apologies or symbolic memorials carry dilemmas of their own. It is questionable whether providing a platform for victims to tell their stories, have them publically acknowledged and receive sympathy for their suffering constitute a form of compensation (Crocker 2003: 47). And furthermore, as Minow (1998: 117) stresses, "nothing should imply that ... [compensations] seal the wounds, make victims whole, or clean the slate".

If means of compensation are a contested issue, so is the conceptualisation of victimhood. Who is to be considered a victim? Making a clear distinction between victims and perpetrators may not always be so simple. Is victimhood the result of acts of criminal nature, such as torture, murder or kidnapping, or should those be included whose civil, political or even economic rights have been violated?

Dealing with the past: national instruments

South Africa

South Africa's dealing with the past was guided by restorative justice philosophy and truth-seeking and reconciliation were prioritised over criminal justice. Under the heading National Unity and Reconciliation, the Interim Constitution of 1993 anchored the negotiated compromise of an amnesty "in respect of acts, omissions and offences associated with political objectives and committed in the course of conflicts of the past" as a means to advancing reconciliation between the people of South Africa and the reconstruction of society (Act No. 200 of 1993).

In July 1995, the South African Parliament enacted the Promotion of National Unity and Reconciliation Act which provided for the establishment of the Truth and Reconciliation Commission (TRC) (Act No. 34 of 1995). It was mandated to

> *a) establish "as complete a picture as possible of the causes, nature and extent of the gross violations of human rights" committed during the period between March 1, 1960 and May 10, 1994; (b) facilitate "the granting of amnesty to persons who make full disclosure of all the relevant facts relating to acts associated with a political objective"; (c) establish and make known "the fate or whereabouts of victims" and restore "the human and civil dignity of such victims by granting them an opportunity to relate*

*their own accounts of the violations of which they are the victims,
and by recommending reparation measures in respect of them";
and d) compile "a report providing as comprehensive an account
as possible of the activities and findings of the Commission [...]
which contains recommendations of measures to prevent the
future violations of human rights" (ibid.).*

The South African TRC had undoubtedly the most elaborate and comprehensive structure and mandate of all the truth commissions to date. Its
work was split between three committees – the Committee on Human Rights
Violations investigated gross violations of human rights mainly by collecting
statements from the victims and witnesses; the Committee on Amnesty
considered and decided about individual amnesty applications; and the
Committee on Reparation and Rehabilitation submitted recommendation on
the reparations of damage to apartheid victims (ibid.).

One of the TRC's unique and unprecedented powers was certainly the
amnesty procedure. Amnesty could be granted for acts, omissions and
offences "associated with a political objective committed in the course of the
past" for which the "applicant has made a full disclosure of all relevant facts"
(ibid.). Of more than 7,112 applications received, the Commission granted
849 amnesties. It also warned against a future "granting of general amnesty
in whatever guise" and recommended further prosecutions "where amnesty
has not been sought or has been denied, prosecution should be considered
where evidence exists that an individual has committed a gross human rights
violation" (TRC Report, Vol. 5: 309).

The Commission made findings on more than 40,000 alleged gross
violations of human rights contained in around 20,300 statements taken from
victims and survivors of these violations. It published a comprehensive, five-
volume *Truth and Reconciliation Commission of South Africa Report* in 1998.
Upon completion of the amnesty process, an additional volume was added in
2003.

Czech Republic

In the Czech Republic, a number of legal instruments were adopted since
1990 to deal with the diverse legacies of communist rule.[1] Unlike in South

---

[1] In the following overview, we only discuss legislation that is most relevant to the ensuing
discussion: the Act on Judicial Rehabilitation, the Lustration Act, the Act on the Unlawfulness
of the Communist Regime and about the Resistance against it, the Act on the Disclosure of
Files Created in the Course of Activities of the Former Security Service and the setting up of
the Office for the Documentation and Investigation of Communist Crimes and the Institute for
the Study of Totalitarian Regimes and the Security Services Archive.

Africa, where the leading role was entrusted to an independent body, the TRC, in the Czech Republic the Parliament played a central role in reckoning with the past.

As early as April 1990, the Federal Parliament adopted the Act on Judicial Rehabilitation (No. 119/1990 Coll.) which repealed all political verdicts pronounced during the Communist era from February 25, 1948 to January 1, 1990 and thus brought full rehabilitation of those unjustly prosecuted and imprisoned. By the end of 1993, 96% of victims had been rehabilitated and 3 billion CZK paid in compensations (Rupnik 2002).

The Lustration Act (No. 451/1991 Coll.) "determining some further prerequisites for holding certain offices in state bodies and corporations of the Czech and Slovak Federative Republic, Czech Republic and Slovak Republic" was ratified in October 1991. It provides a list of senior posts in the public administration and offices of the state, the army, the police and security information service, the judiciary and the prosecutions office, academic institutions, state media and press agencies, state corporations and banks from which people who held certain positions or performed certain activities under the communist regime would be disqualified. These include members of the State Security (StB) and a range of its collaborators, the top echelons of the Communist Party apparatus with the exceptions of those who held it in the period of the so-called Prague Spring (1.1.1968 and 1.5.1969), the political management of the National Security Corps, members of the People's Militias, members of the purge (employment review) committees of 1948 and 1968, and students, scholars or course participants at certain Soviet propaganda and political-security universities. The procedure under the lustration law was based "on the principle of person-by-person specific vetting" (Priban 2007: 311) – any person aspiring to or holding one of the listed posts had to present a negative lustration certificate issued by the Ministry of Interior. The law also provided for the setting up of an Independent Commission charged with reviewing appeals against positive lustration certificates. The major issue that the Commission had to deal with concerned the activities of individual citizens linked to the StB, specifically whether those accused of collaborating with the StB actually had been conscious collaborators or innocent victims of the secret police. Eventually, the Constitutional Court annulled a whole category of persons requiring lustration, namely the "conscious collaborators of StB" (Pl. ÚS 1/92).[2] The

---

[2]The abrogated sections 1(c) and 2 of §2 listed "conscious collaborators of the StB" understood as those listed in the StB files as confidants and candidates for confidential collaboration who was aware of meeting an StB member and giving him confidential information or fulfilling tasks given by him.

law was initially valid for five years but was extended twice – and remains in force to this day.[3] The main rationale for the adoption of the lustration law was to protect the new democracy by preventing the 'old structures' from holding on to or regaining power within key public administration institutions thereby also strengthening its legitimacy and fostering public trust in its institutions.[4] Thus, it was predominantly a forward-looking administrative measure rather than a means of coming to terms with the past. However, "the symbolic power of this practical purpose-oriented legislation has always been very strong and has become a cornerstone of all debates about decommunisation and dealing with past injustices" (Priban 2007: 323).

In July 1993 the Czech Parliament voted in the Act on the Unlawfulness of the Communist Regime and about the Resistance against it (Act No. 198/1993 Coll.) The Act declares the communist regime from February 25, 1948 to November 17, 1989 as well as the Communist Party "criminal, illegitimate and despicable". Popular resistance against the regime is considered "legitimate, morally justified and worthy of respect". Importantly, the period of communist rule was removed from the statute of limitation on crimes previously not prosecuted for political reasons.

An Office for the Documentation and Investigation of Communist Crimes was created in 1995[5] to perform a dual role of investigating and prosecuting cases of crimes committed under the communist regime, and of documenting, collecting and evaluating materials, information and documents concerning crimes of the communist regime and its repressive forces and disseminating this knowledge among the general public (see ÚDV Homepage).[6]

In 1996, the Act on the Disclosure of Files Created in the Course of Activities of the Former Security Service granted access to the files to persons who wanted to read their own file. It was amended in 2002 (107/2002 Coll.) to allow any adult Czech citizen access to the files as well as to make public the lists of StB agents and collaborators.[7]

The most recent additions to the set of legal instruments for confronting the past have been in 2007 the Act establishing the Institute for the Study of

---

[3]The lustration laws were extended in 1995 and then in 2000 indefinitely.

[4]Importantly, it did not apply to any positions contested in the general elections or to the private economy sector. As Priban (2007: 314) observes, the law "thus created a situation in which members of Parliament and local councils could have a secret police record while, for instance, heads of different university departments would be subjected to the lustration procedure".

[5]It was established by merging two separate offices working under the Interior and Justice Ministries respectively.

[6]http://www.policie.cz/clanek/urad-dokumentace-a-vysetrovani-zlocinu-komunismu-679905. aspx

[7]Some limitations apply to make sure the constitutional rights of personal integrity and privacy of other individuals are protected.

Totalitarian Regimes and the Security Services Archive (Act No. 181/2007 Coll.) and the 2011 Act on the Participants in Anti-communist Opposition and Resistance, which provided for their official acknowledgment, rehabilitation and financial compensation.

Facing the past: approaches and dilemmas

Truth

South Africa

The centrality of truth-finding and truth-telling in South Africa is clearly stated in the name and mandate of its main transitional justice institution. Truth was considered to be a vital component on the 'road to reconciliation', expected to restore the dignity of the victims, give the offenders an opportunity to face their own deeds and help all South Africans to understand and overcome the divided past.

The TRC Report distinguishes between four forms of 'truth': 1. factual or forensic truth that brings the information about "whose moral and legal rights were violated, by whom, how, when and where" (Crocker 2003: 44); 2. personal and narrative truth consisting of the stories of individual experiences; 3. social or dialogue truth that emerges from interaction and discussion; and 4. healing and restorative truth which "places facts and their meaning within the context of human relationships" (TRC Report Vol.1 1998: 110–114). What is novel about the TRC is that it recognised these different forms of truth and shifted the focus from the predominantly fact-finding goals of similar bodies that had existed elsewhere in the world.

Concerning factual/forensic truth, it is clear that the TRC process gathered a great volume of information and generated detailed accounts of the 'who', 'what', 'when', 'where' and 'how' questions regarding the gross human rights violations. It had a relatively unobstructed access to information given the full government backing for its work, but it faced many obstructions in gathering evidence from security forces and the army where progress was limited. The victim and witness statements as well as amnesty-for-full-disclosure formula also contributed to uncovering a considerable amount of historical information (Verbuyst 2013: 9). Nonetheless, a significant amount of truth about gross human right violations – those within as well as outside the mandate of the TRC – remained undiscovered. As Verwoerd (2003: 255) admits: "[…] the TRC has indeed only scratched the surface of the whole truth about past human rights violations in South Africa".

Arguably the most unique contribution of the TRC lies in providing a platform both for the individual narrative truth and for practicing the social truth through dialogue and interaction. Gibson (2006: 414) contends that by this it managed to get people "to rethink their views about the struggle over apartheid by creating cognitive dissonance and by mitigating cognitive dogmatism, resulting in changes in the way South Africans feel about each other".

The function of truth as a 'medicine' for healing the nation was the most problematic notion. The idea was captured on one of the banners displayed at the public hearings of the Commission in a slogan 'Healing Our Past'. By linking individual confessions and forgiveness on the one hand and the rhetoric of 'healing the nation' on the other, however, the TRC helped to create the illusion that the national 'body' can be cured with the same 'medicine' as the individual, this medicine being the truth about the past. "The identity of the body in question – whether that of the individual giving testimony before the TRC or of the suffering South African nation – is blurred, suggesting that the healing efficacy of truth-telling operates simultaneously on personal and national levels that are homologous" (Shaw 2007: 190–191). Such continued conflation of individual and national levels was criticised for both placing an unfair burden upon the victims as well as unrealistic expectations from the whole TRC process.

Truth-seeking processes are inevitably linked to history writing. The TRC Report brings the diverse forms of truth together, putting it forth as a "collective memory of the past" (Gibson 2006). While the TRC explicitly states that "it is not the Commission's task to write the history of this country" (TRC Report Vol. 5 1998: 257), it nonetheless engages in constructing a certain historical narrative – one that ought to serve its other key objective, reconciliation. Such "arduous task of writing an account of the past acceptable for all groups previously in conflict in the same society" (Verbuyst 2013: 7) is not without problems, however. The TRC Report was by no means universally accepted: prominent ANC representatives bemoaned what they saw as the TRC's equal treatment of apartheid and liberation movements' crimes, thereby obscuring the moral truth of the past (Verwoerd 2003: 258). Many among white South Africans believed that the TRC was biased in favour of the ANC. Others criticised its narrow focus on gross human rights violations, which gave a prominent place in the historical narrative to the perpetrators and their direct victims, usually political activists, leaving out the everyday discrimination, such as forced removals, sidelined in the narrative. Mamdani (2000b: 61) called it 'a diminished truth': "In its eagerness to reinforce new order […] the TRC created a diminished truth that wrote the vast majority of apartheid's victims out of its version of history".

Czech Republic

None of the instruments adopted in the Czech Republic was explicitly concerned with truth-finding, even less so with truth-telling. This does not mean, however, that there was no demand to 'look into' the past. Indeed, the opening of the secret police files and the publishing of the list of its agents and collaborators was a widely debated issue among the new political representation since the early days of transition. 'Truth revelation' was among the arguments for lustration procedures brought forward in the debate preceding the adoption of the Lustration Law in the Czechoslovak Federal Assembly (David 2003: 392).

From the start, truth was understood in rather narrow terms – as forensic/factual truth, waiting to be discovered in the secret police archives. These were, however, a problematic source of information. For one, the reliability of the "plundered, doctored, manipulated" files of the former secret police was debatable (Rupnik 2002). There were also serious questions about the completeness of the files. The StB materials documented in much detail the activities of the low-level informers but the information on the activities of top-level officers of the security apparatus were much patchier (cf. Rupnik 2002). In spite of these reservations, the broad access to archival records presents an invaluable source of detailed factual information, which, if systematically considered in its broader historical context, can play an important role in the process of reckoning with the past.

Initially, it was chiefly through the documentation role of UDV that the truth from the archives was to be dug up and disseminated. It documented hundreds of injustices and crimes committed by the communist state apparatus and by those who served it, and certainly contributed to improving the knowledge of the workings of the totalitarian state machinery. Later, also individual citizens were given the opportunity to search for the truth in the StB archives when they were opened to the public.

The factual truth of the archives was to be complemented with an 'official' framework for interpreting the past, formulated in a number of legislative acts, such as the Act on the Unlawfulness of the Communist Regime and about the Resistance against it. The enactment of the Institution for the Study of Totalitarian Regimes and the Security Services Archive in 2007 can be seen as a culmination of the state effort to "explore and remember the consequences of the activities of criminal organisations based on Communist and Nazi ideology that between 1938–1945 and 1948–1989 promoted the suppression of human rights and rejected the principles of a democratic state" (Act 181/2007 Coll.). For its proponents, it has both a symbolic purpose as a moral and political discrediting of the communist regime and its active supporters and as an expression of a duty the state has towards its victims and towards preserving the memory of the nation.

These attempts to legislate an official version of the past have raised criticism on a number of points. Kopeček (2013: 4) calls it "usable totalitarianism", a narrative that presents the period of history between 1948 and 1989 as a continuous stretch of totalitarian rule, which is interpreted as 'an aberration' of an otherwise democratic character of the Czech nation. Here, the narrative fulfils the nation-building purpose by "emphasis[ing] the democratic credentials of the new regime and foster[ing] a sense of belonging among Czech citizens" (ibid.). The other feature of this narrative is the conceptualisation of the past through the dichotomy between the oppressors/victimisers and the oppressed/victims, which is problematic given the nature of the regime, so eloquently captured in Vaclav Havel's first address to the Czechoslovak citizens in 1990:

> *When I talk about the contaminated moral atmosphere, [...] I am talking about all of us. We had all become used to the totalitarian system and accepted it as an unchangeable fact and thus helped to perpetuate it. In other words, we are all – though naturally to differing extents – responsible for the operation of the totalitarian machinery. None of us is just its victim. We are all also its co-creators* (Havel 1990).

Sadurski (2003: 13) in his critical account of the Czech approach to dealing with the past expresses concerns about having an authoritative state body such as a Parliament declare an official truth about the past through law:

> *This is a generalised characterisation – accurate, in my view – of the nature of the Communist period, and an interpretation given to that era in the recent Czechoslovak history. As such, it is not the basis for a consensus-seeking establishment of the facts about the past but rather a dissensus-provoking state orthodoxy about the ideological lenses through which the past should be viewed.*

Because it comes from the state's legislative it bears a risk of "leaving those who disagree beyond the pale of a political community" (ibid. 12).

A broader public deliberation on the issue of historical legacy of communism, on how to interpret it and deal with it where space would be provided for the diversity of experiences would have probably benefited the truth-finding process. Instead, the state entirely "repudiates personal testimony as a necessary precondition in the pursuit of 'truth' about the past. [...] the apparatus of the state is fully credited with the capability of unveiling the said 'truth'" (Hladik 2009: 128).

Accountability and punishment

South Africa

The position of the TRC on the issue of accountability reflected its conciliatory philosophy. It strived to apportion the blame and responsibility to all sides in the struggle – the state, its security apparatus and other groups and institutions affiliated to the apartheid government, white right-wing factions, liberation movements engaged both in armed struggle and non-violent resistance and non-state paramilitary formations (TRC Report Vol. 5 1998: 209–210). In spite of the TRC's acknowledgement that "preponderance of responsibility rests with the state and its allies" (ibid.), the even-handedness became the target of much criticism. This mainly focused on the moral problem of presenting the struggle as a war between two equal parties, disregarding the power disparity and character of the apartheid state violence.

Nonetheless, du Bois-Pedain (2008: 70) points out that the TRC accountability findings managed to "pick up the complexity of the 'social production of harms' by manifold agents" through setting the responsibility of the direct perpetrators of violence "in the context of responsibilities of those who controlled their actions through orders or made them possible in other ways". It is evidence of the TRC's effort to steer away from solely criminal accountability towards political and moral responsibility, in order to appeal "to those concerned to accept [such] responsibility and to search for a future course of action that adequately and meaningfully responds to it" (ibid. 80). While this moral appeal largely fell on deaf ears, making some authors doubt its value (cf. Christodoulidis and Veitch 2008), it still serves as a ground for the contestation and exposure of denials of political responsibility (du Bois-Pedain 2008: 85).

The key component of the TRC's approach to accountability was the amnesty process – and the TRC's Amnesty Committee concerned itself with criminal responsibility. Accepting the no crime without law principle, the apartheid system itself did not fall within the scope of the amnesty process as it was legal in terms of South African law (Nerlich 2008: 92). By contrast, some acts of non-violent opposition to apartheid required an amnesty application in order for the offender to be cleared (ibid.).

The TRC's approach to accountability through amnesty has been labelled as a form of restorative justice. Its proponents like Desmond Tutu argued that granting amnesty is not the same as letting the perpetrators to "get off scot-free: they have to confess publicly in the full glare of television lights that they did those ghastly things. And that's pretty tough" (Reid and Hoffman 2000). The public humiliation of the perpetrators was to serve as a form of compensation for the loss of opportunity of criminal prosecution, as a price they had to pay before they could be reintegrated back into the community:

> *By using confessions to perform public shaming rituals, then, the Amnesty Committee's hearings coupled the absolution granted to the perpetrators with the purgation of historical affect for the audience. In more ways than one, the dilemmas of transitional justice were mastered, at least in part, through spectacular effects*
> (Liatsos 2006: 119).

The restorative justice model thus emphasises a form of rehabilitation for both the victim and the offender without, in principle, giving up on accountability altogether.

The amnesty process was not the only approach to criminal accountability. Even before the establishment of the TRC, a number of investigations and prosecutions had focused on the Security Branch of the South African Police (SB) and the secret operations of the South African Defence Force (SADF). The most prominent successful case is the 1996 conviction of Eugene de Kock, a commander in charge of the Vlakplaas based hit squad.[8] On the contrary, all efforts to prosecute crimes committed during the SADF secret operations led to acquittals, which undermined the "assumption that perpetrators would only accept the amnesty carrot if they feared the stick of criminal justice" (Nerlich 2008: 106).

Criminal prosecutions were to follow the amnesty process that generated a list of offenders who failed to apply or persuade the Commission of political motive. In spite of this, the list of post-TRC prosecutions is short. This remains a sensitive issue:

> *The TRC touched a nerve in the South African model of dealing with the past: the integrity of the process depends on the prosecution of those who defied it or were denied amnesty. Failure to do so not only contradicts assurances given and infringes the rights of victims to have perpetrators held accountable, but also bestows an undeserved benefit on those not charged with their crimes* (Nerlich 2008: 109).

---

[8]Prosecution focused on De Kock's non-political crimes – the main aim of the trial was getting off the streets someone who threatened the political stability of the country and not to shed light on the crimes of the apartheid regime (see Nerlich 2008: 99).

Czech Republic

The question of responsibility and accountability was dealt with in different ways in the diverse legislative measures addressing the communist past. On a symbolic level, responsibility for the crimes of communism was explicitly assigned by the 1993 Act on the Unlawfulness of the Communist Regime to all who participated in the communist regime structures. It stated in its Preamble:

> *The Communist Party of Czechoslovakia, its leadership and members are responsible for the system of government in this country in the years 1948–1989, and particularly for the systematic destruction of the traditional values of European civilisation, for the conscious violations of human rights and freedoms, for the moral and economic degradation accompanied by judicial crimes and terror against advocates of different opinions, the replacement of a prospering market economy with command management, the destruction of the traditional principles of ownership, the abuse of training, education, science and culture for political and ideological purposes, and the careless destruction of nature* (Act No. 198/1993).

This was a radically comprehensive formulation of responsibility – political and moral. Paradoxically, the lustration laws both narrowed and extended such broad dealing of political and moral responsibility. As Mayer (2009: 66) observed, the law "inconspicuously shifted the target of stigmatisation from 'communists' to 'agents' and 'collaborators'" (cf. Suk 2010: 35). The growing obsession with revealing the identities of individuals named 'on the lists' of the StB obscured the many other members of the communist state machinery. At the same time, the failure to give attention to historical or individual circumstances led to apportioning a part of the responsibility on the shoulders of those previously victimised by the StB and the communist regime. The blanket nature of the lustration law also precluded a much needed discussion of degrees of responsibility.

Concerning criminal responsibility, some had hoped (and others feared) that the 1993 Act on the Unlawfulness of the Communist Regime opened up a way for investigation and prosecution of communist crimes as it also extended the statute of limitation for crimes previously not prosecuted for political reasons under the communist regime. However, a review by the Constitutional Court of the Czech Republic confirmed its moralising function and declaratory nature and denied any practical enforceability (US 14/1994, cf. Priban 2007; Rupnik 2002). In fact, criminal prosecutions were rare. The

UDV's investigations led to a number of prosecutions but there were many obstacles; only a few ended in courts and even fewer resulted in sentencing those accused.[9]

Lustrations were in the end the closest measure the Czech Republic adopted in terms of retribution, although they are a non-judicial law procedure and not a criminal justice measure. Characteristic of the Czech response is thus a deep contradiction between "the abstract moral imperative of reckoning" contained in the radical verbal condemnation of communism and the limited practical outcomes in terms of meting out punishment (Suk 2010).

Compensation to victims

South Africa

Providing a public platform for victims to come forth and tell their stories as well as making recommendations on compensation were among the key goals of the TRC. The TRC restorative approach is considered victim-oriented and its proponents often argued that the opportunity to have their stories acknowledged made it possible for the victims to have at least part of their dignity restored (Gibson 2006: 425).

According to the TRC Act, victims are defined as those who

> *suffered harm in the form of physical or mental injury, emotional suffering, pecuniary loss or substantial impairment of human rights as the result of a gross violation of human rights or [...] an act associated with a political objective for which amnesty has been granted* (Act No. 34 of 1995).

Du Bois (2008) notes two significant characteristics of such a definition: firstly, victimhood is conceived as caused by gross human right violation based on a list of such violations also provided by the Act. It means that space is opened for reparation claims also for those who suffered from acts not considered crimes under the apartheid law. "In treating the norms of that legal order as irrelevant to reparations, this brings to the fore the TRC's role in asserting the primacy of morality over law and marks out the moral legitimacy of these victims' claims" (ibid. 120). Secondly, it provides for the compensation of those whose right to sue perpetrators for damages in a civil lawsuit is foreclosed by granting amnesty.

---

[9]For an illustrative case on the obstacles of post-communist justice cf. Kauza Uherske Hradiste, dir. Vlachová, Kristina, 57 min., 2006, which follows several years of the failed efforts to convict three StB investigators, Alois Grebeníček, Vladimír Zavadilík and Ludvík Hlavačka, charged with torture of political prisoners. Online: http://www.ceskatelevize.cz/ivysilani/10096386929-kauza-uherske-hradiste/

The proposed compensation measures included individual reparation grants, community rehabilitation programmes, symbolic reparations and institutional reform (TRC Report Vol.5 1998: 175–176). The individual reparations eventually sparked one of the biggest controversies. The Report contained a list of some 22,000 victims eligible for reparations based on either successfully presenting their case of gross human rights violation to the TRC or being affected by an amnesty decision. These victims were eligible for an allowance of R 17-23,000/year over a six years period. First, the closed-list approach that restricted eligibility to individual reparations raised protests (du Bois 2008: 122). A number of victims' groups initiated lists of those who suffered a gross human rights violation but for different reasons did not give statement to the TRC. Second, President Thabo Mbeki's decision in 2003 to reduce the recommended compensations to one off payment of R 30,000 sparked outrage as it was perceived to come short of "morally adequate response" (du Bois 2008: 126).

Both these issues actually relate to a larger problem of the definition of victimhood with which the TRC was working. Mamdani's (2002: 34) sharp criticism reproaches the TRC for individualising the victims, whereby the systematic nature in which the apartheid regime targeted whole communities "for racial and ethnic cleansing and policing" is obliterated. Similarly, it has been argued that given the socio-economic legacy of apartheid, "the TRC's decision not to bother itself with these victims was its biggest flaw" (Verbuyst 2013: 14). According to du Bois (2008: 124), the TRC Act's narrow definition of victim was problematic:

> Again and again cast doubt on the possibility of conceptualising a distinct category of victims of gross human rights violations, pointing not only to the intersection between categories of victims and perpetrators, but also to overlaps between various categories of victims as well as of different yet mutually reinforcing causes of victimhood.

The government's decision to cut the individual grants should be interpreted in this light (ibid. 125). It nonetheless can be seen as a serious setback to the principles underlying the TRC's restorative philosophy based on the premise that distributive justice (compensation) might help victims to accept injustices of forfeiting the right to seek retributive justice (Gibson 2006).

Czech Republic

The Czech Republic adopted the key legal instruments such as the Act on Judicial Rehabilitation shortly after the transition. Its interpretation of victim

– the 'political prisoner' – was rather broad and provided for judicial rehabilitation of all those who were imprisoned on political charges since 1948. Mayer (2009: 62) believes it was a preferred approach as it allowed mending historical injustices "without having to ask the delicate question of who is to blame for them". The victims of communist justice were granted financial compensation for loss of income, health damage and cost of criminal proceedings (Act No.119/1990 Coll.) By the end of 1993, the state paid about 3 billion CZK in compensation and 96% of the victims had been rehabilitated (Rupnik 2002: fn.6).

The question of how 'victimhood' should be conceived of with regard to the communist past resurfaced several times in the controversial debates following the adoption of the lustration legislation as well as the opening of the StB archives to the public. According to critics, the acceptance of the former secret police files at their face value meant that no distinction was made between the oppressors and their victims who were both subjected to the same repercussions following from the lustration process. On these grounds, Priban (2007: 332) called the law "morally repulsive". It has been countered that the law gives the opportunity for appeal and civil lawsuit to review the lustration decision. While this is true, the harm done and the public shaming of those previously targeted and victimised by the StB – such as members of opposition groups and religious circles – was often not undone even if the accusations were eventually cleared and so the moral dilemma persisted (ibid.; cf. also Mayer 2009).

Conclusion

Countries undergoing transitions face many dilemmas with regard to dealing with the legacy of gross human rights violations by the former regime. While each country has to identify its own priorities and approaches that reflect its political, social, cultural and economic histories, it is possible to identify certain general goals that such transitional justice processes ought to address in one way or another. This chapter focused on three of these – truth, accountability and reparation processes as they were framed and performed in South Africa and the Czech Republic.

Uncovering the truth about the past was an important goal in both countries, although the approaches differed significantly. The Czech narrow focus on forensic truth, in which a gradual opening and accessibility of the secret police archives was seen as a central concern, contrasts with the multifaceted understanding of truth promoted by the TRC. Under the TRC process, dialogical truth-telling at public hearings was just as important as truth-finding (which turned out to be a more controversial exercise). As Commissioner Pumla Gobodo-Madikizela put it: "If the public hearings were brutal, seemed heartless or bizarre, they forced the South African public to think about the past, to confront the pain, deep suffering, and sheer survival in the midst of it all" (Doxtader 2001: 250). The Czech predominantly legalistic approach to the past, in which the Parliament took it upon itself to legislate the moral condemnation of the past and emphasised a single mode of historical reflection through uncovering the archives of repressive organs, seems to have inhibited rather than fostered public discussion about the totalitarian past, its political impact, the causes and nature of the 'civic silent obedience' during the normalisation years, or the degrees of responsibility (cf. Mayer 2009; Priban 2007; Vilímek 2010).

Both countries also adopted novel mechanisms for addressing accountability – both the South African amnesty for a full disclosure of truth about politically motivated crimes and the Czech comprehensive lustration process were, in their peculiar ways, radical solutions to dealing with the perpetrators. But their guiding philosophies and their effects were almost the opposite. In South Africa, the main rationale was the inclusion of wrongdoers into the society in the spirit of restorative justice. The net cast was rather narrow as it focused only on perpetrators of gross human rights violations. The resulting weakness was the omission to deal with both the political 'masterminds' of the apartheid system and its beneficiaries, as well as the criminal nature of the regime itself. In the Czech Republic, the main idea was the exclusion of as many as possible of those who actively supported the former regime from participating in the key institutions of the new one, embodying a specific form of retribution. In this case, the net was thrown rather widely in an attempt to reach those who "without being guilty, cannot be called innocent" (Nanda 1998: 391). The unfortunate consequence was a wild 'agentomania' and the public stigmatisation of some of the victims of the StB. In both countries, criminal prosecutions of perpetrators remained rare due to a combination of political and legal reasons.

Rehabilitation of victims of historical injustices was a rather uncontroversial process in the Czech Republic, although the perceived mild attitude to punishing communist crimes and the lack of public acknowledgement of their contribution of the nation's freedom left some of the resistance groups embittered (cf. Mayer 2009; Kopeček 2013). That was, however, to some extent changed with the re-interpretation of 'resistance' through the 2011 Act that officially acknowledged the concept of third (anti-communist) resistance. Given the nature of the apartheid system and the scope of historical injustices in South Africa, it is no wonder that victim rehabilitation became a highly contested issue. The costly compromises made by the TRC were exacerbated by the subsequent failure of the government to follow up on the reparation payments as well as many others of the Commission's recommendations.

Whether or not the benefits of the adopted policies outweigh their flaws is hard to evaluate. The one thing both countries share is that 25 years after the mechanisms were adopted none of them has truly succeeded in "closing the books".[10] For one, different practical issues still emerge – in South Africa, several victims' groups and sympathetic organisations continue to struggle for the reparations' payments. In both countries, calls are still heard for more prosecutions.

But there is also another phenomenon: in both countries, instrumental use of collective identities based on dichotomous categories of us (anti-communists/liberation fighters/blacks) and them (communists/agents/perpetrators/whites) which have roots in the past characterise the discourses of some political actors and is still successfully applied for mobilisation, particularly (but not exclusively) in the pre-election periods. Powered by present-day realities, such as the disillusionment with the results of transformation in the Czech Republic or worsening socio-economic conditions for the majority of the population in South Africa, these discourses contribute to the polarisation of the societies and are a reminder that the reckoning with the past is a long term process that is not quite finished yet.

References

Bloomfield, D., T. Barnes and L. Huyse (ed.) (2003), *Reconciliation after Violent Conflict*. A Handbook, Stockholm: International Institute for Democracy and Electoral Assistance, online: http://www.idea.int/publications/reconciliation/upload/reconciliation_full.pdf (accessed: 4.7.2014).

Christodoulidis, E. and S. Veitch (2008), Reconciliation as Surrender: Configurations of Responsibility and Memory, in: F. Du Bois and A. Du Bois-Pedain (ed.), *Justice and Reconciliation in Post-Apartheid South Africa*, Cambridge: Cambridge University Press, pp. 9–36.

Clark, P. (2008), Establishing a Conceptual Framework: Six Key Transitional Justice Themes, in: P. Clark and Z. Kaufman (eds.), *After Genocide. Transitional Justice, Post-Conflict Reconstruction and Reconciliation in Rwanda and Beyond*, London: Hurst & Company, pp. 191–206.

Constitution of the Republic of South Africa (Interim Constitution) (Act No. 200 of 1993).

---

[10]"Closing the books" is a title of the 2004 book by Jon Elster.

Crocker, D. A. (1998), Transitional Justice and International Civil Society: Toward a Normative Framework, in: *Constellations*, Vol. 5, No. 4, pp. 492–517.

Crocker, D. A. (2003), Reckoning with Past Wrongs: A Normative Framework, in: C. Prager and T. Govier (eds.), *Dilemmas of Reconciliation. Cases and Concepts*, Ontario: Wilfrid Laurier University Press, pp. 39–63.

David, R. (2003), Lustration Laws in Action: The Motives and Evaluation of Lustration Policy in the Czech Republic and Poland (1989–2001), in: *Law & Social Inquiry*, Vol. 28, No. 2, pp. 387–439.

Doxtader, E. (2001), Making Rhetorical History in a Time of Transition: The Occasion, Constitution, and Representation of South African Reconciliation, in: *Rhetoric & Public Affairs*, Vol. 4, No. 2, pp. 223–260.

Du Bois, F. (2008), Reparation and Forms of Justice, in: F. Du Bois and A. Du Bois-Pedain (ed.), *Justice and Reconciliation in Post-Apartheid South Africa*, Cambridge: Cambridge University Press, pp. 116–143.

Du Bois-Pedain, A. (2008), Communicating Criminal and Political Responsibility in the TRC Process, in: F. Du Bois and A. Du Bois-Pedain (ed.), *Justice and Reconciliation in Post-Apartheid South Africa*, Cambridge: Cambridge University Press, pp. 62–89.

Elster, J. (2004), Closing the Books: *Transitional Justice in Historical Perspective*, Cambridge: Cambridge University Press.

Gibson, J. L. (2006), The Contributions of Truth to Reconciliation. Lessons from South Africa, in: *Journal of Conflict Resolution*, Vol. 50, No. 3, pp. 409–432.

Havel, V. (1990), New Years' Address to the Nation, January 1, 1990, online: https://chnm.gmu.edu/1989/archive/files/havel-speech-1-1-90_0c7cd97e58.pdf (accessed: 4.7.2014).

Hayner, P. B. (2011), *Unspeakable Truths. Transitional Justice and the Challenge of Truth Commissions*, New York: Routledge.

Hladik, R. (2009), Between Resentment and Forgiveness: Public Histories in the Czech and South African Transitions, in: *Teorie vědy*, Vol. 31, No. 2, pp. 113–137.

Ignatieff, M. (1996), Articles of Faith, in: *Index on Censorship*, Vol. 25, No. 5, pp. 110–122.

Kopeček, M. (2013), From the Politics of History to Memory as Political Language: Czech Dealings with the Communist Past after 1989, in: *Forum Geschichtskulturen*, Czechia, online: http://www.imre-kertesz-kolleg.uni-jena.de/index.php?id=519&l=0 (accessed: 4.7.2014).

Lambourne, W. (2009), Transitional Justice and Peacebuilding after Mass Violence, in: *The International Journal of Transitional Justice*, Vol. 3, No. 1, pp. 28–48.

Liatsos, Y. (2006), Truth, Confession, and the Post-Apartheid Black Consciousness in Njabulo Ndebele's The Cry of Winnie Mandela, in: J. Gill (ed.), *Modern Confessional Writing: New Critical Essays*, New York: Routledge, pp. 115–136.

Longman, T., P. N. Pham and H. M. Weinstein (2004), Connecting Justice to Human Experience. Attitudes toward Accountability and Reconciliation in Rwanda, in: E. Stover and H. M. Weinstein (eds.), *My Neighbor, My Enemy. Justice and Community in the Aftermath of Mass Atrocity*, Cambridge: Cambridge University Press, pp. 206–225.

Mamdani, M. (2000a), The Truth According to the TRC, in: I. Amadiume and A. An-Naim (eds.), *The Politics of Memory: Truth, Healing and Social Justice*, London: Zed Books, pp. 176–183.

Mamdani, M. (2000b), A Diminished Truth, in: J. Wilmot and L. Van de Vijver (eds.), *After the TRC: Reflections on Truth and Reconciliation Commission in South Africa*, Cape Town: David Philip Publishers, pp. 58–61.

Mamdani, M. (2002), Amnesty or Impunity? A Preliminary Critique of the Report of the Truth and Reconciliation Commission of South Africa, in: *Diacritics*, Vol. 32, No. 3–4, pp. 33–59.

Mayer, F. (2009), *Češi a jejich komunismus* [Czechs and their communism], Praha: Argo.

Minow, M. (1998), *Between Vengeance and Forgiveness*, Boston: Beacon Press.

Nález Ústavního soudu České republiky o návrhu skupiny 41 poslanců Parlamentu České republiky na zrušení zákona č. 198/1993 Sb., o protiprávnosti komunistického režimu a o odporu proti němu (US 14/1994) [Constitutional Court Decision on the Act on the Unlawfulness of Communism].

Nanda, V. P. (1998), Civil and Political Sanctions as an Accountability Mechanism for Massive Violations of Human Rights, in: *Denver Journal of International Law and Policy*, Vol. 26, No. 3, pp. 389–398.

Nedelsky, N. (2003), Divergent Responses to a Common Past: Transitional Justice in the Czech Republic and Slovakia, in: *Theory and Society*, Vol. 33, No. 1, pp. 65–115.

Nerlich, V. (2008), The Contribution of Criminal Justice, in: F. Du Bois and A. Du Bois-Pedain (eds.), *Justice and Reconciliation in Post-Apartheid South Africa*, Cambridge: Cambridge University Press, pp. 90–115.

Priban, J. (2007), Oppressors and Their Victims: The Czech Lustration Law and the Rule of Law. In: A. Mayer-Rieckh and P. De Greiff (eds.), *Justice as Prevention: Vetting Public Employees in Transitional Societies*, New York: Social Science Research Council, pp. 308–346, online: http://www.ssrc.org/

workspace/images/crm/new_publication_3/%7B57efec93-284a-de11-afac-001cc477ec70%7D.pdf (accessed 4.7.2014).

Promotion of National Unity and Reconciliation Act (Act 34 of 1995).

Reid F. and D. Hoffman (dir.) (2000), Long Night's Journey into Day, 95 min.

Roht-Arriaza, N. (2009), Foreword, in: H. Van der Merwe, V. Baxter and A. R. Chapman (eds.), *Assessing the Impact of Transitional Justice: Challenges for Empirical Research*, Washington: United States Institute of Peace, pp. vii-ix.

Rotberg, R. and D. Thompson (2000), *Truth v. Justice. The Morality of Truth Commissions*, Princeton: Princeton University Press.

Rupnik, J. (2002), The Politics of Coming to Terms with the Communist Past. The Czech Case in Central European Perspective, in: *Tr@nsit Online*, No. 22, online: http://archiv.iwm.at/index.php?option=com_content&task=view&id=286&Itemid=464#18 (accessed 4.7.2014).

Sadurski, W. (2003), "Decommunisation", "Lustration", and Constitutional Continuity: Dilemmas of Transitional Justice in Central Europe, *EUI Working Paper* No. 15, online: http://cadmus.eui.eu/bitstream/handle/1814/1869/law 03-15.pdf (accessed 4.7.2014).

Sandoval, C. (2010), Transitional Justice: Key Concepts, Processes and Challenges, *IDCR Briefing paper*, online: http://www.idcr.org.uk/wp-content/uploads/2010/09/07_11.pdf (accessed: 4.7.2014).

Sarkin, J. (2008), Achieving Reconciliation in Divided Societies, in: *Yale Journal of International Affairs*, Vol. 3, No. 2, pp. 11–28, online: http://yalejournal.org/wp-content/uploads/2011/01/083202sarkin.pdf (accessed: 4.7.2014).

Shaw, R. (2007), Memory Frictions: Localizing the Truth and Reconciliation Commission in Sierra Leone, in: *The International Journal of Transitional Justice*, Vol. 1, No. 2, pp. 183–207.

Stan, L. (2009), *Transitional justice in Eastern Europe and the former Soviet Union: Reckoning with the Communist past*, London: Routledge.

Suk, J. (2010), Zjevení komunistické minulosti jako morálního a politického problému [The Emergence of the Communist Past as a Moral and Political Problem], in: *Přítomnost*, No.1 of 2010, pp. 26–36.

Teitel, R. G. (2000), *Transitional Justice*, Oxford: Oxford University Press.

Truth and Reconciliation Commission of South Africa Report, Volume 1, 1998.

Truth and Reconciliation Commission of South Africa Report, Volume 5, 1998.

Vilímek, T. (2010), Několik poznámek k problematice vyrovnávání se s minulostí v České republice a Německu [A Few Notes to the Problem of

Dealing with the Past in the Czech Republic and Germany], in: *Přítomnost*, No. 1, pp. 37–50.

Verbuyst, R. (2013), History, Historians and the South African Truth and Reconciliation Commission, in: *New Contree*, No. 66, pp. 1–26, online: http://dspace.nwu.ac.za/bitstream/handle/10394/9030/No_66%282013%29_Verbuyst_R.pdf?sequence=1 (accessed: 4.7.2014).

Verwoerd, W. (2003), Toward a Response to Criticism of the South African Truth and Reconciliation Commission, in: C. Prager and T. Govier (eds.), *Dilemmas of Reconciliation. Cases and Concepts*, Ontario: Wilfrid Laurier University Press, pp. 245–278.

Vlachová, K. (dir.) (2006), *Kauza Uherske Hradiste* [The Uherské Hradiště Affair], 57 min.

Weinstein, H. M., L. E. Fletcher, P. Vinck and P. N. Pham. (2010), Stay the Hand of Justice. Whose Priorities Take Priority? In: R. Shaw and L. Waldorf (eds.), *Localizing Transitional Justice. Interventions and Priorities after Mass Violence*, Stanford: Stanford University Press, pp. 27–48.

Zákon č. 119/1990 Sb., o soudní rehabilitaci [Act on Judicial Rehabilitation].

Zákon č. 451/1991 Sb., kterým se stanoví některé další předpoklady pro výkon některých funkcí ve státních orgánech a organizacích České a Slovenské Federativní Republiky, České republiky a Slovenské republiky [Lustration Act].

Zákon č. 198/1993 Sb., o protiprávnosti komunistického režimu a o odporu proti němu [Act on the Unlawfulness of the Communist Regime and about the Resistance against it].

Zákon č. 107/2002 Sb., kterým se mění zákon č. 140/1996 Sb. o zpřístupnění svazků vzniklých činností bývalé Státní bezpečnosti, a některé další zákony [Act on the Disclosure of Files Created in the Course of Activities of the Former Security Service].

Zákon č. 181/2007 Sb., o Ústavu pro studium totalitních režimů a o Archívu bezpečnostních složek a o změně některých zákonů [Act on the Institute for the Study of Totalitarian Regimes and the Security Services Archive].

Zákon č. 262/2011 ze dne 20. července 2011, o účastnících odboje a odporu proti komunismu [Act on the Participants in Anti-communist Opposition and Resistance].

Deceived men, kissing women and women with ugly noses: The spectacle of gender transformation politics in South Africa

Thabo Msibi

Introduction

South Africa remains one of the foremost influential countries in the promotion of gender equity and transformation not only on the African continent, but also globally. This is evidenced by the 42 percent women representation in parliament for 2013, compared to a global average of 21.8 percent and 20 percent for the Czech Republic (World Bank 2014). Part of this sustained inclusion and participation of women in national decision making structures has been enabled by decisions made during the transitionary phase from liberation struggle to democratic government (see Erlank 2005; Hassim 2005 and Meintjes 2005) as well as by the pressures globally in post-conflict democracies where "there [has been] an intense concern with the extent to which elected institutions are representative, legitimate and accountable" (Hassim 2014: 85). Intent on distinguishing itself from the dictatorial nationalist government of apartheid, the post-1994 ANC government introduced major institutional structures, with marginalised groups being afforded freedoms previously denied to them. This was mainly achieved through a 'gender machinery' (Shefer et al. 2008) driven largely through Chapter 9 institutions such as the Gender and Human Rights Commissions, as well as through the development of gender sensitive laws.

While the formation of the institutional structures and the promulgation of gender-sensitive laws have resulted in many positive gains for women, many structural challenges remain intact. Women in South Africa continue to be at the receiving end of gender based violence, disproportionate rates of HIV/AIDS infection, poverty and unfavourable work conditions (Jewkes et al. 2010). Although gender inequalities continue to define the lives of women across the racial spectrum in South Africa, the intersection of race and poverty often results in Black South African women being most subject to sexist and misogynistic practices. The inequalities become more pronounced when sexuality is included, with many same-sex loving women being victims of lesbo-phobic rape and physical violence.

In this chapter, while it is acknowledged that these challenges highlighted above still remain major concerns for women, I shift the focus so as to explore the extent to which the discourses that the political elite apply to women cohere with the very progressive South African gender policies. The discursive portrayal of women at a political level by what Ratele (2006) refers to as the "ruling masculinities" or "ANC masculinity(ies)" (Suttner 2003) is important as this can reveal how seriously the gender equity mantra has been taken by the ruling party in South Africa, twenty years after democracy. Linked with the portrayal of women by ruling masculinities is the need to also explore how powerful political women position gender issues as well as the plight for women at the political level. While studies have sought to highlight women's experiences in leadership (De La Rey 2005); the role of values in women leaders (Gouws and Kotze 2007); women in government (Fick, Meintjes and Simons 2002; Goetz and Hassim 2014) and the role of patriarchy in contributing to violence (Gqola 2007), there remains a need for an in-depth analysis focussed on the discursive portrayal of women at a macro, political level by both powerful political men and women leaders.

This chapter deviates slightly from most of the chapters in this book in that it exclusively focuses on the South African context, without directly presenting a comparative dimension to the Czech context. I do this as I am careful to make conclusions about the Czech context without understanding the political dimensions at play. I instead focus on the South African context, a context I am most familiar with, so as to provide a more thorough analysis. Mainly, this chapter seeks to highlight the various ways in which gender politics shape the ways in which women are perceived, constructed, presented and understood at a national political level in South Africa. At this point it is important to distinguish between gender as development (concerned mainly with parity and representation) and gender as personal and structural (concerned with the individual, societal as well as systemic ways which inhibit women's recognition in society). The chapter argues that the South African gender transformation agenda at a national political level has been steeped in a discourse of gender as development, thereby enabling the inclusion and participation of women in higher national decision making structures such as parliament and the executive. This inclusion and participation has sought to present South Africa as a transformed post-conflict, democratic nation, which is a shining example for the entire African continent – a country where men and women have equal opportunity and access to resources in order to succeed in life.

While at a cursory glance this portrayal has been commendable, deeper analysis projects a state in conflict with itself; the male political elite is struggling to reach a balance between the institutional transformation achieved through the development discourse of parity and the individual and structural transformation required to bring about real social transformation for both men and women. Such transformation in essence would require the troubling of traditional conceptions of gender, thereby shifting men's historically inherited positions of privilege. I present evidence through critical incidents from the media, demonstrating the conservative ways in which women are understood, portrayed and used in South Africa. I argue that the employed discourse constitutes a political spectacle. Through this political spectacle, I argue that women continue to be presented as consumables, there to please and maintain the erotic and patriarchal desires of men. I argue that this political spectacle manifests in three forms of consumption: the corporeal consumption (driven by the sexualisation of women); the commercial consumption (informed by the trivialisation of women's work and the drive to generate votes) and political consumption (driven by theatre politics).

In advancing the above arguments I am careful not to construct women as powerless individuals who are at the mercy of powerful patriarchal males. As Foucault's work has shown, power is not located within an actor but rather is a project of discourse, and therefore remains largely fluid. The agency of women is therefore acknowledged. However, I recognise that agency is not necessarily always an act of empowerment. Agency often finds manifestation through normative expectations due to structural limitations inherited though historical means. While women therefore do act, this does not mean often that their actions are to the empowerment of themselves and other women, rather internalised ideals and politics of survival may result in actions directly opposed to the principles of gender transformation.

In the next section I discuss the state of gender equity in South Africa so as to provide some background discussion on the gains made in the last 20 years. This section is followed by a brief discussion on the feminist approach adopted in this chapter. I follow the section with a brief discussion on the critical incident methodology used in the chapter. The arguments advanced in this chapter are then presented, with the focus being on the discourses on gender as espoused by the political leaders in South Africa. I conclude by demonstrating various ways in which substantive transformation could instead be achieved.

The state of gender equity in South Africa

As already alluded to above, there has been a deliberate effort in the post-1994 ruling elite to prioritise gender equity as part of the transformation agenda. Increasingly, more women are participating in political and social processes, with several institutions in place to support and aid women's work. While not wholly successful, a whole ministry for women has been created, there to promote and monitor the issues faced by women, children and people with disabilities. Hassim (2005: 180) presents a fascinating account as to how this women's agenda has been achieved. For Hassim, "the constitutional protections were essentially a bargain struck at the elite level between national women's organisations and the male political leadership; they are not deeply rooted in civil society". The ANC nationalist liberation movement did not in fact perceive women's issues as part of liberation; these were peripheral issues driven by feminism, which was viewed as a dangerously Western pheno-menon (ibid). Tucker (2010) suggests that it is the 'articulation' (using Stuart Hall's reasoning) of equality to other aspects of identification beyond race that was used by activists in order to convince the ANC. Activists were intent on seeing the elimination of all forms of discrimination and therefore equality came to be interpreted and understood beyond the narrow nationalist agenda.

The 'articulation' of equality to other forms of identification and the lack of a civil involvement in the political bargaining process has created several unintended tensions in the post-1994 gender politics. There essentially exists a tension between on the one hand support for gender equality and transfor-mation by ANC leaders and on the other religious, cultural and traditional beliefs which in fact undermine gender equality and transformation. The utterances of President Jacob Zuma (to be discussed at length in the critical incidents below) during his rape trial betray this tension as deep-seated patriarchal ideals and a complete lack of understanding in relation to gender power become evident. We have observed this tension on several occasions, including in 2007 when it was revealed that a senior ANC feminist, Mavivi Myakayaka-Manzini, was being beaten by her husband, Manala Manzini, who happened to be a senior member of government, for refusing to cook for him (see Letsoalo, Majova and Mgibasa 2007). The existing tension relates to the disjuncture between the progressive offerings in the constitution and the tendency to appeal to 'traditional' gender ideals, often in the name of culture. Pregs Govender (2010) argues that some ANC leaders, including Oliver Tambo, even during the liberation struggle, were warning against the use of tradition to mask patriarchy. This masking of patriarchy has continued into the democratic state, with ANC still perceiving women as "mothers of the nation" (see Hassim 2005), a clear indication of the superficial ways in which gender transformation has been understood. Gqola (2007: 115) suggests that

> the discourses of gender in the South African public sphere are very conservative in the main: they speak of 'women's empower-ment' in ways that are not transformative, and as a consequence, they exist very comfortably alongside overwhelming evidence that South African women are not empowered.

While notions of tradition and custom have masked and enabled the continuation of gender inequalities in South Africa, it is too the development agenda which also significantly contributes to the inequalities. In part this is because gender politics based on development use parity as the major marker for equality, forgetting the substantive and more important transformation of structure and self and the role of power in gender relations. This is what Hassim (2005) refers to as 'inclusionary feminism'. As Natasha Erlank has shown, "gender as development is much less of a red-flag issue to conservatives rather than... gender as a power relation established and maintained within the private realm" (2005: 211). While an increasing number of women participate in decision making institutions of the state, the gender power relations remain largely intact with men still very much privileged (see Hassim 2005; Gqola 2007; Hassim 2014). Shefer et al. (2008: 159) attribute the continued marginalisation and victimisation of women in South African society to what they refer to as 'ambivalent sexism'. They note that "ambivalent sexists tend to have polarised images of women. The women they feel the most positive about are those in roles that serve men's needs, such as wives and sexual partners" (ibid. 159–160). An example for this is President Jacob Zuma's sexist assertion after his visit to Venda:

When I was in Venda recently I was so impressed to see how people there express respect for other people... A woman would clap her hands and even lie down to show respect... I was so impressed. If I was not already married to my wives I would go to Venda to look for a woman (Hans 2013).

This is an example of such ambivalent sexism. It becomes clear that while Zuma continues to speak the language of gender transformation, his understanding of what this means in practice is deeply marred by patriarchal ideals embedded in customary, traditional and apartheid practices.

I present the discussion above so as to highlight the various ways in which the limited understanding of gender equality inhibits real transformation, therefore continuing what Gqola (2007) refers to as the 'invisibilisation' of women's issues, lives and work in South Africa. Such a positioning enables patriarchy to remain intact and unopposed as the guise of numbers often tells a more glorified story. It is also partially this flawed understanding of gender equality and transformation that enables the spectacle and trivialisation of women at a political level, an issue I explore at length below.

Theoretical framing of the chapter

This chapter is clearly feminist in its orientation. At the heart of the argument lies the desire to highlight the discourses of power which work to minimise women's lives; in particular black women's lives. I borrow from what Mirza (2009) refers to as black post-colonial feminism. Accordingly (2009: 1) it is argued that

> *Black feminist thought is grounded in an understanding of the nature of power and the way black/othered [women's difference] is systematically organised through social relations. Postcolonial feminist approaches [on the other hand] enable us to situate the silent 'spectral' power of colonial times as it appears in the production and reproduction of marginalised, racialised and gendered others in new contemporary times.*

Combining both black and post-colonial feminism therefore enables a deeper understanding of the intersectional manifestations of gender as they are produced through race, class, sexuality and nation. Like Sara Ahmed (2009), I am concerned about what it means to be doing diversity in relation to gender in a context where conceptions of 'diversity' and 'transformation' mask deeper structural restrictions which remain intact and unchallenged. I am concerned with patriarchy, which intersects with racism, homophobia and sexism in quite profound ways. In reference to how diversity is being perceived in white institutions, Ahmed (2009: 41) writes that

> *The turn to diversity is often predicated on the numbers game, on getting more of us, more people of colour, to add colour to the white faces of organisations. So if we are the colour, then we are what gets added on... We symbolise the hope or promise that whiteness is being undone...Our arrival is read as evidence of commitment, of change, of progress...When our appointments and promotion are taken up as signs of organisational commitment to equality and diversity, we are in trouble. Any success is read as a sign of an overcoming of institutional whiteness. 'Look, you're here!', 'Look, look!' Our talk about racism is read as a form of stubbornness, paranoia, or even melancholia; as if we are holding onto something (whiteness) that our arrival shows has already gone.*

Although Ahmed's irritation is related to the operations of race, it is argued in this chapter that the same applies to gender issues in the context of South Africa. What Ahmed captures therefore is the essence of my theorisation. When numbers come to define the transformation of gender structures, conceptions of diversity and transformation become highly flawed. They only work to sustain the sexist and racist structures inherited through centuries of history.

While I adopt a feminist oriented approach in relation to this study, I am also careful not to be the 'speaking voice' for women. I am cautious about colonising the space yet again: of having yet another man writing about women's struggles and I am fully aware of the dangers this may have in relation to reifying sexist ideas, of constructing women yet again as victims who are powerless in African spaces. I understand how chapters such as this can serve conservative sexist and racist ideas: ideas of a dark, 'oppressed' Africa in need of rescuing. However, I wish to highlight that my hope is for the opposite to happen. It is my hope that this paper will offer a new approach to understanding gender transformation in South Africa. My chapter seeks not to subsume women's voices. Rather, it seeks to contribute in a political agenda, an agenda of understanding women's issues as a concern of femininities and masculinities.

Methodology

This paper uses critical incidents to highlight the various ways in which women are constructed at a political level. Critical incidents can sometimes be viewed as methodologically weak in that they fail to offer detailed, more representative data when used to generalise. However, Jansen (1998) has shown that critical incidents have much to offer to research, particularly scholarship concerned with transformation, as an institution (or perhaps individual) provoked through crisis tells us much more about the nature and extent of transformation than any official documents or quantified outputs. For it is in the response of the institution (or individual) to such critical incidents that important clues are given away about how far that institution (or individual) has travelled in the direction of what it may call 'transformation.' (Jansen 1998: 106)

In the context of this chapter therefore I wish to understand, in the face of claims of a transforming national politics, how women are projected by those in powerful positions. By highlighting particular moments of crisis as presented in the media, and the various responses from politicians, I wish to highlight the tensions which exist in the gender equality discourse of development and the lived experiences of women. Jansen aptly shows how particular events in institutional and individual histories have come to directly counter false narratives of transformation which get presented in the media. In this chapter I capture several important incidents. While the incidents captured are biased in that I selectively choose which to present, I argue, at the very least that these incidents present us with some level of reality and therefore enable us to understand the structural restrictions and challenges experienced by women.

Deceived men, kissing women, and women with ugly noses: The political spectacle

I have argued above that the discursive construction of women at a senior political level is centred on the spectacle, with projections of women being mainly driven by politics of the theatrics. Women are projected at a public level through various scandals, which manifest themselves through public theatre and consumption. It is argued here that consumption takes on both figurative and literal manifestations, with powerful men being caught 'with their pants down' while women are simultaneously undermined through dirty politicking. This consumption manifests in three ways: bodily, commercially and politically. I discuss each of these theatrical consumptions alongside evidence from critical incidents.

The spectacle of the corporeal: the consumption of women's bodies

Perhaps the most spectacular theatrical performance and example of bodily consumption of women is that of President Jacob Zuma's rape trial in 2007. President Zuma, then disgraced and sacked Deputy President of the country, was under immense pressure following corruption charges after being implicated in a corruption trial of his former financial advisor, Shabbir Shaik. While battling the alleged corruption, the country woke to the shocking allegations that the former Deputy President had raped his former friend and comrade's daughter. The woman, known in the media as Khwezi in order to protect her identity, was half the age of Mr Zuma. What followed in the media and across the country was a theatrical spectacle of some sort. The Zuma coalition of supporters went for an all-out attack, accusing Khwezi of having asked for the rape. There were public burnings of her effigies, with signs 'Burn this bitch' clearly on display. Shirts declaring '100percent Zulu boy' were created and worn during gatherings by Zuma supporters. Signs outside the trial declared "How much did they pay you, *nondindwa* [bitch]?" Evans (2006) suggested that the accusations were merely political and that someone was paying the 31-year old to accuse Zuma.

Accompanied by Zuma's signature song, "*Awulethe umshini wami*" (lit. translated: Bring me my machine gun), an image of a patriarch for the struggle for liberation was created publicly. This was a traditional man deserving respect. Such a projection was a direct appeal to Mr Zuma's Zulu conservative base; warrior masculinity was created and publically advanced. Conservative writers like Jon Qwelane came out publicly to attack feminists who were challenging the attacks on Khwezi as well as the outwardly traditional and patriarchal projection of Mr Zuma's conservative ideals. Conservative forces came together to protect Zuma in the theatrics that accompanied the trial (see Ratele 2006).

Perhaps what shocked some in the public the most were Jacob Zuma's own utterances during the trial. We were informed that "compensation" discussions had already begun with the family: with the violence exerted against the woman supposedly meant to be addressed through the traditional ceremony of apologising to, and compensating, the family. Speaking in isiZulu (once again to cement his traditional Zulu masculinity) to testify, Zuma declared that Khwezi had sent him sexual messages. She was wearing a knee-length skirt, and was not wearing any underwear under her *kanga* (wrap). Zuma suggested that he had the cows ready (for *lobola*/bridewealth) in case the woman had decided to marry him after engaging in the sexual act. He had showered to prevent getting HIV and it would have been inappropriate for him as a 'Zulu man' to leave an aroused woman 'unattended' as this would have been tantamount to rape, he claimed (see Mkhwanazi 2008). Throughout the trial Zuma asserted himself as a 'traditional' Zulu man, who simply behaved in accord with Zulu cultural norms governing masculinity. Khwezi on the other hand was not a real Zulu woman as she should have remained silent and followed cultural expectations (ibid).

The incident highlighted above demonstrates the various ways in which women's bodies are consumed for the pleasures of powerful men, together with the ways in which such consumption is discursively constructed as normal and accepted for women. In the above example, Zuma projects himself as someone who cares for his accuser: he was willing to pay compensation; he was willing to pay lobola; he was even willing to marry Khwezi. To him, Khwezi's public revelations on what essentially was a private matter were unacceptable. She should have kept to her culturally accepted role: that of being able to offer pleasure to the man and also of being pleasured by the man. As Zuma himself declared, he could not have left Khwezi as this would have been tantamount to rape, and certainly would have projected him as a weak man. It is important to note that this is a man who was the Deputy President of the country; the very man who was elected President of South Africa for two terms.

Certainly, the above has as much to say about how women are discursively constructed and understood at a political level as it does about how society understands gender issues. Zuma appealed to traditional masculinity as this was what the general public would accept. The failure to have a feminist agenda driven by civil society has meant that the constitutional offerings are often rejected at a social level. Zuma understood this, hence the spectacle that followed and the crowds that accompanied the trial. Apart from a few voices from activists and academics, very few people spoke out against the victimisation of Khwezi. Even the ANC Women's League, the very body that should have come out to support Khwezi, remained silent – no doubt due to the political climate that prevailed at the time, but also for purposes of self-preservation (as I will discuss later).

Apart from the physical consumption of Khwezi's body through the sexual engagement, consumption also took on a figurative meaning through the images that were publically consumed during the demonstrations. Khwezi's body was seen as open to consumption and torture not only by men but also by women. She became a 'bitch', someone who easily gives away her sexuality for the pleasure of men. Her humanity was taken away from her. She needed to be burnt. She had asked for it through her provocative clothing. At the end of the trial, Zuma was found not guilty through some very problematic judgement which continues to be challenged by many legal minds to date. Khwezi was thereafter forced to emigrate in fear for her life.

The consumption of women's bodies and the accompanying spectacle in the political space were also evident in the sexual harassment accusation levelled against the current secretary of the very powerful Congress of South African Trade Unions (COSATU), the largest trade union movement in South Africa, at the climax of the organisation's near implosion in 2013. Mr Vavi, a former supporter of President Zuma, was accused of rape and sexual harassment by a co-worker he had hired. Mr Vavi conceded to having hired the co-worker after she had competently handled his flight booking (the co-worker was previously employed by South African Airways). He recruited his accuser to work for COSATU and began having an affair with her. He had never once harassed nor raped the accuser; the sexual encounters in the COSATU office were all consensual, he claimed.

Just like the Khwezi case, what followed was yet another attack on the woman for having lured innocent Vavi into a sexual relationship. Mr Vavi, who until this stage had been seen as a critical and independent thinker, alongside his 'supportive wife', accused the woman of attempting to ruin their marriage and being used for political means. Although Vavi had conceded to having an affair with the woman, Vavi's wife, who happens to be a well-known business woman, indicated that she fully supported her husband and that they would work through the issue of the affair in their own way. Mr Vavi presented sms conversations as evidence of having had a relationship with the woman. He claimed that the woman was trying to extort R2 million from him, and that the accusations were baseless. In political rallies that followed in support of Mr Vavi, the rape accuser continued to be vilified, with Mr Vavi referring to the 26-year old as 'that girl' who was '*nopatazana*' (bitchy) (Matlala, Macupe and Merten 2013). The same Vavi would go on later, however, to ask South African's to stand up against gender inequality, arguing that "Patriarchy, gender based violence, poor access to skills development and decent employment" (SAPA 2013) continue to cloud women's experiences in South Africa. This suggests, as argued above, that at a political level, gender equality and transformation are an ethical concern so long as they do not threaten the ruling masculinities.

While I do not wish to enter the merits of the arguments that Mr Vavi was being attacked for political reasons, it is once again the very public theatrics I wish to highlight. Like the previous incident, the woman becomes trivialised and constructed as a 'bitch'. She becomes a docile actor who needed to appreciate the job she was given and accept the affair or rape (depending on whose version one believes). While the woman went on to withdraw the accusations due to the distress the entire matter was causing her and her family, it became clear that, like Khwezi, it was she who was being questioned, and that men's politics resulted in the trivialisation of her experiences. She was the 'loose' one; Vavi was the innocent actor.

While there has been the sexual consumption of women's bodies, there has also been the reduction and trivialisation of the work of women in higher office, especially women critical of the ANC. Such attacks have primarily focussed on their bodies too, often using the ANC's junior affiliates. Women have been objectified, seen as mainly there to look beautiful, and crudely sexualised if they play a more challenging role. The Public Protector, Thuli Madonsela, who has been a bastion against corruption in the country, has for instance been at the receiving end of attacks on her body image and her work. Vulgarities and statements determined to undermine her work have been hurled her way. The intentions have been to undermine her work, with gendered innuendos driving the attacks. The ANC was for instance forced earlier this year to summon and reprimand publically both the ANC Youth League and the Congress of South African Students, an ANC affiliate, after their public attack on the Public Protector. The COSAS Secretary-General referred to Ms Madonsela as "that woman with the big, ugly nose". While the ANC Youth League noted the report on the wastage which occurred during President Jacob Zuma's homestead security upgrades "with sheer disgust", pointing out that Ms Madonsela was "poisoning the public against the ANC" (see Letsoalo 2014). Here, patterns witnessed during Khwezi's attack once again emerge. The discourse used is to sexualise Ms Madonsela's body (referring to her nose as 'ugly'), while also trivialising her work and competencies as a woman (she's referred to as *that* woman', clearly gendering her competencies). Madonsela is also constructed as a witch – hence the reference to her 'poisoning' the nation.

The spectacle of the market: the commercial consumption

Much has been written in the literature about how working class women are used as cheap labour for the advancement of men (see Bair 2010; see also the collection of essays by Waylen, Celis, Kantola and Weldon 2013). While existing work has given us insights into the systemic, cultural and structural ways in which women's lives are limited through the market, the assumption often is that it is women who are in the working classes who are at the receiving end of being consumed by the market. I wish to challenge this thinking in this chapter by arguing that women across the spectrum experience commercial consumption, but that the manifestations of this consumption takes different forms depending on the intersectional relations of different identity markers. For women in positions of power, I submit that commercial consumption mostly works to retain patriarchal and capitalistic conditions. Instead of men driving the trivialisation of women, it is women themselves who often engage in such processes mainly through internalisation and co-option. By commercial consumption in this instance, I do not refer directly to the financial (monetary) market place. Rather, what I refer to as commercial consumption is mainly the deep desire to generate votes and establish a political base, no matter the ethical implications involved, at the national political level. The public become the market, with ideology and appeal becoming the central products on offer.

In providing evidence to my claim of the commercial consumption of women, I wish to use as example Ms Helen Zille, leader of the Democratic Alliance – South Africa's biggest opposition party – when she was elected Premier of the Western Province in 2009. Apart from herself, Ms Zille chose no other woman to be part of her cabinet. All her cabinet members were men. This was despite the fact that during the election campaign, all three faces that appeared on the party's main election posters were that of women. Following the uproar from South Africans, including several women's groups criticising her decision, Ms Zille responded by attacking President Zuma noting that "Zuma is a self-confessed womaniser with deeply sexist views, who put all his wives at risk by having unprotected sex with an HIV-positive woman" Mail and Guardian, 2009), therefore failing to provide a clear and justifiable rationale behind her decisions. The ANC and its affiliates went on a determined attack on Zille, criticising her poor decision-making and sexist approach for failing to choose a more representative cabinet. In response, Zille argued that her chosen cabinet was not based on quotas, but rather on competent individuals who could get the work done.

I wish to suggest here that in political theatrics, matters of gender equity and transformation take on political meaning, with parties competing to show who can best represent women's issues. While the ANC's attack on Zille appeared at cursory glance to deplore Zille's inability to think in a more representative manner, the manner in which the attacks were levelled were no more than politicking, with the South African voters being perceived as the market which needed to be exploited (or attracted). For instance, the ANC Youth League demonstrated very little sensitivity towards gender equality and transformation responded by noting that:

> *Zille has appointed an all male cabinet of useless people, majority of whom are her boyfriends and concubines so that she can continue to sleep around with them, yet she claims to have the moral authority to question our President. If the fake racist girl Zille continues to speak hogwash like she has been doing during elections, we will take militant action against her, and demonstrate to her that she does not have monopoly over the Western Cape. The fake racist girl who was dropped on a head as child should understand that South Africa will never be a Mickeymouse Republic like she wants to portray it* (de Vos 2009).

The above comments are not only sexist; they also show very little regard for Zille's person and abilities in office, furthering the sexist notion that women sleep their way to success. At the heart of the response is less of a concern about the lack of gender transformation in Zille's cabinet, but rather an attempt to protect Mr Zuma, thereby attracting voters. This of course is the danger of gender equity when understood to represent numbers: it enables patriarchs and sexists to claim to speak on behalf of women when in fact they speak for patriarchy.

Apart from the concerning actions from the ANC, Zille's actions truly undermined women. While one can at cursory argue that Zille's position was to shift away from an affirmative action approach in appointing senior politicians, the fact that she saw no woman fit to take up any position in the cabinet did much to project women as unable to handle the political space, thereby grossly undermining women. I wish to argue here that what transpired was in fact part of the commercial consumption noted above, in that Zille had to appeal to her base, a base which, although claiming liberal roots, still very much remains conservative. The overbearing question within gender politics of the market is 'what will sell'. Within politics one ought to ignite one's base so as to ensure growth. Zille's choice of cabinet therefore had very little to do with women's inabilities than it did with the sustainability of the patriarchal base within the Democratic Alliance.

It is when women are co-opted into patriarchal projects that commercial consumption becomes more glaring. This has also been witnessed in the last presidential elections when the ANC Women's League President, Angie Motshekga, publicly declared that no woman was ready to be president, all because of the League's interests in being seen as supportive of President Jacob Zuma, who enjoyed overwhelming popular support among the ANC voters and the public at large. Ms Motshekga noted that:

> *We know the ANC, we understand the ANC, we understand the ANC processes, and no one wants to go into a futile battle. There are traditions, there are processes, and those processes have a long, long life... We want to have a female president in the near future. We are just not prepared for it now. We do not have capable leaders* (Seale 2013).

When focus becomes more on 'what will sell' to the public instead of what is ethically correct, gender transformation become heavily compromised. This becomes clear from Motsekga's assertions as patriarchy remains fully intact, all due to processes of history and fear of challenging the status quo. The embeddedness of patriarchy therefore becomes strengthened and women continue to be side-lined.

The public theatre: political consumption

The last consumption I wish to explore is that of political consumption. This links directly with the two types discussed above in that this type of consumption concerns not only the trivialisation of women's work in the political space, it is also deeply driven by politics of the theatre, i.e. public political drama primarily concerned with the projection of women's political actions as trivial, objectifying them and their bodies and also creating 'fun' out of women's serious political efforts. All these aspects come together to construct an image of women as incompetent and pseudo politicians, in-habiting a space 'naturally' preserved for men. Of course, the tactics used by those seeking to undermine women are often covert, disguised often as genuine political concerns which require genuine political attention.

An example of the theatrical political consumption of women I wish to highlight concerns the botched merger between South Africa's leading opposition party (the Democratic Alliance) and AGANG SA (a new political party that was until recently under the acclaimed struggle hero, academic and business woman, Mamphela Ramphele). A media launch was held by the leaders of both parties to announce the political marriage. During the media conference, the two leaders embraced each other with a kiss, and congra-tulated each other for what they termed the 'realignment of opposition politics in South Africa'. After the launch, newspaper headlines were splurged with images of the two women kissing each other. However, within five days, the deal had completely collapsed, causing much harm to the reputations of both women, particularly Ramphele.

It is the mockery following the collapse of the deal I wish to particularly highlight. The very same image of the two women kissing was used to mock their political attempts and their efforts were constructed as a joke both in public forums and in the media. The image of the two women kissing was instrumentally used to 'feminise' and trivialise their attempts of being big political players in a shrewd, masculine political environment. The Minister of Higher Education and Training, Dr Blade Nzimande, as well as the current Minister for Human Settlement, Ms Lindiwe Sisulu, (both in the ANC) took a photo kissing each other to mock the flawed attempts of the two women. The entire political attempt was turned into a public spectacle with questions like 'what were they thinking' reverberating in the public space. Apart from the flaws in the approach of the two women (AGANG SA members for instance knew nothing about the merger until it was announced publicly through the conference), the entire mockery produced an image of incompetent women who 'bit more than they could chew'. Such a projection had direct intents: that of constructing the political space as too cumbersome for women and of constructing women as not being serious about politics. Of course Zille and Ramphele did not do much to help their project; however the discursive projections grossly undermined their political competencies as women.

Another brief example I wish to highlight is that of current ANC Women's League President and Minister of Education, Angie Motshekga's case against the South African Democratic Teachers Union (SADTU), South Africa's biggest teacher union, during a strike in 2013. The striking members of SADTU, an organisation that projects itself as so concerned with gender matters that it has gender officers in all its structures, launched a public stunt on Moteskga's body as a woman. Carrying a gigantic women's underwear, mounted on wire, with "puluma ya Angie" (Angie's panty) inscribed on the front, two men marched with their SADTU compatriots demanding for Motshekga's resignation. Women and other marchers were seen in images captured by journalists laughing at this theatrical display of sexism, with no immediate objections. The intention was clear: to dehumanise the Minister by drawing attention to her body size while simultaneously sexualising and objectifying her. Publicly, the act constituted the spectacle that has come to define women's politics. The office that the Minister occupied and her dignity were grossly undermined through the objectification. When these images were seen in newspapers across the country, Motsekga, quite correctly, took serious offense at the gross violation of her rights as a woman and reported the matter to the Commission for Gender Equality. In her open letter to SADTU, she noted that she wanted to register her "very profound revulsion about [the] nauseating displays" and that the display of women's underwear was "disgusting and [certainly had] no place in our democratic order" (Motshekga 2013). She went into history showing how women, in particular, black women had been "denigrated and objectified objects whose primary reason for existence was to the man's wanton desires and pleasures". The manner in which Motsekga was treated demonstrates clearly not only just how trivialised women's bodies, work and lives come to be in politics, but also the role of 'fun' in such trivialisation. The fact that SADTU members saw nothing wrong with this public denigration of the Minister, demonstrates just how ingrained patriarchy is in the daily experiences of South Africans.

The surprising seriousness with which Motsgekga reacted to the panty theatrics demonstrated just how commercialising, sexualisation and politics come together to shape women's lives at a political level. Had Motsekga reacted with the same level of disgust to the many sexist and misogynistic scandals in the ANC and in government, the plight for gender equity and transformation would be far more visible. However, politics of identification and power often play a powerful role in rendering objection towards sexism as not just a matter of ethics, but rather a matter of convenience and survival. When speaking out against sexism may mean losing your job, ethics are often compromised.

Conclusion

This chapter has sought to highlight the discursive construction of women at a political national level. I have argued that while much has been achieved in South Africa in relation to gender equity, the fact that South Africa's approach appears to be driven by politics of development (and therefore concerned with parity in the main) undermines the plight of gender equity and transformation in South Africa, as it often allows conservatives the space to project a pro-women disposition while in fact they are concerned with the reification of patriarchy. Given the already established literature on the intersection of gender, race and poverty, I sought to shift focus in this paper to the political space of privilege, focusing in the main on men and women in power. I argued that at a political level, traditional tactics of gender which undermine women take on more covert forms, driven by the competing tension between constitutional democracy and traditional values, but that due to the space in which all of this occurs (i.e. the political space) spectacles and theatrics are often created to undermine women. Further, I suggested that women are undermined through three tactics/ consumptions: bodily/corporeal (sexualisation), commercial and political consumptions. Also, I showed that these tactics then shift gender away from being a matter of ethics to being a matter of convenience and survival.

For radical transformation to occur within South African's political space, focus has to shift away from developmental gender politics of representation, to politics of personal and structural transformation. This means that both men and women need to engage in processes of troubling cultural and social historical learnings so as to understand how power is implicated in the experiences and relations of both men and women. Unless the focus shifts to personal and structural transformation, the endemic violence, abuse and marginalisation of women will continue unabated. For it is through the transformation of structure and the individual that patriarchy can in part be uprooted.

References

Ahmed, S. (2009), Embodying diversity: problems and paradoxes for Black feminists, in: *Race Ethnicity and Education*, Vol. 12, No. 1, pp. 41–52.

Bair, J. (2010), On Difference and Capital: Gender and the Globalization of Production, in: *Signs*, Vol. 36, No. 1, pp. 203–226.

De la Rey, C. (2005), Gender, women and leadership, in: *Agenda*, Vol. 19. No. 65, pp. 4–11.

De Vos, P. (2009, May 12), 2009 May 12 – Constitutionally Speaking, online: http://constitutionallyspeaking.co.za/2009/05/12/ (accessed 2.8.2014).

Erlank, N. (2005), ANC positions on gender, 1994–2004, in: *Politikon*, Vol. 32, No. 2, pp. 195–215.

Evans, J. and R. Wolmarans (2006, March 21), *Timeline of the Jacob Zuma rape trial*, online: http://mg.co.za/article/2006-03-21-timeline-of-the-jacob-zuma-rape-trial/ (accessed 24.8.2014).

Fick, G., S. Meintjes and M. Simons (2002), *One Woman, One Vote: The Gender Politics of South African Elections*, Johannesburg: The Electoral Institute of South Africa.

Foucault, M. (1977), *Discipline and Punish*, London: Penguin.

Foucault, M. (1979), *The Will to Knowledge: The History of Sexuality One*, London: Penguin.

Goetz, A.-M. and S. Hassim (2003), *No Shortcuts to Power: African Women in Politics and Policy Making,* Johannesburg: Zed Books.

Gouws, A. and H. Kotzé (2007), Women in Leadership Positions in South Africa: The Role of Values, *Politikon*, Vol. 34, No. 2, pp. 165–185.

Govender, P. (2010), *When "traditional values" are a stick to beat women*, online: http://www.timeslive.co.za/opinion/editorials/2010/02/28/when-tradi-tional-values-are-a-stick-to-beat-women (accessed 24.8.2014).

Gqola, P. D. (2007), How the 'cult of femininity' and violent masculinities support endemic gender based violence in contemporary South Africa, in: *African Identities*, Vol. 5, No. 1, 111–124.

Hans, B. (2013), *Zuma's Venda women comments slammed*. IOL News, online: http://www.iol.co.za/news/south-africa/kwazulu-natal/zuma-s-venda-women-comments-slammed-1.1625004#.U-5xqmO8PA0 (accessed 20.8. 2014).

Hassim, S. (2005), Voices, Hierarchies and Spaces: Reconfiguring the Women and Movement in Democratic South Africa, in: *Politikon*, Vol. 32, No. 2, pp. 175–193.

Hassim, S. (2014), Persistent Inequalities: A Comparative View of Indian and South African Experiences of Local Government Quotas for Women, in: *Politikon*, Vol. 41, No. 1, 85–102.

Jansen, J. D. (1998), But our natives are different! Race, knowledge and power in the academy, in: *Social Dynamics,* Vol. 24, No. 2, pp. 106–116.

Jewkes, R. K., K. Dunkle, M. Nduna and N. Shai (2010), Intimate partner violence, relationship power inequity, and incidence of HIV infection in young women in South Africa: a cohort study, in: *The Lancet,* Vol. 376, pp. 41–48.

Khuthula, N. (2013, July 30), *Cosatu may still pursue rape case against Vavi*, online: from http://mg.co.za/article/2013-07-30-cosatu-may-still-proceed-with-rape-inquiry-against-vavi (accessed 24.8.2014).

Letsoalo, M. (2014, March 24), *Mapisa-Nqakula defends Madonsela against "sexist" remark*, online: from http://mg.co.za/article/2014-03-24-mapisa-nqakula-defends-madonsela-against-sexist-remarks (accessed 24.8.2014).

Letsoalo, M., Z. Majova and M. Mgibasa (2007), *NIA boss in abuse claim,* online: http://mg.co.za/article/2007-10-26-nia-boss-in-abuse-claim/ (accessed 24.8.2014).

Mail and Guardian (2009, May 12), *ANC, allies lay into Zille*, online: from http://mg.co.za/article/2009-05-12-anc-allies-lay-into-zille/ (accessed 24.8. 2014).

Matlala, G., Macupe, B., and Merten, M. (2013, September 15), *Vavi hits out at "that girl."* IOL News., online: http://www.iol.co.za/news/politics/vavi-hits-out-at-that-girl-1.1577733#.U_pP42NhIyg, (accessed 24.8.2014).

Meintjes, S. (2005), Gender equality by design: The case of South Africa and commission on gender equality, in: *Politikon*, Vol. 32, No. 2, pp. 259–275.

Mirza, H. S. (2009), Plotting a history: Black and postcolonial feminisms in "new times", in: *Race Ethnicity and Education,* Vol. 12, No. 1, pp. 1–10.

Mkhwanazi, N. (2008), Miniskirts and Kangas: the Use of Culture in Constituting Postcolonial Sexuality, *Darkmatter Journal*, online: http://www.darkmatter101.org/site/2008/05/02/miniskirts-and-kangas-the-use-of-culture-in-constituting-postcolonial-sexuality/ (accessed 24.8.2014).

Motsekga, A. (2013, April 26), SADTU must apologise for underwear stunt, online: http://www.politicsweb.co.za/politicsweb/view/politicsweb/en/page71654?oid=373055andsn=Detailandpid=71616 (accessed 20.8.2014).

News 24 (2013, August 10), *Stand against gender injustice: Vavi*, online: http://www.news24.com/SouthAfrica/News/Stand-against-gender-injustice-Vavi-20130809 (accessed 24.8.2014).

Ratele, K. (2006), *Ruling masculinity and sexuality*, in: *Feminist Africa*, Vol. 6, pp. 6–64.

Seale, L. (2013, October 9), *SA not ready for female president – ANCWL*, IOL News, online: http://www.iol.co.za/news/politics/sa-not-ready-for-female-president-ancwl-1.1589121#.U_pRiGNhIyh (accessed 24.8.2014).

Seedat, M., A. Van Niekerk, R. Jewkes, S. Suffla and K. Ratele (2009a), Violence and injuries in South Africa: prioritising an agenda for prevention, in: *The Lancet,* Vol. 374, pp. 1011–1022.

Shefer, T., M. Crawford, A. Strebel, L. C. Simbayi, N. Dwadwa-Henda, A. Cloete and S. C. Kalichman (2008), Gender, Power and Resistance to Change among Two Communities in the Western Cape, South Africa, in: *Feminism and Psychology*, Vol. 18, No. 2, pp. 157–182.

Suttner, R. (2012), The African National Congress centenary: a long and difficult journey, in: *International Affairs*, Vol. 88, No. 4, pp. 719–738.

Tucker, A. (2009), *Queer Visibilities: Space, Identity and Interaction in Cape Town*, West Sussex: John Wiley and Sons.

Waylen, G., K. Celis, J. Kantola and L. Weldon (eds.) (2013), *The Oxford handbook of gender and politics*, New York, USA: Oxford University Press.

World Bank (n.d.), *Proportion of seats held by women in national parliaments (percent),* online: http://data.worldbank.org/indicator/SG.GEN.PAR (accessed 20.8.2014).

The position of women in post-communist Czech Republic

Petra Ahari

In the Czech Republic, the events of 1989 and the collapse of the communist regime were the beginning of profound political, economic and social changes. The Czech Republic and other Central and Eastern European communist countries had to face radical transformations at that time and find ways of replacing the communist value system with democratic aspirations. A political reform introduced a multiparty democracy and economic reforms resulted in a shift from a centrally planned to a market economy. The many new phenomena and changes occurring after 1989 have affected both women and men and both in a positive and negative sense. Social stratification and mobility previously restrained by the communist regime was now set in motion. New opportunities for social advancement have appeared. Conversely, some population groups in particular were faced with the rise of unemployment, poverty and social exclusion. Everyone had to adapt to new conditions and try to find their place in the new system.

This chapter will explore the consequences of transition on women's positions as citizens and as workers by comparing the status of women during the socialist period and after 1989. The following question will be the focus of this chapter: What exactly are the consequences of the transition for the development of gender inequality? In order to analyse the impact of these transformations, I have chosen to focus on the following elements: women's employment, remuneration and work-life balance. To be able to understand and compare the situation of women in the current times, it is necessary to get a glimpse of the period before 1989, the period of so-called socialism.

There is a scarcity of studies dealing with social and gender inequality and its development in ex-communist countries. But the topics and issues dealing with the post-communist transformation have been more often of a political nature. Nonetheless there is a body of research that emerged on gender issues in the related country: Čermáková (1995), Kuchařová (2009), Pollert (2003), Hraba et al. (1997), and most recent Havelková and Oates-Indruchová (2014). Some scholars had predicted that gender inequality in the post-communist European countries would grow simultaneous to the rooting of capitalism (Watson 1993; Haney 1994). Čermáková (1995: 16) for instance notes that market oriented economy puts women in particular at risk of unemployment and inequality, caused by gender divisions on the labour market. Pascall and Lewis (2004: 374) believe that the dual worker model of Central and Eastern

European (CEE) countries has been undermined by economic insecurity, with higher unemployment bringing an increase in women's dependence on men's income, and by changes in the state, especially reduction in legitimacy and in collective spending. Individualisation of personal and public life is a key trend east and west, and challenges the structures that supported child care in state and family. The decrease in state intervention has brought reduced spending on child care, education, health, pensions, and child benefits. We examine here whether and to what extent this has indeed been the case in the Czech Republic.

The chapter is structured as follows: In the first part, I analyse the trends in female labour force participation. This is followed by an assessment of the dual-earner system. Attention then turns to the gender pay gap, in particular to factors that contribute most to income disparities. Finally, the gender roles at the level of the family are reviewed, followed by an evaluation of work-life balance. In the conclusion the possibilities for change are discussed.

Women's employment

During the socialist era, women's participation in the labour market was very high since this trend was in line with the socialist emancipation and homogeneity. The fabricated illusion of gender equality was of course less convincing when factors such as wage disparities, and genderisation of jobs are considered. Theoretically though, unemployment did not exist. The regime presented itself as the absolute employment and social security regime. The Law dictated the obligation to work to all eligible adults and if unemployed, one would not only be looked down upon, but could be subject to a criminal prosecution. Czechoslovakia in particular had high rates of women's labour force participation and women were almost equally represented in the labour force as men. The numbers far exceeded those in the West, with the exception of the Scandinavian countries. 60.8% of women above the age of 15 were economically active in 1980 (ILO).

Government officials would employ an "arsenal of scientific techniques and procedures", in order to promote a dual-earner family model, with an emerging image of women as a "new socialist man" (Gal and Kligman 2000: 47). The dual-earner model typical for CEE countries under socialism stands in contrast to a male breadwinner-female housewife model, which in Lewis's (1992: 162) view would, in its pure form, find married women excluded from the labour market, firmly subordinated to their husbands for the purposes of social security entitlements and tax, and expected to undertake the work of caregiver (for children and other dependents) at home without public support.

By making participation in the labour force mandatory, socialism successfully removed the male-breadwinner model of the family. It should be noted that to thrive as a one-income family under conditions of a socialist economy was hardly possible. Two sources of income were needed in order to maintain an average standard of living. Perhaps what women tend to take for granted today is the fact that the dual-earner system typical for socialist countries made women less dependent on their husbands and allowed them to be more economically autonomous. However, the dependency was transferred onto the state as it was the state that provided family-related supports and benefits to women in order to support them in their effort to combine dual roles as employees and mothers. State support aimed at women included a generous amount of maternity leave with guarantee of job security, a system of child allowances, and a state sponsored system of kindergartens. From some of these family benefits, such as childcare leave, men were legally excluded. The lack of economic prosperity was balanced out by relative material security.

Some predictions were made that the artificial over-employment and state-controlled redistribution economy demise would bring mass unemployment and growth of gender inequality. In the Czech Republic with exception of the economic slowdown in 1997 and the few following years when unemployment rose, the high employment rate in general has been maintained. The hypothesis of dual-earner model decline has not been confirmed and the continuous high female employment rates show that the dual-earner model has withstood the transition from socialism. Furthermore the institutional setting and state support for childcare was not fundamentally challenged either, the state has not withdrawn from the involvement in childcare. Even though after the transition, there has been a slight drop in the number of pre-school facilities and fees have increased, the kindergartens are still accessible. According to the Ministry of Education, Youth and Sports in the Czech Republic (2013), 90.4% of children aged five attended formal childcare in 2012/2013.

In 1995 Czech labour market analysis Čermáková concludes that less than 4% (of women) have fallen through the employment net, while more that 10% of Czech women have markedly improved their positions. At the cost of adaptation, a greater effort and retraining they have partly improved their position within structural labour relations (women's increasing penetration of the working elite; number of women leaving traditionally-feminised occupations) (Čermáková 1995: 24–27). The Lisbon Strategy aim to attain 60% employment of women by 2010 has been largely met in the Czech republic and in recent years the employment rate for women aged 20–64 is at around 63% which is slightly above the EU 28 average (62.5% in 2013, see Table 2).

Even taking the above information into consideration, on closer analysis, there are various important concerns. The period from 1997 was characterised by rising unemployment (from 4.8% in 1997 to 8.8% in 2000). Even though this dramatic rise affected both men and women, it was women who suffered more from the rise in unemployment. Female unemployment ranged from 5.5% in 1993 to 10.60% in 2000 – its highest value over the past 20 years (comparing to men 7.3% in 2000, see Table 1). Večerník (2001:8) reports that women, in particular those up to age 34, have been significantly affected, as employers are concerned about issues of maternity leave and absence due to child care.

Table 1: Unemployment rates by sex, age group 15–74.

	Male, age group 15–74				Female, age group 15–74			
	1993	2000	2012	2013	1993	2000	2012	2013
EU-28		7.9	10.4	10.8	10.1	10.5	10.9	10.9
Czech Republic	3.4	7.3	6	5.9	5.5	10.6	8.2	8.3

Source: Eurostat 2014a (online data code: tsdec450)

Compounding this imbalance is the fact that the difference in employment between women and men in the Czech Republic is one of the highest in the EU. And in the table below we can see that the difference between female and male employment rate has not decreased. The difference in 2012/13 was still around the same as 10 years earlier. As these statistics show little if any improvement has occurred during the last decade.

Table 2: Employment rates by sex, age group 20–64.

	Male, age group 20–64				Female, age group 20–64			
	2002	2007	2012	2013	2002	2007	2012	2013
EU-28	75.4	77.7	74.5	74.2	58	62.1	62.4	62.5
Czech Republic	80.9	81.5	80.2	81	62.3	62.4	62.5	63.8

Source: Eurostat 2014b (online data code: tsdec420)

Even though women do not participate in the labour market to the same degree as men, the transition from state-controlled redistributive economy to a market-oriented economy has not severely affected women's work force participation. The transformation did not cause any major mass withdrawal from the labour force or transformation of women into full time homemakers, and women remain to be an important part of the labour force. Nonetheless, more focused efforts are required to move from the currently stagnant participation of women in the labour force to achieve greater parity.

Gender pay gap

The gender pay gap (GPG) is the difference between women's and men's remuneration, based on the average difference in hourly earnings of all employees. Opposed to the alleged economic inequalities of the capitalist systems, the economic system of state socialism equalised the benefits for the masses. Wages were set by the state according to a centrally-determined wage grid. Irrespective of input and efficiency, everybody was equal or rather equally poor. According to Večerník the very small differences in the equalised wages were caused more by demographical factors (gender and age) than market factors (qualification, skills). In addition, some industries were favoured by the system (mining, metallurgy and heavy manufacturing) and so were few selected categories of workers (top government and Communist Party officials, army and police officers). Since 1950s the demographic factors became increasingly influential, favouring of so-called productive industries grew, whilst remuneration of educated people declined and the younger generation was disadvantaged in favour of the older one (Večerník 2009: 87). As far as the labour market is concerned, the gender regimes of the state-socialist era appeared on the surface similar to Scandinavian ones, with women's high labour market participation and small GPG restricted by the occupational wage grid. Despite the equality proclaimed by the socialist regime, the reality and informal social relations did not fully mirror these claims. The results of socialist policies were mixed and women's work continued to be considered second class compared to that of men. Below the surface, the GPG was significant. In former Czechoslovakia in 1988, the average salary of women working full time amounted to 71% of the average wage of their male colleagues (Večerník 2001: 27). This put women in socialist Czechoslovakia in a similar position to those in the West. Even though, socialist Czechoslovakia had one of the highest wage equality systems in the world, a gender was the strongest explanatory variable with respect to wage disparity in comparison to other communist countries. The hierarchy of earnings fell into two parts, the bottom for women and the top for men (Večerník 2009: 78; Večerník 1991: 244).

Market reforms in the Czech Republic after 1989 included wages liberalisation and privatisation, and newly allowed the former artificially egalitarian
system to transform. People have gained the flexibility to respond to opportunities offered by market forces. The job prospects and remuneration became
more dependent on education, skills and occupational category. For many
workers that meant being able to explore and take advantage of new opportunities and consequently increase their earnings, for others it meant worsening
of their situation. Hand in hand with greater wage dispersion, the earnings
inequality began to rise.

Although the gender wages inequality research has shorter tradition in
post-communist countries comparing to West, a number of studies investigating male-female income difference in post-socialist countries has been
published over the last twenty years. Sometimes these studies bring contradictory results due to analysing different years or using different methodology.
Brainerd (2000:158) provides an overview of the evolution of the gender wage
gap in Russia and Ukraine within one to two years of the introduction of
market reforms. She concludes that while the gender wages gap diminished
in Eastern Europe, it has increased substantially in Russia and Ukraine.
According to Brainerd women in Russia and Ukraine have borne an unequal
burden of the economic restructuring. On the other hand, Ogloblin (1999)
analyses gender pay differences in Russia during mid 1990s and in 2000–02
(Ogloblin 2005) and conversely concludes that after a decade of radical
economic reforms, the gender pay gap in Russia remains fairly close to its
levels during the late Soviet era. Hunt focused on East Germany and
documented that, during 1990–94 the average monthly wages of full time
female workers in Eastern Germany have risen from 81% to 91% of male
wages. This would suggest that the transition has been extremely beneficial
for women in East Germany. However the author demonstrated that 40% of
this gain could be attributed to the selective withdrawal of low-skilled women
from employment (Hunt 1998: 1). In the case of Eastern Germany the
evolution of GPG was 'positively' affected by the decline in employment
rates of low-wage women. A considerable amount of studies on the GPG in
the Czech Republic has been published by Jurajda (2000, 2003, 2005 and
2007) who is mainly concerned about the gender occupational segregation
and within-occupation within-establishment pay discrimination.

The statistics of early transition years in the Czech Republic indicate slight
convergence in the gender gap in wages. As reported by Večerník (2001: 27)
the female-male average wage ratio was 71% in 1998, in 1996 it increased to
76% and in 1998 declined back to 72%. Čermáková (1995: 19) believes that
the inequalities just continue as in during the pre-89 period. Statistics of the

last few years (see Table 3) support this notion; in 2012 the GPG was still high at 22% in favour of man. Lower remuneration of women comparing to men is not specific to the Czech Republic, it appears in all countries. According to European Commission's Report, women in Europe in 2013 still worked 59 days 'for free' until they matched the amount earned by men (EC 2014). As can be seen from Table 3 at present the Czech Republic has higher GPG than is the EU average and actually ranks among countries with the widest gap in EU alongside Estonia, Austria, Germany and Slovakia (Eurostat 2014).

Table 3: The difference between men's and women's average gross hourly earnings as percentage of men's average gross hourly earnings.

	2007	2008	2009	2010	2011	2012
EU27:		17.3	16.6	16.1	16.2	16.4
CZ:	23.6	26.2	25.9	21.6	22.6	22.0

Source: Eurostat 2014c (Code: tsdsc340)

The GPG is a complex issue and the explanatory factors behind it are multiple, interrelated and extend beyond direct discrimination. The EU report names as major underlying causes for high GPG in Europe different jobs and sectors, discrimination in the workplace, workplace practices and pay systems, undervaluing of women's work and skills and presence of few women in senior and leadership positions (EC 2014a: 5–6). In order to establish which part of the gender gap in earnings can be attributed explicitly to direct or indirect discrimination it is necessary to first identify and eliminate other explanatory factors. This is not a simple task as a whole range of other factors may affect the figures. The remaining part of the gender income difference could be then associated with discrimination. Different decomposition methods are being used for this purpose.

The occupation segregation by industry or job status is often used as a key explanation of the gender wage gap. The overrepresentation of women in particular occupations is not unique to the Czech Republic or the EU countries. Ogloblin (1999) observes that in Russia work experience and education cannot explain the GPG alone, most of the gap is ascribable to occupational segregation. It is found to account for 75–80% of the gender wage gap in Russia. According to Kunze (2000), women in general are most likely to comprise the majority of workers in the service occupations and industries, while men are more likely to work in manufacturing jobs and industries. Similarly, in the Czech Republic the differences in remuneration are tied to gender-determined segregation in the labour market and are not merely a product of differences in the qualifications, experience and responsibilities required for each profession. Čermáková (1997: 403–4) believes that the gender-based differences discriminate against the female workforce, and consequently result in lower social and job positions for women as well as lower earnings. As a result, women operate within their own female sector in the labour market, "floating under the surface" of the male sector. Czech females are more likely to be employed in clerical or sales and elementary occupations, while Czech males are more likely to be employed in manual or craft occupations and also in managerial occupations (Jurajda 2007). It is evident that irrespective of the change from a centrally-planned economy the occupational segregation of women into lower paid occupations and sectors continue throughout the periods of transition until the present. Women in the Czech Republic continue to lag behind in securing top-level positions, while the better-paid positions continue to be disproportionately occupied by men.

Jurajda (2005) analysed gender pay difference and occupational segregation in Czech and Slovak Republics using employer-employee data sets including wage records in 1998. After considering age, education, job type and category the result shows that one third of the wage gap appears due to segregation of women into low-paying occupations, firms and job cells[1]. Furthermore, in the non-public sectors of the Czech Republic, about two thirds of the wage gap appears due to gender differences in wages that remain after accounting for most forms of workplace segregation as well as for other explanatory variables. He points out that it is not the occupational segregation that is to blame for most of the GPG, but rather within-occupation within-establishment phenomena (Jurajda 2000: 22–23). In his 2003 study, Jurajda compares the wage gap structure in the Czech Republic to the one in the USA and concludes that the main difference in the structures of the gap is in the importance of its unexplained part. In the non-public sectors of the Czech Republic, almost two thirds of the wage gap is unexplained and potentially related to discrimination, which compares unfavourably to less than one-third unexplained component in the USA. In this regard the situation in the Czech Republic with two thirds of the wage gap unexplained and potentially related to discrimination is much less favourable comparing to other western countries. Jurajda's findings on within-occupation possible discrimination are consistent with Čermáková's study concluding that the difference in GPG is not only due the segregation of women into certain jobs. She finds out that more educated Czech women in particular are more likely to receive unequal pay.

---

[1] Job cell is defined as a group of workers with the same occupation within a firm.

For example, women doctors earn on average only 76% the salary of their male colleagues, while for women university lecturers the figure is only 85%. The figure for lawyers is 91%, for directors of large companies it is 56%, for directors of small organisations 43% etc. (Čermáková 1999). What is clear from the figures shown above is that attention should be paid to violations of equal pay clause in particular.

Unquestionably, there still remains a notable male-female income disparity both in the Czech Republic and in Europe in 2014. The stagnating high gender pay gap in the Czech Republic reflects ongoing discrimination and inequalities in the labour market. The underlying causes of the wages gap, such as undervaluation of women's work, occupational gender segregation, and discriminatory treatment in the work place, persist. Women continue to be over-represented in female-dominated occupations and sectors, and subsequently receive lower pay influenced by the feminisation of particular jobs. In the Czech Republic alongside the gender job segregation, the within-establishment pay discrimination is very important determinant of the wages differential. This suggests that employers are more influenced by the patriarchal stereotypes to a greater extent and continue to perceive women as less productive labour force. Equal pay still has many obstacles in its way: lack of transparency in pay systems, lack of legal clarity in the definition of work of equal value, and lack of clear information for workers that suffer inequality. To create a more equal society, wage transparency in companies along with gender neutral job classification has to be promoted. Fairer valuing of women's work and skills will increase their motivation, productivity and consequently the business performance.

Work-life balance

During the socialist era, in public life, work, studies, culture, and politics, women had become (almost) equal, and they may have felt (almost) equal. But in the private sphere, in relationships, within the family and the interpersonal arena, traditional ways of constructing men and women's roles remained, by and large, untouched (Ferge 1998: 221). In the CEE countries women had to put in long hours of work at home as well – a "double burden" averaging close to 70 hours per week (Unicef 1999: 14). Besides being full time employed women simultaneously bore the main responsibility for the care of the family and household. The state had affected the women's participation in the labour market by promoting a dual-earner family model and providing childcare facilities, but the gender stereotypes in the private sphere were not addressed. This placed women under great pressure trying to combine full time jobs and most of the domestic labour as well. Also, house-hold time saving appliances utilised in the West were not available.

At present, despite the continuously high level of women's employment, the traditional idea of men and women as having complementary roles is still firmly embedded in the Czech Republic. Kuchařová observes that men recognise the rights and ability of women to self-realisation outside the home, but on the other hand they do not wish to 'relieve' them of their domestic roles of women-partner and women-mother of their children (Kuchařová 1999: 184). Furthermore, Hohne et al. (2008) observe that in the Czech Republic in particular there is a high degree of identification with the current state of the division of family and work roles between partners. This is in conformity with a study conducted by the Sociological Institute of the Czech Academy of Science "Family 1994 – Social Survey of the Czech Family". The study indicated that, seen through the lens of a male, the exchange of roles in the family is out of the question. But surprisingly even women do not seek a simple shift of roles. Everyone feels that it would not be beneficial. According to the study contradiction is present in two circumstances: "While men would not miss women at work, women on the contrary feel the absence of men in families" (Čermáková 1997: 26). Čermáková (ibid.) argues that this dispute has an individual, but also social dimension. Binding family strategy with the sphere of employment, in which the model "men more at work – women more in the family" is unilaterally favoured – reinforces gender inequality in the private sphere of the family as well. Kuchařová (2009: 1305) considers a general sense of complacency to be the reason for not fighting for gender equality. There is not enough pressure put on the relevant subjects, in particular employers and local authorities, to pursue the goal of attaining greater gender equality.

The fact that state has maintained its high level of involvement in childcare provision as well as in providing support allowances connected with childcare is positive. But it could also be argued that the long paid childcare leave may on the contrary reinforce the traditional gender division of labour. It may also become a reason for employers to be reluctant to hire women entitled to take up their long maternal and childcare leave. Furthermore, the longer women are out of the labour market, the more difficult it will be for them to find a job. Javorník observes that the work-family policies of post-socialist countries differ: between 2000 and 2008, Slovenia and Lithuania incentivised women's continuous employment and gender equity, and had provided gender-neutral parental leave with father quotas as well as public childcare options. By contrast, Hungary, Czech Republic and Estonia supported and reinforced conventional gendered care giving; they financially supported stay-at-home mothers, whilst Poland, and to some extent also Slovakia and Latvia, left parents nearly without public support (Javorník 2012: 2). According to the OECD report, among European countries, the Czech Republic has one of the lowest employment rates of mothers with dependent children up to the age of 3 (OECD 2014). It is likely that the generous financial support provided to families with young children in combination with one of the lowest day-care coverage for children up to three years of age, considerably limits the labour participation options of women in question and may have de-motivating effect on female employment. While by international standards, the Czech Republic offers a long maternity leave, so far, no paternity leave has been established. With regards to parental leave entitlements, according to 2013 data from the Ministry of Labour and Social Affairs of the Czech Republic, only 5,200 Czech fathers received parental allowance (1.8% of all recipients) compared with 288, 500 Czech mothers (MPSV 2014).

For the Czech Republic the impact of parenthood is high on female employment in particular. To equalise the disproportionate impact of a presence of a child on male and female, employment organisational changes have to be made. Not only abandoning of long maternity leave and instead increasing investment into the development of accessible child care services (with particular relevance to children up to three years old), but mainly promoting share of caring duties. Greater acceptance of flexible work schedules would also help to balance work and family responsibilities. Measures to support the right work-life balance including flexibility in employment are implemented very slowly in the Czech Republic. The number of people – both men and women employed on a part time bases are still very low comparing to EU member states average. Women's part time employment rate in 2013 was 11% whereas the EU28 average was 32.7% (Eurostat 2014d). As the low numbers of part time employment suggest, the work flexibility is still hardly ever offered or used. Since the two worlds of work and family are very much interconnected in both women's and men's lives, the importance of finding the best solutions is ever more important. Implementing the above changes would enable both parents to achieve improved levels of reconciling their professional and family roles.

Čermáková calls for women not to ignore the discrepancy (hypocrisy) between the inflicted stereotyped form of gender relations and roles and the real social position of the female population in our culture. The consequence may be at best, ending up in the suburbs as a comfortably well-off wife caring for children and the house; in the worst case, as a single parent with children, dependent on social support. Rationalisation of options that includes independence and achievement of the highest social status is associated with the realisations of one's own educational and social needs (Čermáková 2003: 1).

Conclusion and outlook to the future

It was the main purpose of this chapter to draw attention to the changes in women's positions that the transformation processes after 1989 have brought about. Summing up the results, it can be concluded that while there has been some progress towards equality for men and women in the Czech Republic, there is still a lack of fairness in many areas. Equality in remuneration and balancing professional and family life in particular has not been reached. As economic independence leads to ability to make one's own choices and be able to act upon them, achieving greater equality in remuneration is particularly important for women.

Women's work force participation remains relatively high but is still characterised by horizontal and vertical job segregation.[2] It is necessary to decrease a gender-based segregation of the labour market, connected with devaluation of predominantly female work. The number of women in managerial or similar higher-level jobs is still low and prevents women from equal access to decision making and rewards. Also the male-female income disparity remains evident. Reducing the gender job segregation and discriminatory treatment in the work place, calling for wage transparency in companies along with gender neutral job classification will undoubtedly lead to narrowing of the gender pay gap.

The impact of parenthood on labour market participation is still hugely different for women and men and continues to correspond with social stereotypes. Only 42.1% of women with children under 6 worked in the Czech Republic versus the average in EU of 59% in 2013 (Eurostat 2014e). This reflects the unequal sharing of family responsibilities, but also often signals a lack of childcare and work-life balance opportunities. More accessible child care services for children up to three years old as well as more flexible forms of employment including part time jobs need to be created for both men and women. Simultaneously it is necessary that these positions are not treated less favourably than equivalent full time positions regarding both the pay rates and privileges. The gender inequality is still evident especially in the domestic sphere with the unequal division of labour in the family. The traditional idea of men and women as having complementary roles is firmly embedded in Czech society. A high degree of identification with the present situation seems to lie behind the lack of struggle for greater gender equality in the family.

There is no single solution to achieve gender equality. Is there will enough to question the equality of women's engagement and participation in labour

---

[2] Horizontal segregation refers to the under/overrepresentation of women and men in occupations or sectors, whilst vertical segregation indicates men's domination of the highest status jobs.

market and their remuneration? Are women prepared to question the current situation and the position of men as the head of the family? Are they willing to question the discrimination on the bases of motherhood and are they ready to defend their rights? The political, economic and societal changes presented women with the opportunity to be more creative, active and opportunity to strengthen their societal rights. Therefore also women themselves need to be more critical and inquiring of their situation and relation with men in society. Awareness needs to be increased and wider discussions leading to further improvement of the current situation encouraged.

References

Brainerd, E. (2000), Women in transition: Changes in gender wage differentials in Eastern Europe and the former Soviet Union, Industrial and Labor Relations Review, in: *ILR Review*, Cornell University, ILR School, Vol. 54, No. 1, pp. 138–162.

Čermáková, M. (1995), Gender, Society, Labour Market, in: *Czech Sociological Review*, Vol. 31, pp. 7–24.

Čermáková, M. (1997), Postavení žen na trhu práce [The position of women in the labour market], in: *Sociologický časopis*, Vol. 33, pp. 389–404.

Čermáková, M. (1999), Gender Differences among Economically Active University Graduates, in: *Czech Sociological Review*, Vol. 7, No. 2, pp. 127–144.

Čermáková, M. (2003), Genderové identity – ekonomické a sociální souvislosti [Gender identities – economic and social connection], in: *Gender, rovné příležitosti, výzkum*, Vol. 4, No. 1–2, pp. 1–2.

Český statistický úřad (2014), Zaměstnanost a nezaměstnanost od roku 1993 [Czech Statistical Office, Employment and unemployment since 1993], online: http://vdb.czso.cz/vdbvo/tabparam.jsp?voa=tabulka&cislotab=PRA1010CU && kapitola_id=3 (accessed 4.7.2014).

Český statistický úřad (2012), Harmonizace rodinného a pracovního života [Czech Statistical Office, Harmonization of family and work life], online: http://www.czso.cz/csu/csu.nsf/ainformace/7887002B6B23 (accessed 4.7.2014).

European Commission (2014), Tackling the Gender Pay Gap in the European Union, online: http://ec.europa.eu/justice/gender-equality/files/gender_pay_gap/140227_gpg_brochure_web_en.pdf (accessed 4.7.2014).

European Commission (2014b), Gender Pay Gap: Women in Europe still work 59 days 'for free', Commission report finds, online: http://europa.eu/rapid/press-release_IP-13-1227_en.htm (accessed 18.8.2014).

Eurostat (2014a), Unemployment rate, by sex, online: http://epp.eurostat.ec.
europa.eu/tgm/refreshTableAction.do?tab=table&plugin=1&pcode=tsdec450
&language=en (accessed 18.8.2014).

Eurostat (2014b), Employment rate, by sex, online: http://epp.eurostat.ec.
europa.eu/tgm/refreshTableAction.do?tab=table&plugin=1&pcode=tsdec420
&language=en (accessed 18.8.2014).

Eurostat (2014c), Gender pay gap in unadjusted form, online: http://epp.euro-
stat.ec.europa.eu/tgm/table.do?tab=table&init=1&language=en&pcode=tsdsc
340&plugin=1 (accessed 18.8.2014).

Eurostat (2014d), Persons employed part-time, online: http://epp.euro-
stat.ec.europa.eu/tgm/refreshTableAction.do?tab=table&plugin=1&pcode=
tps00159&language=en (accessed 18.8.2014).

Eurostat (2014, Employment rate of adults by sex, age groups, highest level
of education attained, number of children and age of youngest child, online:
http://appsso.eurostat.ec.europa.eu/nui/submitViewTableAction.do (accessed
18.8.2014).

Ferge, Z. (1998), Women and Social Transformation in Central-Eastern
Europe: the Old Left and the New Right, in: *Social Policy Review*, Vol. 10,
pp. 217–36.

Gal, S. and G. Kligman (2000), *The Politics of Gender After Socialism:
A Comparative-Historical Essay*, Princeton: Princeton University Press.

Haney, L. A. (1994), From Proud Worker to Good Mother: Women, the State,
and Regime Change in Hungary, in: *Frontiers Editorial Collective*, Vol. 14,
pp. 113–50.

Havelková, H. and L. Oates-Indruchová (eds.) (2014), *The Politics of Gender
Culture under State Socialism: An Expropriated Voice*, London and New
York: Routledge.

Hohne, S., K. Svobodová and A. Šťastná (2008), Význam partnerství pro
harmonizaci rodiny a zaměstnání [The meaning of partnership for the
harmonisation of family and career], in: T. Sirovátka and O. Hora (eds.),
Rodina, děti a zaměstnání v České společnosti [Family, children and career
in Czech society], Brno, František Šalé-Albert, pp. 119–144.

Hraba, J., A. L. McCutcheon and J. Večerník (1996), *Gender Differences in
Life Chances During the Post-Communist Transformation of the Czech and
Slovak Republics: Trends from Eight National Surveys, 1990–1994*. Paper
presented at the 1996 meeting of the American Sociological Association, New
York.

Hunt J. (1998), The Transition in East Germany: When is Ten Per Cent Fall
in the Gender Pay Gap Bad News, in: *CEPR Discussion Paper Series in
Transition Economies*, No 1, p. 805.

Javorník J. (2012), State Socialism: Dismantling the male-breadwinner family model in Central and Eastern Europe? In: *Working Paper* 14.

Jungbauer-Gans, M. (1999), Der Lohnunterschied zwischen Frauen and Männers, in: Selbständiger und abhängiger Beschäftingungen. *Kölner Zeitschrift für Soziologie and Sozialpsychologie*, Vol. 51, No. 2, pp. 364–390.

Jurajda, Š. (2000), Gender Wage Gap and Segregation in Late Transition, in: *William Davidson Institute Working Papers Series* 306, William Davidson Institute at the University of Michigan.

Jurajda, Š. (2003), Gender Wage Gap and Segregation in Enterprises and the Public Sector in Late Transition Countries, in: *Journal of Comparative Economics*, Vol. 31, No. 2, pp. 199–222.

Jurajda, Š. (2005), Gender Segregation and Wage Gap. An East-West Comparison, *Journal of the European Economic Association*, Vol. 3. No. 2–3, pp. 598–607.

Jurajda, Š. and M. Franta (2007), Occupational Gender Segregation in the Czech Republic, in: *Czech Journal of Economics and Finance* (Finance a úvěr), Vol. 57. No. 5–6, pp. 255–271.

Kuchařová, V. (1999), Women and Employment, in: *Czech Sociological Review*, Vol. 7, pp. 179–194.

Kuchařová, V. (2009), Work-life Balance: Societal and Private Influences, in: *Czech Sociological Review*, Vol. 45, No. 6, pp. 1283–1310.

Kunze, A. (2000), The determination of wages and the gender wage gap: a survey, in: *IZA Discussion Paper*, No. 193, online: http://www.iza.org/teaching/empirische_wirtschaftsforschung/iza-dp193.pdf (accessed 4.7.2014).

Lewis, J. (1992), Gender and the development of welfare regimes, in: *Journal of European Social Policy*, Vol. 2, No. 3, pp. 159–173.

MPSV (2014), Počet příjemců rodičovského příspěvku podle pohlaví [Number of family allowance recipients according to sex], online: http://www.mpsv.cz/cs/10543 (accessed 4.7.2014).

MŠMT (2014), Výroční zprávy o stavu a rozvoji vzdělávání v České republice v roce 2013. Praha: MŠMT, online: http://www.msmt.cz/vzdelavani/skolstvi-v-cr/statistika-skolstvi/vyrocni-zpravy-o-sta-vu-a-rozvoji-vzdelavani-v-ceske-1(accessed 4.7.2014).

OECD (2014), OECD Family database 2014, LMF1.2: Maternal employment rates, online: http://www.oecd.org/els/family/LMF1_2_Maternal_Employment_14May2014.pdf (accessed 4.7.2014).

Ogloblin C. G. (1999), The Gender Earnings Differential in the Russian Transition Economy, in: *Industrial and Labor Relations Review*, Vol. 52, No. 4, pp. 602–27.

Ogloblin, C. G. (2005), The Gender Earnings Differential in Russia After a Decade of Economic Transition, in: *Applied Econometrics and International Development*, Vol. 5. No. 3, pp. 5–26.

Pollert, A. (2003), Women, Work and Equal Opportunities in post-Communist Transition, in: *Work, Employment and Society*, Vol. 17. No. 2, pp. 331–57.

Pascall G. and J. Lewis (2004), Emerging gender regimes and policies for gender equality in a wider Europe, in: *Journal of Social Policy*, Vol. 33. No. 3, pp. 373–394.

Statistical Office of the European Communities (2012), EUROSTAT: Gender pay gap statistics, online: http://epp.eurostat.ec.europa.eu/statistics_explained/index.php/File (accessed 18.8.2014).

UNICEF (1999), Women in Transition, Florence, The MONEE Project: Regional Monitoring Report, No. 6.

Večerník, J. (1991), Earnings distribution in Czechoslovakia: temporal changes and international comparison, in: *European Sociological Review*, Vol. 7, pp. 237–252.

Večerník, J. (2001), *Mzdová a příjmová diferenciace v České republice v transformačním období* [Wages and income differentiation in the Czech Republic in the transformation era], Praha: Sociologický ústav Akademie věd České republiky.

Večerník, J. (2009), *Czech Society in the 2000s: a report on socio-economic policies and structure*. Prague: Academia.

Watson, P. (1993), Eastern Europe's Silent Revolution: Gender, in: *Sociology*, Vol. 27, No. 3, pp. 471–87.

HIV/AIDS in South Africa and beyond: Pulling the epidemic 'out of the box'

Júlia Lampášová

Introduction

The beginning of the 1990s saw coinciding liberation in different parts of the world. Then still Czechoslovakia, which split into two separate countries just few years later, finally set forth the route of liberal democracy already in 1989. The Republic of South Africa followed two years later by abandoning almost fifty years of the apartheid system.

The freedom, however, has brought its own challenges, which the new society and the new governments had to handle themselves. The situation in South Africa has become far more complicated by the recent emergence of HIV/AIDS, a silent killer of its citizens, of which nobody would have known much during the days of apartheid. The position of the Czech Republic has been vastly different in this respect. Surrounded by countries with relatively higher prevalence of the disease, both to the East and to the West, it has nonetheless managed to retain one of the lowest rates worldwide.

After two decades from the transition towards democracy, the situation has not changed to a large degree. The HIV/AIDS epidemic with its sub-stantial human and economic repercussions is perceived to be "one of the most significant developments of South Africa's post-apartheid period" (Horton 2005: 113). The disease still claims more than 4,000 lives each day worldwide, with 35.3 million people currently living with HIV globally (UNAIDS Report on the Global AIDS Epidemic 2013). The region of sub-Saharan Africa has remained disproportionately affected by 70% of all new HIV infections in 2012 and falling slightly below that rate in the number of people living with HIV. Moreover, the recent trend of anti-retroviral therapy provided to a larger amount of citizens brings new challenges, particularly the economic ones, when more people are currently living with the disease than dying of it.

South Africa is struggling hard to keep the epidemic under control, which requires enormous financial resources that could otherwise be invested into the education of the future labour force and to enhancing the overall quality of life of its citizens. At the same time, the Czech Republic is showing a discrepancy in the rates of HIV and AIDS between the heterosexual and homosexual community with the latter constituting 80% of all the cases

(Czech Republic's Report on the Global AIDS Epidemic 2013). Unlike the official status of homosexuals as equal members of the society, with the right to enter into registered partnerships, the community is still being ostracised by mainstream society not willing to conduct a dialogue about their partner lives (see, for example, Baťa 2011), which leads to the negligence of the problems that may be caused by their sexual activities if practiced in an unsafe way.

This chapter is based upon the comparative analysis of the HIV/AIDS epidemiological patterns, along with the socio-demographical ones, of the Republic of South Africa and the Czech Republic indicating the current state of affairs of the emerging Global Health Governance. The Republic of South Africa is at the centre of interest, and later it is compared with the situation in the Czech Republic, thus posing a rather intriguing question what can the international society get from the comparative analysis of two countries with one of the highest and the lowest prevalence of HIV/AIDS.

The aim of the analysis is to prove that the regional differences generate diverse challenges and that the epidemiological patterns in sub-Saharan Africa are too specific to give the researchers a significant chance to elaborate widely applicable measures of a global security strategy concerning HIV/AIDS. Nevertheless, placing two diverse HIV stories side by side may be a promising way to unveil certain tendencies of the disease which may have been neglected thus far and the lessons already learned in South Africa may lead us to set up more universal tools for further progress worldwide.

The analysis begins with the socio-demographic comparison of the countries, as both demographers and public health specialists suggest that the spread of HIV/AIDS reflects behavioural and socioeconomic conditions of the population (Horton 2005). The comparative analysis in this chapter is based on the statistics provided by both countries, which are put next to each other in order to form the grounds for the following comparative analysis of the current epidemiology of HIV/AIDS.

A subsequent epidemiological comparison focuses on the recent epidemic trends in both countries and analyses political steps undertaken thus far to combat the disease and its further spread, with the participation of all kinds of stakeholders interested in finding efficient solutions. Within the provided epidemiological profile of the countries, the paper also conceptualises their geographical position in a wider region where they are situated to analyse how the cross-boundary coexistence and cooperation with the neighbouring countries affect the spread of the HIV epidemic. Both primary and secondary sources of information are applied throughout the analysis. The primary sources consist of the national reports on the progress in their response to the epidemic as well as various national statistics, put into critical comparison with the more independent ones provided by various international organisations and academic researches (particularly Horton 2005; Natrass 2011; Posel 2008).

It is necessary to understand the sociocultural patterns of the disease in order to understand the efficiency of the current solutions and political steps put in place. Positioning of the infected and affected within the society, their quality of life, these are crucial questions that matter for the new stage of the epidemic in which most of the countries have already stepped when the AIDS-related mortality finally decreased and the lifespan of those infected has increased. The cultural issues also have their significant place in the overall picture, evidencing the attitude of the society as such to the epidemic driven by traditions, both rigid and evolving over time.

Before moving to the outlined analysis, however, it is useful to operationalise some of the crucial terms applied throughout this chapter.

Operationalisation of terms

Human Immunodeficiency Virus (HIV) is a retrovirus allegedly transmitted to humans from chimpanzees in west central Africa, more specifically southeastern Cameroon, dating back to the beginning of the twentieth century (Sharp and Hahn 2011). The virus has later been transferred between humans through various types of body fluids. The most common means of transmission is thus unprotected sexual intercourse with an HIV-positive partner, but it can also be transmitted through contact with infected blood or vertically from mother to child during pregnancy, childbirth or breast-feeding.

Within the host organism, the virus infects vital cells of the immune system, mainly CD4 positive T lymphocytes, which help the body fight diseases. Based on their number in the organism, it is possible to diagnose **Acquired Immunodeficiency Syndrome** (AIDS) when the CD4 cell count per mm^3 of blood drops below 200, as defined by the United States (US) Centers for Disease Control and Prevention in 1993.[1] The term AIDS thus applies to the most advanced stages of HIV infection, which is its causative agent by one or more of a variety of direct and indirect means (Weiss 1993: 1273). The main problem with the spread of HIV is that there are no symptoms until the virus reaches the advanced stages. As a result, many HIV-

---

[1]The anti-retroviral treatment to prevent the burst of AIDS is provided already with a higher count of CD4 cells. New guidelines by the World Health Organization (2013) suggest a CD4 threshold of 500 for initiation of HIV treatment, while the older guidelines of 2010 recommended the treatment at a count of 350 CD4 cells/mm^3.

positive individuals do not know about their infection status for years until AIDS is already diagnosed in them.[2]

Both HIV and AIDS are widely referred to as an epidemic, commonly named HIV/AIDS. **Epidemic** is generally defined, deriving from the Stedman's Medical Dictionary, as the occurrence of an illness "in excess of normal expectancy in a community or region" (Merrill 2012: 6). The epidemic of HIV/AIDS has already managed to spread to all the regions of the world, although its prevalence greatly varies. The region of sub-Saharan Africa still remains the most heavily affected (UNAIDS 2012). The severity of the epidemic is measured based on its prevalence among the given population. While *prevalence* informs us about the percentage of the population living with HIV infection, *incidence* represents the annual number of new infections that occur in that population (Brookmeyer 2010: 27).

In the Second generation surveillance for HIV, the World Health Organization (2002) defines that if the prevalence of HIV among the general population is lower than one per cent, we talk of a *low-level* epidemic. If, however, in such an environment the epidemic is being spread within a certain sub-population with more than 5-per cent prevalence, the epidemic is considered to be *concentrated*. The respective communities consist of people who mostly engaged in high risk behaviour, such as men who have sex with men (MSM), injecting drug users (IDUs), sex workers or prisoners. In certain parts of the world, namely sub-Saharan Africa as well as parts of Asia, Central America and the Caribbean, the HIV prevalence has overcome one per cent within the general population, thus being considered a *generalised* epidemic. Throughout the article, the term *epidemic* is preferred to *pandemic*, since the meaning of the latter has not yet been agreed upon officially (Morens et al. 2009; see also Kelly 2011).

Acknowledging that "there seem to be more definitions of epidemiology than there are epidemiologists," Rothman, Greenland and Lash (2008: 32) attempt to define **epidemiology** "as the study of the distribution of health-related states and events in populations." Within the chapter, the view of epidemiology is defined as a set of patterns that indicate how the disease is

---

[2]Without treatment, the infected can live for some ten years until AIDS develops in them. It took indeed whole decades to acknowledge the relationship between HIV and AIDS, which was first clinically recognised only in 1981 in the US where the disease was brought from the African continent and further spread within the community of men having sex with men. It should also be noted that people do not die of AIDS as such, but of the acquired life-threatening opportunistic infections and cancers when the immune system of the patients progressively fails. Although there has been no cure discovered, the progression of the infection may be dramatically slowed down by providing antiretroviral treatment (ART) to the patients.

spread within a country, followed by a cross-boundary transmission to a sub-region or a larger region, as well as globally. Since the analysis tackles two specific countries from diverse regions, the state-level is at the centre of focus. Epidemiology is mainly indicated by the current general prevalence on the specific territory and by a projected prevalence curve that shows how the prevalence has changed through years, when the disease was first identified and when, if already, the prevalence reached its peak.

It is also important to analyse the means of transmission, both horizontal and vertical (from mother to child), and enumerate the groups at higher risk, if present. One should not neglect even the overall health status of the population, by examining the life expectancy and other indicators, since it has already been proven that other diseases, such as herpes-simplex or syphilis, may be co-factors in acquisition of HIV (Steen et al. 2009).

The last term to be discussed is **Global Health Governance**, which has emerged as a natural evolution of transnational endeavour to combat health challenges present worldwide. Focusing on the health impacts of globalisation, it aims to suppress the persisting gap in the development of the individual world regions. Although its architecture is still being shaped, it has already succeeded in interlinking the health of the world population with major political issues and health has progressively become a significant agenda for the international society. "Recognising that domestic action alone is not sufficient to ensure health locally," global health risk management is being constituted via cross-border activities (Dodgson et al. 2002: 2).

With the first intimations of a global health cooperation dating back to the early twentieth century, namely the post-World War I period when the Red Cross network was established, one can see the real beginning of the cooperation in the emergence of the World Health Organization (WHO) right after the following World War II. As Youde (2012: 3) puts it, currently "there exists no single global health governance hierarchy and no single solution for global health concerns." UNAIDS as the Joint United Nations Programme on HIV/AIDS is thus merely one of many examples of the global cooperation that aims to concentrate all efforts and resources on joint advancement.

Comparative analysis

Socio-demographic comparison

With five times higher population inhabiting more than fifteen times larger area than the Czech Republic, the challenges faced by the government of South Africa in case of any security threat to its citizens are strikingly different. The impact of HIV/AIDS in South Africa is mostly apparent on the upper part of the population pyramid shown below in the Figure 1. The life expectancy currently reaching 59.6 years is slowly increasing again after a considerable fall in the early 1990s, which has "negated gains made during the past few decades on the pandemic" (Mba 2007: 201). In the absence of the disease, the life expectancy is prospected to be 26 years more. The life expectancy prospect according to the World Factbook issued by the US Central Intelligence Agency (CIA) is even much lower – 49.56 years for 2014.

Figure 1.

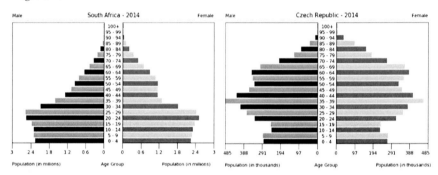

Source: The CIA World Factbook 2014

With a slowly increasing fertility rate in the Czech Republic, currently estimated to 1.43 per woman, the future population basis is still lower by almost one child when compared to the Republic of South Africa, where the current rate reaches 2.3 children per woman. This comparison should be taken into account by reflecting the infant mortality factor as well, which is approximately 42 deaths per 1,000 live births in South Africa, whereas the Czech Republic accounts for approximately 2.63 deaths. As WHO warns, "the toll that HIV/AIDS is taking is already retarding progress in reducing child mortality" (World Population Prospects 2012: 19).

The economic strength of the countries, required to be able to independently combat the disease efficiently while retaining relatively the same quality of life for its citizens, is yet another important indicator to be analysed. The gross domestic product (GDP) per capita in South Africa, rated as an upper middle income economy with an emerging market, is estimated to be 11,500 US dollars by the CIA, which is slightly less than a half of that in the Czech Republic. However, if we compare the rate of the countries' gross external debt to their GDP, the position of South Africa is twice as positive as in the Czech Republic.[3]

Unemployment, poverty and inequality in South Africa, which are among the highest levels in the world, remain a challenge that has further been complicated by the implications of the global financial crisis. The official unemployment rate currently remains at 25.2%, but runs significantly higher among black youth, reaching estimated 55% (*The Economist* 27 April 2013), which is also reflected in a direct correlation with the prevalence of HIV. Hand in hand with this gloomy trend, the rate of people living below the food poverty line develops according to the same scenario. Just in comparison, the general unemployment rate issued by the Czech Statistical Office in the first quarter of 2014 was 6.9% and the Czechs at risk of poverty reached 15% in 2012, which was the lowest ratio across the European Union, together with the Netherlands (European Commission 2013).

Malnutrition is another challenge in the combat of HIV/AIDS in South Africa. One in five children is suffering from stunting according to UNICEF, as of the most prevalent forms of malnutrition in South Africa. Yet another associated factor is the number of orphans, estimated to 3.7 million. More than 60% of them have lost one or both parents due to AIDS, being mostly raised by their grandparents. Furthermore, about 150,000 children are believed to be living in child-headed households (UNICEF 2013). Due to the epidemic patterns in the Czech Republic, none of these factors is directly connected to the HIV-infected population.

Epidemiology

Epidemic trends

While South Africa has the world's largest HIV-positive population in the world (UNAIDS 2013: Annex 14), the HIV epidemic in the Czech Republic can be described as "low and slow" (Czech Republic's Global AIDS Response Progress Report 2012: 12). The total number of South Africans living with HIV is about 5.26 million (Statistics South Africa)[4], which is half of the population of the Czech Republic. The general prevalence among adults (aged 15 to 49 years) is currently at about 16%, while some 400,000 children below the age of 15 live with the disease. (South Africa's Global AIDS Response Progress Report 2012). Estimated deaths due to AIDS decreased to 240,000 in 2012 (Global AIDS Response Progress Report 2012).

[3]The South African Reserve Bank (2014) has calculated the current debt to be over 138 billion US dollars, which is approximately 23% of its GDP, while the indebtedness stated by the Czech National Bank (2014) is close to 35% of GDP exceeding 108 billion US dollars.
[4]The last official estimates by UNAIDS from 2012 indicate 6.1 million infected.

In South Africa, the epidemic of HIV in terms of its prevalence is closely linked to the incidence of tuberculosis (TB), which has increased by 400% over the past 15 years. It is estimated that 80% of the population is currently infected by it, which does not explicitly mean progressing to the active tuberculosis disease (National Strategic Plan on HIV. STIs and TB 2012–2016, Republic of South Africa 2011). Nevertheless, the people living with HIV are among the groups particularly vulnerable to TB. According to the South African 2012 Global AIDS Response Progress Report, the proportion of TB-HIV co-morbidity is as high as 60%.

In the Czech Republic, the HIV virus is mostly transmitted between men having sex with men. While the prevalence among the Czech population stays constantly low, with the last official estimate of 0.014% in 2011 (country's Global AIDS Response Progress Report 2012)[5], the prevalence among the MSM community has reached almost 5%. The Czech Republic may thus soon fall within the category of countries with a *concentrated* epidemic of HIV. Currently, the community counts for more than 70% of new epidemic incidence cases. Nevertheless, the prevalence of HIV within this community is still half of that in South Africa, where the prevalence among men having sex with men is officially 9.9% (South African 2012 Global AIDS Response Progress Report).

The spread of the disease among the MSM community in the Czech Republic is closely connected to the spread of syphilis, which had reached a five-fold incidence increasing among men as of 2009 (Czech Republic Global AIDS Response Progress Report 2012). On the other hand, the South African Report evidences the decrease of the syphilis prevalence in most provinces over the past 10 years.

The Progress Reports further suggest that the highest prevalence within the South African population is concentrated among young adults of the age 20 to 24 years, reaching 13.6%. The rate of men and women infected, however, is strikingly different. While the percentage among men of this age is 5.1%, the prevalence among women is as high as 21.1%, which means the difference of the whole 16%. Another dividing line occurs in terms of racial population groups, with black Africans being unevenly hit by the disease when compared to the other population groups (Statistics South Africa 2013). Such a discrepancy in both indicators has much to do with the sociocultural dimensions of the disease, which are discussed later in the chapter. In the Czech Republic, the situation is exactly opposite. Due to the concentration of

---

[5]According to the latest number of 2,268 infected, the current prevalence may be calculated to present 0.0215%.

both incidence and prevalence inside the MSM community, men represent more than 80% of the infected cases in the Czech Republic.

In the Czech Republic, the epidemic is additionally concentrated in urban areas, with the capital city hosting almost half of all the incidences. In South Africa, the prevalence is also generally lower in rural areas, but not as significantly. In fact, "there is evidence of a parallel spread of the epidemic in urban and rural areas" (Van Donk 2006: 1). On one hand, rural areas are distinguished by greater isolation and closer family (and moral) bonds. On the other hand, the awareness about the spread of HIV/AIDS is sometimes poor due to the stated isolation. When we look at the prevalence from the provincial perspective, the region around the capital city is not indeed the one that would experience the highest rates. According to the state's Department of Health (2010), the province of KwaZulu-Natal followed by Gauteng is most affected by the disease in the long term, while the lowest rates can be found in Western Cape, Northern Cape and Limpopo. The disease is spread further afield mainly via roads connecting the individual centres, frequently used by truck drivers.

When it comes to HIV testing, South Africa reports approximately 20% of its population being tested thus far. For the Czech Republic, no such statistics are available, only the cumulative number of tests conducted thus far which is reported monthly by the National Institute on Public Health. Nevertheless, due to the risk of horizontal transmission from mother to child, all pregnant women attending antenatal care are being tested for HIV in both studied countries. The prevention of the mother-to-child transmission (MTCT) has still been a challenge in South Africa. 30% of the pregnant women are HIV positive,[6] even though the trend has been moderate for the recent years. The South African government has achieved much success in cutting MTCT rate from 8.5% in 2008 through 3.5% in 2010 to less than 2% reported in May 2011. According to another significant statistics, close to two-thirds of the pregnancies among HIV-infected women are unplanned (Global AIDS Response Progress Report 2012).

Providing antiretroviral therapy (ART) nationwide in South Africa has indeed been highest in the world, with over 2 million citizens currently having access to the treatment. When compared to the number of the individuals eligible for the treatment, the country has already managed to surpass the 80% threshold defined by the World Health Organisation (WHO 2013). The coverage of ART to prevent mother-to-child transmission is even higher, currently reaching 87%. In the Czech Republic, thanks to the low HIV

---

[6]Compared to only 4 cases in the Czech Republic, not even being the country's citizens.

prevalence, the government has been able to provide the treatment to almost 100% of the eligible citizens (96.9% in 2011 according the Czech Progress Report), with all infected mothers and their infants receiving ARV prophylaxis.

Orphanhood is another serious issue connected to the effects of the HIV/AIDS epidemic in South Africa. More than 2 million AIDS orphans were indicated in the last 2011 Census in South Africa, with the international estimations, including UNAIDS, suggesting a higher number of almost 2.5 million children. Despite these unfavourable figures, the country attempts to reduce the number of AIDS related deaths below 200,000 annually (South Africa's Global AIDS Response Progress Report 2012).

Policy steps

An attempt to handle the burden of HIV/AIDS politically has become an unprecedented security challenge to multiple countries, including the Republic of South Africa. As Posel (2008: 13) puts it, "the international visibility of post-apartheid South Africa has, unfortunately, had a lot to do with its highly politicised controversy about AIDS." The disease was so uncommon and strange to the population that hardly anybody could understand its origins and means of transmission for many years. Such an environment of unconsciousness led the responsible representatives to either neglect the seriousness of the situation or provide their own insights and explanations.[7]

The official response to the epidemic came in 1992 by establishing the national coordinating committee that would develop an HIV/AIDS strategy. After the initial optimism, though, the situation developed otherwise. The presidency of Thabo Mbeki was, unfortunately, marked by the environment of denialism of the direct causal relationship between HIV and AIDS. This attitude was officially supported by the outcomes of the established Presidential Advisory Panel regarding HIV/AIDS. The policy finally led to estimated preventable deaths of more than 300,000 citizens (Chigwedere et al. 2008). Even Mbeki's predecessor, Nelson Mandela, was able to speak out loud on the problem the country faced due to the epidemic only when he lost his own son to AIDS in 2005.

Despite the overwhelming silence, South Africa succeeded to launch the largest anti-retroviral campaign worldwide in 2003. Within the latter decade, the country implemented the largest national HIV Counselling and Testing campaign in the world in 2010, already reaching 13 million individuals. The

---

[7]One of many examples may be former Health Minister Manto Tshabalala-Msimang officially advocating the supplementation of certain vegetables instead of ART.

campaign achieved this success by being promoted through mass events, and not only at health facilities.

All the steps taken to combat HIV/AIDS have for long been hindered by the problematic health care services. Nevertheless, South Africa has recently overcome the biggest challenge to the mass deployment of anti-retrovirals by reducing the price of the drugs by more than a half through a new tender signed in 2011 and by additional almost 40% at the end of 2012 (South African Government News Agency 2012). This achievement was the result of a price competition that started in the early 2000s by the introduction of generic drugs onto the market. However, as it has already been mentioned, the treatment still does not reach all of those eligible for it, despite the significant progress.

The network of South African bodies responsible for the state's response to the epidemic is becoming quite dense, with a multitude of projects initiated externally by UNAIDS. The Know-Your-Epidemic/Know-Your Response is just one to be mentioned. The South African National AIDS Council (SANAC) is a voluntary association of institutions established by the national cabinet of the South African Government to build multi-stakeholder consensus. Currently, the second five-year National Strategic Plan is being in its half period. In addition, each province conducts a Provincial Strategic Plan, co-ordinating the response on a micro-level and formulating the regionally based specific plans. The annual spending of the country on HIV and TB has been increasing annually, already reaching some 1.6 billion US dollars.[8]

When it comes to education, South Africa has already succeeded to put into place measures that ensure the awareness of the disease among the young generation. The biggest challenge in this respect remains breaking the stereotypes among the educators (as well as within families), which has led to the need for special educational programs targeted at teachers themselves, such as Higher Education and Training HIV/AIDS Programme. A special National Action Plan for Orphans and Vulnerable Children has also managed to secure education of orphans, all of them reported to attend primary schooling (Global AIDS Response Progress Report 2012). In the same report, however, the government acknowledges the persisting lack of social workers.

The Czech Republic, as a country with the low HIV prevalence, is conducting its policy steps only within the framework of the international commitments towards the UNAIDS or the European Union in eliminating the disease through its own National Action Plan. In reflection to this current

---

[8]This data for the fiscal year 2009/10 was provided in the recent National AIDS Spending Assessment (2013) and shows that the Government of the United States of America still remains the largest external contributor.

situation, the first challenge articulated in the country's Global AIDS Response Progress Report (2012: 19) is "more political will and investments". The disease remains rather a public health concern, while its social dimensions are not taken into account considerably.

Awareness in the media is also very important in order to ensure the prevention of the disease among the population. In the Czech Republic, however, a wider campaign outside schools is missing. The only advertisement tackles free testing and is placed in the public transportation in the capital city in the form of A4-format leaflets with a contact to the hotline.

Participation of the non-governmental sector

It has already been widely acknowledged (see Gavian et al. 2006) that multisectoral stakeholder approach is needed to efficiently combat the spread of HIV/AIDS and the negative impacts of the epidemic on the population. Each government as such should, of course, take the responsibility for the quality of life of its own citizens into its own hands. At the same time, however, without the participation at the communitarian level, the centralised policy may become costly and less efficient.

The first Czech non-governmental organisation (NGO) focused on the HIV epidemic, the Czech AIDS Help Society, was established already at the end of 1989, with the initial impulse coming directly from the families and close friends of those infected to help them struggle over the disease. Within a short period of time, the society expanded its activities also to prevention and education, including free HIV testing. In the late 1990s, it also managed to establish the "Lighthouse", a centre for housing the infected and their families with a wide range of services, including the legal issues connected to their discrimination.

Despite the promising timely non-governmental engagement in the problematic across the Czech Republic, a body targeting the specific issue of the high prevalence among MSM is still lacking, which may be an effect of the persisting neglecting of this community within the Czech society, being perceived at the individual level as 'sick' or at least 'unnatural'.

When examining the situation in South Africa, Williams et al. (2002: n.d.) suggest that "echoing the history of the struggle against Apartheid, responsibility for dealing with HIV/AIDS is falling increasingly on society's NGO sector." According to their observation, NGOs specifically concerned with HIV/AIDS began to emerge in the late 1980s, and by 1997 more than 600 organisations were directly involved in HIV/AIDS. The first indication of a larger grassroots level engagement was so-called NACOSA, the Networking

HIV/AIDS Community of South Africa, launched in 1991, which participated in the formulation of the first National AIDS Plan. However, this network is currently being sponsored by the Global Fund. The leading civil society force behind the battle with HIV/AIDS in South Africa has thus become the Treatment Action Campaign founded in 1998, soon becoming "the most assertive and prominent social movement of the post-apartheid era" (Posel 2008: 14). The campaign has been focused specifically on the comprehensive access to ART and prevention literacy. It opposed the denialism of Thabo Mbeki's era by confronting the government with the reality of the epidemic, including the lawsuit against the government raised in 2001 (see more at www.tac.org.za).

NGOs in both countries are slowly managing to shift the attention also on empowerment of those affected. Besides the NGOs as such, the community-based organisations (CBOs) in most of the corners of South Africa include churches, which is not so common in the Czech Republic, being one of the most atheist countries in the world. Engagement of the church in the HIV/AIDS problematic in South Africa may be seen in two dimensions. While it has strongly campaigned against the use of condoms as the means of HIV prevention (see Noonan 2012), it has also provided significant help to the diseased ones and contributed to the education of the South African youth.

Sociocultural patterns of the disease

The current social environment in South Africa can be seen as both a trigger for the HIV/AIDS spread and a factor making the lives of those already infected or affected even more gruesome. According to Williams et al. (2002: n.d.), "the 1990s provided fertile ground for the spread of HIV" due to "the social unrest and civil disorder that marked the dying years of Apartheid. (…) The advent of freedom of movement (…) meant that people, and so also diseases, could move about as never before." In addition, the Minister of Women, Children and People with Disabilities has recently recognised "on-going discriminatory and stereotypical beliefs towards persons with disabilities" (ibid.). For a very long time, the society lacked the ownership of the epidemic, living in an environment of denial, naming AIDS, among other terms, a 'four-letter disease'. Self-identification was not promoted even by publicly known personalities who refused to admit their status, although apparent from the first sight.[9]

---

[9]One of the first who tried to encourage the society was DJ Fana Khaba who announced his status in 2003 and died of the disease one year later. Makgatho Mandela, the last living son of Nelson Mandela, died in 2005. Two other examples were children of Mangosuthu Buthelezi, the leader of Inkatha Freedom Party.

Acknowledging that culture has "both positive and negative influences on health behaviour", Leclerc-Madlala et al. (2009: 13–14) point out that due to the multi-cultural nature of the country, "there is no single sociocultural context on which the HIV/AIDS epidemic is occurring." According to them, South Africa is situated in a dualistic belief system consisting of the predominant Christian influence hand in hand with the traditional witchcraft practices. Traditions are shaping many of the attitudes towards HIV/AIDS and its spread, particularly to the (risky) sexual behaviour, such as male circumcision, polygamy or virgin cleansing. At the same time, HIV status has for long been seen as a shame to the whole family and even wider community, perceived as a result of promiscuity (Deacon et al. 2009).

Another pattern of the South African society nowadays, which explains the discrepancy of HIV prevalence among women compared to men (Jewkes et al. 2003; Jewkes et al. 2010; Wood et al. 1997), is increasing sexual violence, particularly in the urban areas with higher level of detachment from traditional communitarian bonds. The culture of sexual violence has almost become a new norm in certain larger cities, even within long-term partnerships. "Refusing sex, inquiring about other partners, or suggesting condom use have all been described as triggers for intimate partner violence; yet all are intimately connected to the behavioural cornerstones of HIV prevention" (Maman et al. 2000: 459).

The epidemic of HIV/AIDS does not affect only the individuals infected by it, but the whole families and communities that struggle both to save their beloved ones and beat the widespread stigma. With the alarming number of AIDS orphans, it is mostly grandparents who become the care-takers of the children. While caring the burden of their advanced age, they have to safeguard the vulnerable youth at the same time. What is more gruesome, multiple research conducted by Cluver (2007, 2009) reveals a lower quality of life of AIDS orphans, who experience bullying and ostracism and even exhibit promiscuous behaviour, thus increasing their own chance of contracting the disease and continuing the cycle (Operario et al. 2007). The sociocultural patterns of HIV/AIDS in the Czech Republic are much different. Due to the low prevalence of the disease among the general population, people do not often know anybody who is infected. As the epidemic is concentrated within the MSM community, stigmatisation is mostly directed towards the community as such, and it is not even recognised as the one that spreads HIV most in the country. The focus of the society's attention is rather on the sexual behaviour of homosexuals, which is still not tolerated much on the public even in the central urban areas (Platforma pro rovnoprávnost, uznání a diverzitu 2013). In recent years, however, there have been attempts to break the notional barriers through organising the Prague Pride festival, which officially celebrates human differences of all kinds. The festival has been organised under auspices of the Prague mayor, which indicates at least some ulterior official support for the minority. The attitude towards homosexuals is slightly different among the young community in urban areas, where this orientation is understood more as natural and even *trendy*.[10]

Despite the low HIV/AIDS prevalence in the Czech Republic, the country has attempted to contribute to the international resolution of the problem via its scientific achievements. The pioneering personality in the research of AIDS treatment was Antonín Holý. In cooperation with American colleagues, he was able to invent Truvada, thus far the most effective antiretroviral therapy on AIDS, significantly prolonging the lives of AIDS patients with apparently lower side effects. He died that very day when the US health regulators for the first time approved the usage of the treatment (*Reuters* 2012).

Impact of the neighbouring countries

Immigration from neighbouring countries represents a challenge to suppress the spread of HIV/AIDS both in South Africa and the Czech Republic. The HIV prevalence is higher both to the east and west of the Czech Republic. Western neighbours, namely Germany and Austria, are evidencing higher rates of HIV due to comparatively more intensive fluctuation of its citizens worldwide and intensified connections with other nations, where they can potentially acquire the disease. Along the Czech borders with these countries, prostitution is quite frequent. Although its frequency has fallen by half in 2013 due to conducted criminal proceedings, "it remains to pose significant risks" (Ministry of Interior 2014: 5). Nevertheless, the Ministry does not rank HIV among prostitutes.

The fluctuation of people from the East presents a significant risk of increasing the HIV incidence in the Czech Republic. While the biggest minority in the country consists of Slovaks, once the members of the same state entity, these are residing mostly legally thanks to the common Schengen territory with lowered control and restrictive mechanisms towards its members. A much more worrying situation is that of Ukrainians and citizens of other post-Soviet countries, who frequently seek a relatively better paid job than back at home with a smaller chance to get longer working visas, which is reflected in the official statistics of disclosed illegal workers (Czech Statistical Office 2013). These are not only seasonal construction workers,

---

[10]According to the Public Opinion Research Centre (2013), homosexuals are better tolerated by the right-wing oriented atheist respondents of lower age residing in Prague.

but also prostitutes, either voluntary or the victims of human trafficking. As it has already been mentioned, apart from the capital city, prostitution is concentrated along the former borders with Germany and Austria. This fact gives rise to a collision of the higher rates of HIV from both sides, although no monitoring has tackled this issue explicitly yet. As stated in the Czech Global AIDS Report (2012), clear statistics concerning the prevalence among foreigners staying in the Czech Republic illegally are lacking due to the substance of this black market. At the same time, however, foreigners officially form a significant portion of all the HIV positive cases in the country.[11] Moreover, the current political crisis in Ukraine may potentially even worsen the current trend.

When positioning South Africa in a wider region, the epidemic entered the country later than the rest of sub-Saharan Africa, as well as tighter southern Africa, due to the relative political and economic isolation during the 1980s (Grimond 2001 cited in Liamputtong 2013). The following post-apartheid freedom has brought about increased migration, both internal and international, which presents once again a co-factor in the spread of HIV. "It is not so much movement per se (…) but the social and economic conditions that characterize migration processes that puts people at risk for HIV" (Crush 2004: 1). Lessened ties to the homeland are characteristic especially for men doing migrant work, mostly being truck drivers and mine workers, who use condoms for occasional sexual intercourse less frequently. When they come back home, they usually spread the epidemic even within their own community. Horton (2005) enumerates also other significant factors, namely mass population resettlement to homelands and urban townships during apartheid, the arrival of refugees from other parts of Africa, the return after 1990 of exiles and combatants from liberation armies.

Conclusion

As indicated in the title of the chapter, its aim was to think of the HIV epidemic 'out of the box' by providing a comparative analysis of two purportedly incomparable HIV stories. The major difference, with no doubt, is the HIV prevalence in the analysed countries, which are highly disproportionately affected. However, while the statistics from South Africa suggest that the HIV epidemic has already reached a plateau in the country, the Czech Republic has still not reached the peak in the infection rate, only in the

---

[11]According to the recent statistics of the National Reference Laboratory for HIV/AIDS (2014), foreigners count for 17% of all cumulative findings of HIV in the Czech Republic, with the highest proportion from the region of Eastern Europe, followed by sub-Saharan Africa.

epidemic incidence. We thus need to wait for the data within the upcoming years to reveal the following trend.

When it comes to the epidemiology of HIV, the countries also remarkably differ in the key populations exposed to the highest risk, with primarily (black) young women in South Africa and homosexual men in the Czech Republic. Despite the various epidemic burdens, we may find certain mutual or parallel patterns. In both cases, the epidemic of HIV/AIDS is closely connected to other severe diseases, namely tuberculosis and herpes-simplex in South Africa and syphilis in the Czech Republic. This reminds us that the problem of HIV/AIDS cannot be tackled separately. All the potential suspected co-factors of its spread have to be taken into consideration worldwide.

Some of the problems are rooted in the traditions of both societies, naming at least (forced) sexual practices in South Africa and homophobia against the gay community in the Czech Republic, to which the HIV/AIDS agenda in the country should be aimed first and foremost.

Moreover, the Republic of South Africa has been positioned in a rather peculiar situation nowadays. With one of the worst cases of HIV/AIDS world-wide heavily burdening the state budget, it should act, at the same time, as an example of an efficient development to the whole region due to its economic status of the leader across Africa.

Both countries indicate progressive emergence of grassroots-level engagement in the absence of a clear policy action conducted by the government. Mass awareness of the problematic is the key for the future elimination of the disease. Although the role of the in-school education seems to work well in both countries, the sexually active population in the Czech Republic lacks the perception of HIV as something that could anyhow strike them. The epidemic affecting whole communities, thus being not only the health security issue, should not be handled only at the health care facilities, but rather be brought at the light.

The Czech Republic should also prepare for the effects of persistent immigration, particularly illegal immigration, on the hidden spread of the epidemic. This issue, however, has not yet been addressed directly even in the Republic of South Africa. The problems may thus become one of the future agendas for the emerging Global Health Governance.

References

Baťa, J. (2011), Jaké postavení má vlastně homosexualita ve společnosti? Aneb jak to vidí Nejvyšší soud, in: *Britské listy*, 6 June 2011, online: http://www.blisty.cz/art/58879.html#sthash.4Mb5B0lz.dpuf (accessed 21.9.2014).

Brookmeyer, R. (2010), Measuring the HIV/AIDS Epidemic: Approaches and Challenges, in: *Epidemiologic Reviews*, Vol. 32, No. 1, pp. 26–37.

Centers for Disease Control and Prevention (1992), 1993 Revised Classification System for HIV Infections and Expanded Surveillance Case Definition for AIDS among Adolescents and Adults, 41(RR-17), online: http://www.cdc. gov/mmwr/preview/mmwrhtml/00018871.htm (accessed 14.7.2014).

Central Intelligence Agency (2014), The World Factbook, online: https:// www.cia.gov/library/publications/the-world-factbook/ (accessed 13.7.2014).

Chigwedere, P., G. R. Seage, S. Gruskin, T. H. Lee and M. Essex (2008), Estimating the Lost Benefits of Antiretroviral Drug Use in South Africa, in: *JAIDS Journal of Acquired Immune Deficiency Syndromes*, Vol. 49, No. 4, pp. 410–415.

Cluver, L. and M. Orkin (2009), Cumulative risk and AIDS-orphanhood: Interactions of stigma, bullying and poverty on child mental health in South Africa, in: *Social science & medicine*, Vol. 69, No. 8, pp. 1186–1193.

Cluver, L., F. Gardner and D. Operario (2007), Psychological distress amongst AIDS-orphaned children in urban South Africa, in: *Journal of Child Psychology and Psychiatry*, Vol. 48, No. 8, pp. 755–763.

Crush, J. (ed.) (2004), Migration, Sexuality, and the Spread of HIV/AIDS in Rural South Africa, in: *Southern African Migration Project*, Migration Policy Series, No. 31.

Czech AIDS Help Society (n.d.), A Short Guide to the History of CSAP, online: http://www.aids-pomoc.cz/english.htm (accessed 13.7.2014).

Czech National Bank (2014), The Czech Republic's international investment position and external debt, online: http://www.cnb.cz/en/statistics/bop_stat/ investment_position/iip_commentary.html (accessed 13.7.2014).

Czech Statistical Office (2013), Foreigners in the Czech Republic 2013, online: http://www.czso.cz/csu/2013edicniplan.nsf/engpubl/1414-13-eng_r_ 2013 (accessed 21.9.2014).

Czech Statistical Office (2014), Employment and unemployment as measured by the LFS – First Quarter 2014, online: http://www.czso.cz/csu/csu.nsf/ enginformace/czam050514.docx (accessed 13.7.2014).

Deacon, H., L. Uys and R. Mohlahlane (2009), HIV and stigma in South Africa, in: *HIV/AIDS in South Africa 25 Years On*, New York: Springer, pp. 105–120.

Dodgson, R., K. Lee and N. Drager (2002), *Global Health Governance: A Conceptual Review*, Geneva: World Health Organization, Dept. of Health and Development.

European Commission (2013), At risk of poverty or social exclusion in the EU28, Eurostat news release 184/2013, online: http://epp.eurostat.ec.europa.eu/cache/ITY_PUBLIC/3-05122013-AP/EN/3-05122013-AP-EN.PDF (accessed 13.7.2014).

Gavian, S., D. Galaty and G. Kombe (2006), Multisectoral HIV/AIDS Approaches in Africa: How Are They Evolving? in: S. Gillespie (ed.), *AIDS, Poverty, and Hunger: Challenges and Responses*, Washington, D.C.: International Food Policy Research Institute, pp. 221–243.

Government of South Africa (2011), Know Your Epidemic, Know Your Response: Summary Report 2011, online: http://dutblogs.dut.ac.za/hivaids/wp-content/uploads/2013/09/Know-Your-Epidemic-Report.pdf (accessed 13.7.2014).

Horton, M. (2005), HIV/AIDS in South Africa, in: M. Nowak and L. A. Ricci (eds.), in: *Post-Apartheid South Africa: The First Ten Years*, International Monetary Fund, pp. 113–129.

International Organization for Migration (2005), HIV/AIDS, Population Mobility and Migration in Southern Africa. Defining a Research and Policy Agenda, online: http://www.sarpn.org/documents/d0001632/ (accessed 13.7.2014).

Jewkes, R. K., K. Dunkle, M. Nduna and N. Shai (2010), Intimate partner violence, relationship power inequity, and incidence of HIV infection in young women in South Africa: a cohort study, in: *The Lancet*, Vol. 376, No. 9734, pp. 41–48.

Jewkes, R. K., J. B. Levin and L. A. Penn-Kekana (2003), Gender inequalities, intimate partner violence and HIV preventive practices: findings of a South African cross-sectional study, in: *Social science & medicine*, Vol. 56, No. 1, pp. 125–134.

Kelly, H. (2011), The classical definition of a pandemic is not elusive, in: *Bulletin of the World Health Organization*, Vol. 89, pp. 540–541.

Khumalo, G. (2012), HIV Patients to Take One ARV Tablet Daily, in: *South African Government News Agency*, 29 November 2012, online: http://www.sanews.gov.za/south-africa/hiv-patients-take-one-arv-tablet-daily (accessed 15.7.2014).

Leclerc-Madlala, S., L. C. Simbayi and A. Cloete (2009), The sociocultural aspects of HIV/AIDS in South Africa, in: *HIV/AIDS in South Africa 25 Years On*, New York: Springer, pp. 13–25.

Liamputtong, P. (2013), *Stigma, discrimination and living with HIV/AIDS: a cross-cultural perspective*, New York: Springer.

Maman, S., J. Campbell, M. D. Sweat and A. C. Gielen (2000), The Intersections of HIV and violence: directions for future research and interventions, in: *Social Science & Medicine*, Vol. 50, No. 4, pp. 459–478.

Mba, C. J. (2007), Impact of HIV/AIDS mortality on South Africa's life expectancy and implications for the elderly population, in: *African Journal of Health Sciences*, Vol. 14, No. 3–4, pp. 201–211.

Merrill, R. M. (2012), *Introduction to Epidemiology*, 6th ed., Burlington, Massachusetts: Jones & Bartlett Learning.

Ministry of Health of the Czech Republic (2012), Czech Republic Global AIDS Response Progress Report, online: http://www.unaids.org/en/data-analysis/knowyourresponse/countryprogressreports/2012countries/ce_CZ_Na rrative_Report[1].pdf (accessed 15.7.2014).

Ministry of Health of the Czech Republic (2012), Národní program řešení problematiky HIV/AIDS v České republice na období 2013–2017, online: http://www.mzcr.cz/obsah/narodni-program-reseni-problematiky-hiv/aids_ 1688_5.html (accessed 13.7.2014).

Ministry of Interior of the Czech Republic (2014), Zpráva o stavu obcho-dování s lidmi v České republice za rok 2013, online: http://www.mvcr.cz/ clanek/obchod-s-lidmi-dokumenty-982041.aspx (accessed 21.9.2014).

Mlcochova, J. (2012), HIV drug creator Antonin Holy dies at 75, in: *Reuters*, 17 July 2012, online: http://www.reuters.com/article/2012/07/17/us-czech-scientist-death-idUSBRE86G0HX20120717 (accessed 15.7.2014).

Morens, D. M., G. K. Folkers and A. S. Fauci (2009), What is a Pandemic? in: *The Journal of Infectious Diseases*, Vol. 200, No. 7, pp. 1018–1021.

Nattrass, N. (2011), AIDS Policy in Postapartheid South Africa, in: I. Shapiro and K. Tebeau (eds.), *After Apartheid: Reinventing South Africa?*, Charlottesville and London: University of Virginia Press, pp. 181–198.

Noonan, M. (2012), The Catholic Church versus HIV/AIDS in Africa, in: *Consultancy Africa Intelligence*, 2 October 2012, online: http://www.consul-tancyafrica.com/index.php?option=com_content&view=article&id=1135: the-catholic-church-versus-hivaids-in-africa-&catid=61:hiv-aids-discussion-papers&Itemid=268 (accessed 21.9.2014).

Operario, D., A. Pettifor, L. Cluver, C. MacPhail and H. Rees (2007) Prevalence of parental death among young people in South Africa and risk for HIV infection, in: *JAIDS Journal of Acquired Immune Deficiency Syndromes*, Vol. 44, No. 1, pp. 93–98.

Platforma pro rovnoprávnost, uznání a diverzitu (2013): Report on implementation by the Czech Republic of the Recommendation CM/Rec (2010)5 of the Committee of Ministers of the Council of Europe on measures to combat discrimination on grounds of sexual orientation or gender identity, online: http://ilga-europe.org/home/guide_europe/council_of_europe/lgbt_rights/ recommendation_com_lgbt (accessed 21.9.2014).

Posel, D. (2008), AIDS, in: N. Shepherd and S. Robins (eds.), *New South African Keywords*, Ohio University Press, pp. 13–24.

Procházka, I., J. Novotný, P. Kaňka and D. Janík (2005), *HIV infekce a ho-mosexualita*, Česká společnost AIDS pomoc.

Republic of South Africa (2011), *National Strategic Plan on HIV, STIs and TB 2012–2016*, online: http://www.sanac.org.za/nsp/the-national-strategic-plan (accessed 20.9.2014).

Republic of South Africa (2012), Global AIDS Response Progress Report 2012, online: http://www.unaids.org/en/dataanalysis/knowyourresponse/country-progressreports/2012countries/ce_ZA_Narrative_Report.pdf (accessed 15.7. 2014).

Rothman, K. J., S. Greenland and T. J. Lash (2008), *Modern epidemiology*, Philadelphia: Williams & Wilkins.

Sharp, P. and B. H. Hahn (2011), Origins of HIV and the AIDS Pandemic, in: *Cold Spring Harbor Perspectives in Medicine*, Vol. 1, No. 1.

Sociologický ústav AV ČR (2013), *Postoje veřejnosti k právům homosexuálů*, online: http://cvvm.soc.cas.cz/media/com_form2content/documents/c1/a7023/f3/ov130604.pdf (accessed 21.9.2014).

South Africa Government (2012), Minister concerned about slow progress in empowering people with disabilities, speech, online: http://www.gov.za/speeches/view.php?sid=25958 (accessed 14.7.2014).

South African National AIDS Council (2013), South Africa's National Aids Spending Assessment Brief (2007/08–2009/10), online: http://www.sanac.org.za/resources/aids-spending/cat_view/6-aids-spending (accessed 13.7. 2014).

South African Reserve Bank (2014), Gross External Debt – First Quarter 2014, online: https://www.resbank.co.za/Lists/News%20and%20Publications/Attachments/6296/Gross%20External%20Debt%20%20%E2%80%93%201st%20Quarter%202014.pdf (accessed 13.7.2014).

Statistics South Africa (2013), Mid-year population estimates 2013, Statistical Release P0302, online: http://beta2.statssa.gov.za/publications/P0302/P03022013.pdf (accessed 13.7. 2014).

Statistics South Africa (2013), Mortality and causes of death in South Africa, 2011: Findings from death notification, Statistical Release P0309.3, online: http://beta2.statssa.gov.za/publications/P03093/P030932011.pdf (accessed 13.7.2014).

Statistics South Africa (2013), The 2012 National Antenatal Sentinel HIV & Herpes Simplex Type-2 Prevalence Survey in South Africa, online: http://www.health-e.org.za/wp-content/uploads/2014/05/ASHIVHerp_Report2014_22May2014.pdf (accessed 21.9.2014).

Statistics South Africa (2014), Poverty Trends in South Africa, Press Statement, online: http://beta2.statssa.gov.za/?p=2591 (accessed 13.7.2014).

Statistics South Africa (2014), Quarterly Labour Force Survey, First Quarter 2014, Statistical Release P0211, online: http://beta2.statssa.gov.za/publications/P0211/P02111stQuarter2014.pdf (accessed 13.7.2014).

Steen, R., T. E. Wi, A. Kamali and F. Ndowa (2009), Control of sexually transmitted infections and prevention of HIV transmission: mending a fractured paradigm, in: *Bulletin of the World Health Organization*, Vol. 87, pp. 858–865.

UNAIDS (2012), Regional Fact Sheet 2012. Sub-Saharan Africa, online: http://www.unaids.org/en/media/unaids/contentassets/documents/epidemiolog y/2012/gr2012/2012_FS_regional_ssa_en.pdf (accessed 20.9.2014).

UNAIDS (2013), UNAIDS Report on the global AIDS epidemic, online: http://www.unaids.org/en/media/unaids/contentassets/documents/epidemiolog y/2013/gr2013/UNAIDS_Global_Report_2013_en.pdf (accessed 20.9.2014).

UNICEF (2013), Towards an AIDS-Free Generation – Children and AIDS: Sixth Stocktaking Report online: http://www.unicef.org/publications/files/ Children_and_AIDS_Sixth_Stocktaking_Report_EN.pdf (accessed 10.10. 2014).

UNICEF (n.d.), Nutrition, online: http://www.unicef.org/southafrica/survival_ devlop_755.html (accessed 13.7.2014).

United Nations Department of Economic and Social Affairs, Population Division (2013), World Population Prospects. The 2012 Revision, ESA/P/ WP.228, United Nations, New York, online: http://esa.un.org/wpp/Documen-tation/pdf/WPP2012_HIGHLIGHTS.pdf (accessed 13.7.2014).

Van Donk, M. (2006), "Positive" urban futures in sub-Saharan Africa: HIV/AIDS and the need for ABC (A Broader Conceptualization), in: *Environment and Urbanization*, Vol. 18, pp. 155–175.

Weiss, R. A. (1993), How Does HIV Cause AIDS? in: *Science*, New Series, Vol. 260, No. 5112, pp. 1273–1279.

Williams, B., E. Houws, J. Frohlich, C. Campbell and C. Macphail (2001), Lessons from the Front: NGOs and the Fight Against HIV/AIDS in South Africa, in: *Voices from Africa*, No. 10.

Wood, K. and R. Jewkes (1997), Violence, rape, and sexual coercion: Every-day love in a South African township, in: *Gender & Development,* Vol. 5, No. 2, pp. 41–46.

World Health Organization (2002), *Initiating Second Generation HIV Surveillance Systems: Practical Guidelines*, online: http://www.who.int/hiv/ pub/surveillance/ guidelines/en/ (accessed 15.7.2014).

World Health Organization (2013), *Consolidated Guidelines on the Use of Antiretroviral Drugs for Treating and Preventing HIV Infection: Recommen-dation for a Public Health Approach*, online: http://www.who.int/hiv/pub/ guidelines/arv2013/download/en/ (accessed 14.7.2014).

World Health Organization (2013), *Global Update on HIV Treatment 2013: Results, Impact and Opportunities*, online: http://www.unaids.org/en/media/

unaids/contentassets/documents/unaidspublication/2013/20130630_treatment
_report_en.pdf (accessed 15.7.2014).
Youde, J. (2012), *Global Health Governance*, Cambridge: Polity Press.
Youth unemployment: Generation jobless (2013), in: *The Economist,* 27 April
2013, online: http://www.economist.com/news/international/21576657-
around-world-almost-300m-15-24-year-olds-are-not-working-what-has-cause
d (accessed 15.7.2014).

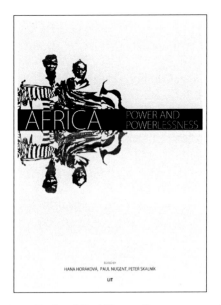

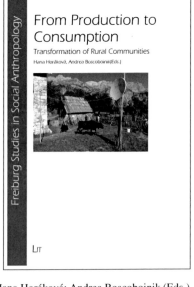

Hana Horáková; Paul Nugent; Peter
Skalník (Eds.)
Africa – Power and Powerlessness
In Africa the distribution of power and powerlessness seems to be more rigid than on other continents. Political power is in the hands of narrow elites
while the overwhelming majority has hardly any
access to decision-making. The common denomi-
nator of this book is the notion of power. It follows
the analytical differentiation between the concept
of power-over that is largely used by mainstream
political science, and the concept of power as social
practice. The authors ask pertinent questions on
how power is composed, created and used on the
African continent.
Afrikanische Studien/African Studies, vol. 43, 2011,
184 pp., 29,90 €, br., ISBN 978-3-643-11187-6

Hana Horáková; Andrea Boscoboinik (Eds.)
From Production to Consumption
Transformation of Rural Communities
Up to a few decades ago the anthropology of tourism was regarded as a way to become involved in
effortless researches in pleasant settings. Moreover, tourism was portrayed as a sinister carrier of
westernization, thus as a menace to the subaltern
societies that had to endure it. Nowadays anthropological studies on tourism have established their
own legitimacy due also to the considerable socioeconomic significance of tourism in this age of
hectic global mobility. This book points up new and
important research perspectives showing the impact
of tourism on the rural world. The articles presented
are a major and groundbreaking contribution to the
analysis of the new rurality in global society.
Freiburger Sozialanthropologische Studien, vol. 35, 2012,
184 pp., 29,90 €, br., ISBN-CH 978-3-643-80124-1

LIT Verlag Berlin – Münster – Wien – Zürich – London
Auslieferung Deutschland / Österreich / Schweiz: siehe Impressumsseite